Dan Pilcher

Other books in the Jossey-Bass Public Administration Series
and the Jossey-Bass Nonprofit Sector Series include:

Collaborative Leadership, *David D. Chrislip, Carl E. Larson*

Creating and Implementing Your Strategic Plan,
John M. Bryson, Farnum K. Alston

The Drucker Foundation Self-Assessment Tool for Nonprofit
Organizations, *The Peter F. Drucker Foundation for Nonprofit
Management*

Handbook of Practical Program Evaluation, *Joseph S. Wholey,
Harry P. Hatry, Kathryn E. Newcomer, Editors*

Handbook of Public Administration, Second Edition,
James L. Perry, Editor

How Do Public Managers Manage? *Carolyn Ban*

The Jossey-Bass Handbook of Nonprofit Leadership and
Management, *Robert D. Herman and Associates*

The Leader of the Future, *Frances Hesselbein,
Marshall Goldsmith, Richard Beckhard, Editors*

Marketing Social Change, *Alan R. Andreasen*

The Organization of the Future, *Frances Hesselbein,
Marshall Goldsmith, Richard Beckhard, Editors*

The Quickening of America, *Frances Moore Lappé,
Paul Martin Du Bois*

Strategic Planning for Public and Nonprofit Organizations,
revised edition, *John M. Bryson*

Transforming Public Policy, *Nancy C. Roberts, Paula J. King*

Trustworthy Government, *David G. Carnevale*

Understanding and Managing Public Organizations,
Hal G. Rainey

Grassroots Leaders
for a New Economy

Douglas Henton, John Melville,
and Kimberly Walesh

Foreword by Edward R. McCracken

Grassroots Leaders for a New Economy

How Civic Entrepreneurs Are Building Prosperous Communities

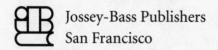

Jossey-Bass Publishers
San Francisco

Substantial discounts on bulk quantities of Jossey-Bass books are available to corporations, professional associations, and other organizations. For details and discount information, contact the special sales department at Jossey-Bass Inc., Publishers (415) 433–1740; Fax (800) 605–2665.

For sales outside the United States, please contact your local Simon & Schuster International office.

 Manufactured in the United States of America on Lyons Falls Turin Book. This paper is acid-free and 100 percent totally chlorine-free.

Library of Congress Cataloging-in-Publication Data

Grassroots leaders for a new economy: how civic entrepreneurs are
  building prosperous communities / Douglas Henton . . . [et al.].
      p. cm. — (A joint publication in the Jossey-Bass public
  administration series and the Jossey-Bass nonprofit sector series)
    Includes bibliographical references and index.
    ISBN 0–7879–0827–4 (acid-free paper)
      1. Social responsibility of business—California—Santa Clara
  County. 2. Community development—California—Santa Clara County.
  I. Henton, Douglas C. II. Series: Jossey-Bass public administration
  series. III. Series: Jossey-Bass nonprofit sector series.
  HD60.5.U52S364   1997
  338.973—dc21   96–51203

FIRST EDITION
HB Printing   10 9 8 7 6 5 4 3 2 1

A joint publication in

*the Jossey-Bass Public Administration Series
and the Jossey-Bass Nonprofit Sector Series*

—⟋⟍— Contents

We dedicate this book to our parents,

who taught us about community,

and to our families,

who remind us every day why it matters.

To Carol, Wade, and Elizabeth

Susan and Sam

Stu and Jerrie, and David

⸺ᴡᴠ⸺ Foreword

In Silicon Valley, the world's center of high-technology innovation, business executives, government officials, educators, and community leaders have created a new regional organization—Joint Venture: Silicon Valley Network. Joint Venture is built on a platform of civic entrepreneurship and community collaboration.

The authors of this stimulating book, *Grassroots Leaders for a New Economy,* were deeply involved in developing the conceptual framework for our new Silicon Valley organization. Their combined experience is extraordinary, and their academic, corporate, and public policy credentials are impressive. I have enjoyed working closely with them at Joint Venture.

The writers describe civic entrepreneurs as new links between the economy and the community. Understanding who these civic entrepreneurs are and why they do what they do is a core objective of this book.

Civic entrepreneurs understand the importance of collaboration, the authors say. They bring business and community together and are driven to achieve results. They come from all levels of business, government, education, and community organizations. They know that a dynamic economy depends on building a strong community.

This building is precisely what is happening in Silicon Valley. The authors' original concepts are unfolding in the real world of a dynamic, innovative, and resourceful community. As chief executive officer of Silicon Graphics Computer Systems and a cochair of Joint Venture, I believe that this pioneering effort exemplifies, among other things, the differences between the old industrial age and the new information age.

In the industrial age, large, vertically integrated organizations followed a highly centralized and paternalistic philosophy. Employees enjoyed stable, one-company careers. Community relationships were nurtured with philanthropic grants and direction from strong corporate owners or executives.

In the information age, employees have unlimited mobility. The community is a tremendously important asset for the happiness of employees and the prosperity of businesses. Community relationships are conducted by talented and motivated people—civic entrepreneurs—at all levels of their organizations.

Employees of information age companies are really freelancers and independent entrepreneurs. They just happen to work inside corporate boundaries. In fact, they can choose to work anywhere and bring their intellectual skills to the job. As freelancers, they can live anywhere, so they are intensely interested in their communities.

Business executives in this new information age are concerned with their communities for both business and civic reasons. We have four constituencies: shareholders, customers, employees, and community. If we run our companies properly and profitably and provide a reasonable, long-term return for shareholders, we can, and must, get involved in the community and have an impact on its direction.

Why? We must get involved because information age businesses like Silicon Graphics rely on partnerships with other companies in the community to do things quickly at a world-class level. We work together to be competitive in the global economy. We have worked with thousands of companies in Silicon Valley. They are right next door. To retain these relationships in the Valley, we have to develop world-class educational opportunities and other elements of a world-class quality of life for our employees.

Until a few years ago, Silicon Valley had neither a feeling of "family" nor an understanding of the interconnections that are necessary to develop a successful place to live and work. The economic downturn of the early 1990s and rapid globalization of the economy, however, jolted Silicon Valley with a severe reality check about its future.

That jolt started the creative juices flowing among people in business, government, education, and community. It generated a determined group of more than a thousand leaders in these areas to take destiny into their hands. *Grassroots Leaders for a New Economy* describes the process that created this business-community interconnection.

So far, so good. Joint Venture's experiment in regional collaboration is delivering a higher level of cooperation, new ways to think and act about our common interests, and positive results.

It is fair to ask, however, whether civic entrepreneurship in Silicon Valley—this new paradigm—will last. Is it just a short-term response to the economic difficulties Silicon Valley faced a few years ago? Now that our economy is "hot" again, will we revert to being just business entrepreneurs? Have we, as one of Joint Venture's directors asked, just cherry-picked the fruit from low-hanging branches in terms of the issues we have dealt with (the relatively easy ones), and the really tough ones will be beyond our grasp?

I do not think so. Our regional, collaborative approach to the link between business and community in Silicon Valley will continue, principally because it is rooted in reality and necessity.

The authors are right when they say we need civic entrepreneurs to help lead our new global economy and community through continuous restructuring of every institution in our society. And we must have new regional institutions like Joint Venture to bring us together in a neutral forum. As the authors put it, "The task is no less than creating economic communities for the twenty-first century."

I am pleased to write this foreword, because *Grassroots Leaders for a New Economy* has an important message for people who want to strengthen the economy and the quality of life in the communities where they live and work. And I appreciate what the authors have done to help us accomplish that goal in Silicon Valley.

Mountain View, California EDWARD R. McCRACKEN
March 1997 Chairman and Chief Executive Officer
Silicon Graphics Computer Systems

He is certainly not a good citizen who does not wish to promote, by every means in his power, the welfare of the whole society of his fellow-citizens.

—*Adam Smith,* The Theory of Moral Sentiments

⎯⎯ **Preface**

Across America, a new type of grassroots leader is building communities for a new economy. These civic entrepreneurs are helping communities collaborate to compete in the information age. From all walks of life, they are a new generation of leaders who forge new, powerfully productive linkages at the intersection of business, government, education, and community. *Grassroots Leaders for a New Economy* is the story of people building vital, resilient economic communities in turbulent times. It is the story of what they have to teach us, as a nation struggling to rebuild our civil society.

ECONOMIC COMMUNITIES
COLLABORATE TO COMPETE GLOBALLY

Americans will remember the last twenty years of the twentieth century as a transition period ushering in a new era focused on America's communities. As people in Washington, D.C., debate how to reinvent the federal government, people in communities are struggling to understand and respond to real and fundamental shifts. Big companies undergo massive restructuring and layoffs; new companies and industries spring forth in their wake. Traditional pillars of community stability (banks, utilities) are bought out by outsiders or are shaken by deregulation and consolidation. Companies are rethinking their role in a more networked, real-time world. Demographic shifts are bringing the boomer generation to the forefront and proliferating a diversity of new power groups. And devolution is sure to push responsibility, if not resources, down to the local level.

As these forces play themselves out, we are all asking ourselves, What will happen to our communities, to our companies, to us as individuals? How will we sustain what we have and build for the future?

In the past fifteen years, we have watched more than thirty communities struggle with this emerging new environment and helped them develop and implement strategies for regional economic competitiveness. From Austin, Omaha, and Wichita to Los Angeles, Silicon Valley, and Hong Kong, communities have participated out of necessity in the same experiment: finding ways to stay competitive. Along the way, we faced a very basic and powerful set of questions: Why do some regions succeed while others fail? Why do regions with similar assets perform differently? Why do some regions rebound from economic hardship, while their counterparts continue to decline? Why do some communities seize new economic opportunities, while the world passes others by? Why do some communities sustain steady progress, while others emerge, then recede?

Over time, we have come closer and closer to an answer. At first, we thought it might be technology—high-tech regions would do better than those with low tech. But we realized that today, technology permeates every industry and provides no easy formula for success. So, then we looked at the presence of education and research institutions and of wealth—and we saw regions with exceptional institutions and assets and unexceptional economies. Then we thought the silver bullet might be industry clusters: networked firms that competed and cooperated together. But we saw places whose clustered companies could not sustain success—and so on, and so on.

After a decade of exploration, we have observed a recurring pattern that offers the best explanation for why regions succeed. The communities that are most optimistic and ready for the new world practice "collaborative advantage." They enjoy tight relationships at the intersection of their business, government, education, and community sectors, which provide regional resiliency and a unique ability to set and achieve longer-term development goals. As AnnaLee Saxenian of the University of California, Berkeley, notes, the important part is not the ingredients—what they have or do not have. The important part is how communities leverage their community assets, processes, and relationships to support the changing needs of their economy. We call these communities "economic communities." They are places that collaborate in order to compete globally.

At the center of every one of these collaborative communities, we observed a team of civic entrepreneurs. Civic entrepreneurs provide collaborative leadership to bridge the economy and the community. Often, these leaders hail from business, whether global, entrepreneurial, or small. They act on their belief that the long-term health of their organization is tied to the long-term health of their region. But civic entrepreneurs also come from the public sector, education, labor, and the nonprofit sector. Where others see problems and gridlock, civic entrepreneurs see opportunity and mobilize their communities on a path forward. When others practice antagonistic tactics and produce gridlock, civic entrepreneurs build consensus and move diverse communities ahead, patiently and without formal authority or position. When others give up and walk away, civic entrepreneurs persist to help their communities not just cope with but thrive on change.

They are neither philanthropists nor do-gooders, nor are they business lobbyists. Civic entrepreneurs appear to be a special class of individuals in certain types of communities who have emerged at this point in history—in the globalizing regions of the late twentieth century.

Who are these people? What do they do? Why do they do what they do? What results have they achieved? What does it all mean for America? These are central questions that we address in this book.

RESTORING CIVIL SOCIETY

As we approach the next century, a widening debate asks how to restore civil society—the arena that is not business and not government but between the market and politics. It is in this space where, historically, America has pioneered the institutions, relationships, and individual initiative to advance the common good. Civil society is the essential middle ground that helps to link business and government within successful economic communities.

A growing body of literature describes the decline of civil society, looking at the nation from the top down. Harvard philosopher Michael Sandel (1996) bemoans the loss of community and civic engagement essential for self-government. He argues that civil society can only be restored at the community, not the national, level. Political scientist Robert Putnam (1993b), also of Harvard, tracks the decline of social capital and links high stocks of social capital to economic performance. Historian Francis Fukuyama (1995) points to a lively civil society based on trust as critical to an advanced capitalist economy. Even political leaders are beginning to focus on civil society. Former senator Bill Bradley writes that "the failure to appreciate the importance of civil society lies at the core of our policy dilemma" (Bradley, 1996, p. 413).

The problem is that there is no how-to book for reinvigorating civil society and jump-starting community self-governance. Success is likely to come from the bottom up, one economic community at a time. We have found that it is the civic entrepreneurs who are rebuilding civil society from the grass roots. Moving beyond re-engineering the corporation and reinventing government, their task is nothing less than to forge a new collaborative civil society that can help build a bridge between business and government. They restore civil society by helping people work together on specific projects to improve their economy and community—reforming education systems, streamlining permitting processes, fostering business connections, revitalizing urban centers, and leveraging the information infrastructure. *Grassroots Leaders for a New Economy* makes a unique contribution to the emerging literature on civil society and social capital. It demonstrates what people in American communities today are doing to create a civil society that enhances regional economic performance.

PURPOSE AND METHODOLOGY

The purpose of *Grassroots Leaders for a New Economy* is to describe and explain the nature of leadership necessary for regions to compete in the twenty-first century, based on observation of effective civic entrepreneurs. We focus on the critical role of civic entrepreneurs, what they have been able to achieve in specific circumstances, and, by implication, what civic entrepreneurship might be able to achieve on a more widespread basis. By sharing what civic entrepreneurs do and why they do what they do, we aim to inspire more people to become civic entrepreneurs and to support the work of these new leaders.

The book builds on our experience working with public and private leaders in communities in the United States, Europe, and Asia. It also closely examines the practices of civic entrepreneurs in regions that have enjoyed some success with the new collaborative model. Three communities (Cleveland, Austin, and Wichita) are "early adopters" that began operating under the collaborative leadership paradigm in the early 1980s. Two states, Arizona and Florida, launched major state and regional efforts to unite the private and public sectors around a new vision of economic progress in the late 1980s. And in 1992, a team of Silicon Valley entrepreneurs turned to transforming their region into a community collaborating to compete globally.

Grassroots Leaders for a New Economy uses the words and stories of civic entrepreneurs to convey their motivation, purpose, lessons learned, and advice. Jim Morgan, CEO of Applied Materials, and

Lionel Alford, former senior vice president of Boeing, talk about why global corporations care in new ways about local economic regions. The mayor of Orlando, Glenda Hood, describes the importance of linking established and next-generation leaders. Alan Hald, vice chairman and cofounder of MicroAge, Inc., recounts how he helped mobilize Arizona's emerging technology economy and thousands of citizens to choose their future. Ed McCracken, chairman of leading-edge Silicon Graphics, and John Kennett, a San Jose printer, explain why they and others from all walks of life invest countless hours creating a world-class Silicon Valley community to sustain its world-class economy. And Al Ratner and Richard Pogue, Cleveland business leaders, describe how they fought back with others and rebuilt Cleveland rather than leave the city they loved.

This book does not attempt to explain regional differences in economic performance fully or to present a full-blown, explanatory theory of regional economic development. Regional economic development is a complex, multidimensional challenge. We are not offering a complete theoretical paradigm for why regions succeed or fail. Nor are we claiming that the mere absence of civic entrepreneurs is the only reason why a region's economic performance may be weak. Rather, we are sharing from the ground level what corporate and community leaders believe has been the secret to their region's success.

WHO SHOULD READ THIS BOOK?

"All these complex issues can be addressed with leadership. We have great leaders, but need more. This must be our legacy." This message from civic entrepreneurs in Austin is repeated by others across America. Challenges and opportunities cry out for leaders with the collaborative skills necessary for the diverse, complex, and fast-moving information age.

Anyone who wants to be a civic leader for the twenty-first century should read this book. So should people who want to spark civic entrepreneurship and economic renewal in their community.

- *Business executives* will learn why and how civic entrepreneurs from business integrate into local communities, the varied roles they could play, and what the payoff could be for business and communities.

- *Elected officials and public managers* will learn how their counterparts have collaborated with private sector civic entrepreneurs to provide community leadership for the long haul and how public leaders themselves transform into civic entrepreneurs.

- *Community and nonprofit leaders* will see the power of a new top-down/bottom-up model for community renewal—one based on participation, good process, and results.

- *Economic and community development practitioners* will find out how they can become civic entrepreneurs and foster civic entrepreneurship in their community, leveraging talent and resources.

- *Citizens* will learn how they can be leaders and how new intermediary institutions can help people make a difference in their community's economic future.

Although the primary audience for this book is current and potential leaders, we hope its grassroots perspective will contribute to the lively debate about the role of leadership in rebuilding civil society.

STRUCTURE OF THE BOOK

Like civic entrepreneurs, this book operates at two levels. Civic entrepreneurs are both people of vision and pragmatists who get things done. *Part One* introduces the framework for economic community and the facts about civic entrepreneurs. *Part Two* describes specifically how civic entrepreneurs build economic community and offers advice for others trying to do the same. The final chapter in the book provides an agenda for accelerating the change process in American communities.

Readers who want big concepts and implications should read Chapters One, Two, Three, and Eight.

Readers seeking practical advice and specific examples should focus on Chapters Four through Seven.

PART ONE: COMMUNITY LEADERSHIP FOR THE INFORMATION AGE

Chapter One describes how four forces (globalization, information technologies, demographic shifts, and devolution) heighten the importance of cross-sector collaboration at the community level. The chapter provides a historical perspective on why a new type of leader and a new focus on community are emerging now. We are in the midst of a fundamental transition period as big business, big government, and national orientation shift to nimble, networked businesses, to devolution, and to community. The final section outlines the three central features of these emerging economic communities—engaged clusters of specialization, responsive community competencies, and civic entrepreneurs linking economy and community.

Chapter Two describes the phenomenon of civic entrepreneurship in depth. Where do civic entrepreneurs come from? They can come from all sectors, but many come from the new economy, particularly from global companies and homegrown entrepreneurial companies that view their long-term future as tied to regional habitats. How do civic entrepreneurs work? They work in teams but with no formal power or authority. Why do they do what they do? Civic entrepreneurs say they get involved for enlightened, long-term economic interest, to make a unique difference, and for the personal challenge. Civic entrepreneurs overcome barriers that stop other communities cold: too much government, too much business, a culture of blame, outside ownership of companies, and a legacy of poor process.

PART TWO: HOW CIVIC ENTREPRENEURS BUILD COMMUNITY

Chapter Three describes how civic entrepreneurs build economic community, introducing the eight roles of civic entrepreneurship. The chapter explains how these roles are played across four stages of community building—initiation, incubation, implementation, and improvement or renewal. At various stages of a community's development, civic entrepreneurs act as motivators, networkers, teachers, conveners, integrators, drivers, mentors, and agitators.

In *Chapter Four,* at the initiation stage, we show how civic entrepreneurs serve as motivators and networkers to organize their communities for action. They help communities accept responsibility for their future and make clear breaks with the past. They lend their personal credibility and networks to get collaborative efforts off the ground.

Chapter Five, at the incubation stage, shows civic entrepreneurs serving as teachers, helping their communities localize global challenges and opportunities and recognize interdependence. We also describe how and why they practice the politics of inclusion and safe-guard the integrity of the collaborative process.

Moving from strategy and consensus building to implementation is even harder for communities than it is for companies and other organizations. *Chapter Six* focuses on the hard work of implementation. It shows how civic entrepreneurs assemble the people and resources to get things done, how they drive for measurable results, and how they persist when the going gets tough.

In *Chapter Seven*, civic entrepreneurs confront the big question: How can regions sustain cross-sector collaboration over the long haul? The key is in continuously reaching out and pulling in new leaders. Some groups are experimenting with new types of intermediary organizations to sustain collaboration. All fight complacency daily, along with the danger of becoming ingrown or irrelevant. In the end, building economic community is a process of ongoing renewal.

Finally, in *Chapter Eight* we lay out an agenda for sparking civic entrepreneurship across America. The agenda includes roles for all of us—business people, public officials, economic development practitioners, foundation and nonprofit executives, the media, and ordinary citizens who want a better community.

We have learned from some phenomenal Americans, and we believe that their work in building economic community is our best hope for the future. We hope you enjoy and are inspired by their stories.

Palo Alto, California   Douglas Henton
March 1997   John Melville
                                          Kimberly Walesh

─── Acknowledgments

Like building community, this book has been a truly collaborative effort. We have been fortunate to be able to work with a group of leaders who come from all walks of life and all kinds of communities. They have taught us about civic entrepreneurship and how it works at the grassroots. While it is impossible to acknowledge everyone who has been part of the learning process, we would like to acknowledge a few people who have been a special inspiration to us over the years.

William F. Miller, professor at the Graduate School of Business at Stanford University, has been our intellectual partner for more than 15 years. As president of SRI International, where we first met him, and then as a leader in Smart Valley and Joint Venture: Silicon Valley Network, Bill taught us about the dynamic and mutually supportive relationship between technology, business, and society. We tested our ideas with Bill's business school classes and met monthly for more than a year to discuss our evolving book themes. Bill has been generous with his time and ideas and has served as a mentor to us all.

Jim and Becky Morgan, chairman and CEO of Applied Materials, Inc., and president/CEO of Joint Venture: Silicon Valley Network, respectively, have provided inspiration, encouragement, and support for our efforts over the years. Both are archetypal civic entrepreneurs who have given deeply of themselves for their community. Their style of leadership is what this book is all about and has served as an inspiration to many in Silicon Valley.

Several long-time collaborators around the country have provided invaluable assistance during the writing of this book. In particular, we would like to thank those who helped to organize the civic entrepreneur roundtables that provided a key source of insights for this book. Tom Keating of Florida and Mary Jo Waits of Arizona have been catalysts to help bring a new approach to economic development in their states. Susan Engelking of Austin and Dan Berry of Cleveland have worked tirelessly to build teams of civic entrepreneurs to help their communities succeed. All have contributed to our thinking over the years and made special efforts to help make our book a success.

We want to thank all of the civic entrepreneurs who were willing to share their experiences in this book. Their optimism and persistence have been an inspiration. Their stories give us hope that America can rebuild its communities. We appreciate their willingness to be so open about their experiences, sharing both the good and the bad. Our hope is that the sharing of lessons learned can provide the type of best practice information that leaders in other regions can use to move ahead.

We also want to thank Alan Shrader and Susan Williams of Jossey-Bass Publishers for providing us with helpful guidance in the development of this book and ensuring that we created a book that will be useful to others.

Finally, we appreciate the contributions of our colleagues at Collaborative Economics—Indrani Kowlessar, Brendan Rawson, and Frances Horonia. They have been essential members of our team, helping us with the research and managing a complex writing, review, and approval process for the manuscript. Thanks for all the long hours and your commitment to our shared vision.

D. H.

J. M.

K. W.

⸻ᴡᴡ⸻ The Authors

Douglas Henton, John Melville, and Kimberly Walesh are the founders and directors of Collaborative Economics. Based in California's Silicon Valley, Collaborative Economics helps public and private leadership groups develop and implement collaborative strategies for creating high-performing economic communities. Collaborative Economics has assisted leaders in more than thirty regions in the United States, Asia, and Europe.

Douglas Henton has more than twenty years experience in economic development at the national, regional, state, and local levels. Henton is nationally recognized for his work bringing industry, government, education, and community leaders together around specific collaborative projects to improve competitiveness. He has a bachelor's degree in political science and economics from Yale University and a master's degree in public policy from the University of California, Berkeley.

John Melville has expertise in human resource and education and training issues and strategies, especially their role in regional economic development. Melville has helped launch state and local education, training, and economic development strategies in diverse regions. He holds a bachelor's degree with honors in political science from Stanford University.

Kimberly Walesh is recognized for her expertise in industry engagement and participatory regional strategy. She has led successful processes to engage business leaders in developing and implementing regional economic strategies with their communities. Walesh holds a bachelor's degree in economics from Valparaiso University and a master's degree in public policy from Harvard University.

Prior to founding Collaborative Economics in 1993, Henton, Melville, and Walesh worked together at SRI International.

Collaborative Economics
350 Cambridge Avenue, Suite 200
Palo Alto, CA 94306
E-mail: info@coecon.com

Phone: (415) 614–0230
Fax: (415) 614–0240
http://www.coecon.com

Grassroots Leaders
for a New Economy

PART ONE

Community Leadership
for the Information Age

The combined forces of globalization, information technologies, changing demographics, and devolution are increasing the importance of collaboration at the community level. A new kind of leader, the "civic entrepreneur," has emerged to help communities respond to the fundamental transition from big business, big government, and action at the national level toward nimble, networked businesses collaborating with local communities to compete globally. Successful places have learned how to connect their clusters of economic specialization with responsive community competencies such as education, infrastructure, and quality of life. Part One describes this new economic community and the characteristics of the civic entrepreneurs who build them. It answers these questions: Where do civic entrepreneurs come from? Why do they do what they do? Why are they so important at this point in our nation's history?

CHAPTER ONE

Communities Meet the New Economy

When I became CEO of Applied Materials in 1976 to implement a corporate turnaround, the company fought with its customers, fought with its suppliers, and fought with itself. Today, we work as a team. Silicon Valley must transform in the same way.

—Jim Morgan, Chairman and CEO, Applied Materials, the world's largest semiconductor equipment company

We all live in communities, whether we notice them or not. Community surrounds us like water surrounds fish. As business people, we rely on the community for the talent, resources, and suppliers that we need to succeed. As citizens, we need community to provide the quality of life, the education, and the environment that keep us healthy and happy.

Yet new waves of forces are constantly transforming communities. Global competition, continuous industry restructuring, government cutbacks, and growing diversity are forces big and fundamental enough to knock people, companies, and communities off course. How do communities respond to the forces of change? How well do communities meet the ever-changing needs of its citizens and its businesses?

As American regions struggle to advance in a time of rapid change, they are experimenting with new ways for public, private, and community interests to advance together. The four communities that this book profiles—Austin, Texas, Cleveland, Ohio, Wichita, Kansas, and Silicon Valley, California—and the two states, Arizona and Florida, raise a lot of questions and provide some interesting answers.

• *Austin.* In the early 1980s, Austin was a sleepy college town and state capital, like many others. It was a quiet, low-cost place to live, study, work, or make policy. Within a decade, a team of business, university, and community leaders catapulted their branch plant economy into an internationally renowned technology powerhouse. Its performance statistics and team spirit would become the envy of communities worldwide. Visitors would ask, What happened there? Who made it happen? Why?

• *Cleveland.* A team of business and community leaders decided to stand and fight for Cleveland's future when the city went into fiscal default, its manufacturing economy was being decimated by global competition, and racial tension was high. Business leaders joined with local government and with the community to turn Cleveland into "The Comeback City." What did these leaders do? What makes Cleveland tick now? How will the region sustain its success?

• *Wichita.* Leaders from business and local government believed that Wichita could lessen its dependence on the ups and downs of the aircraft industry. They created a nationally recognized initiative that combined business, city, and county leaders to address the community's diversification, education, transportation, and downtown challenges. Despite remaining cyclicality, Wichita has consistently enjoyed unemployment rates below the national average. What is going on? Why did it happen? What can we learn from Wichita's decade of collaborative experience?

• *Silicon Valley.* The world's premier high-tech region found itself in midlife crisis in the early 1990s, plagued by a stagnant economy and a festering "culture of blame." Hundreds of people from high-tech and small businesses, education, labor, and government developed local solutions to pressing problems in education, regulation, and business retention. Why do these people contribute their time and resources to this regional effort? What have they learned?

• *Arizona.* Buzzards circling for prey were depicted on the cover gracing the *Barron's* issue about the real estate bust in the late 1980s, the savings and loan scandal, and the virtual collapse of the powerful Phoenix 40. While many longed for the good old days, a group of local entrepreneurs along with some established leaders saw new opportunity. They rallied people statewide around an entrepreneurial economy based on technology and talent rather than on the traditional cotton, citrus, copper, and construction. Why did Arizonans follow their leadership? How has it paid off?

• *Florida.* Leaders at the Florida Chamber of Commerce believed that Florida could have a high-value economy with high-paying jobs. Their state did not have to settle for the consistently declining standard of living that was accompanying population growth. They helped spark an effort to remake economic development at the state and community levels. New public-private institutions, new attitudes, and higher-quality growth are the result. Why did businesses get involved? What did they do? What have they learned for the future?

A COLLABORATIVE APPROACH FOR REGIONAL RESILIENCE

Diverse in geography and culture, as well as politics and economics, these regions share a common secret to their success: they are practicing a new, collaborative model for regional resilience led by a new type of civic leader. Although these communities represent some of the most interesting examples, they are not alone.

Communities across America are figuring out that world-class economies need world-class communities. They are experimenting with new types of public-private relationships and organizations to keep moving forward in a time of change. They are building a new type of community—an economic community. Economic communities are places with strong, responsive relationships between the economy and community that provide companies and communities with sustained advantage and resiliency. Economic communities integrate the economy (the world of work) and the community (the world of living). These communities have learned that the secret of successful regions is effective collaboration among business, government, education, and community leaders in addressing new challenges and opportunities.

In contrast with other communities, economic communities take responsibility for their future. They are marshaling their resources, leveraging their assets, and embracing change. They are not trying to turn back the clock to a simpler, more certain time. They are not waiting for Washington, D.C., to bail them out. In fact, they are not turning to government at any level for the answer.

Rather, a new kind of leader is emerging to help American regions become strong economic communities. The civic entrepreneur is the catalyst for building economic community. Civic entrepreneurs build relationships between the economy and the community. They provide the leadership that brings people and institutions together across sectors and jurisdictions to work on the long-term development of their region. In some cases, this work means solving complex problems. In others, it means being the first to see and seize opportunities. Civic entrepreneurs often come from business, but they can come from government, education, or other sectors. They contribute their time, experience, and personal networks to help their regions collaborate to compete in the global economy.

This new model is regional and collaborative, and it depends on a new kind of leader. It contrasts with the established perspective that is more national and adversarial and driven by political leaders or special interests. What has changed to cause the new model to take shape?

FORCES SHAPING
ECONOMIC COMMUNITY

The confluence of four forces in the last two decades of the twentieth century is increasing the importance of economic community and sparking civic entrepreneurship. Fundamental economic, technological, demographic, and political shifts push collaboration at the regional level to the center of a new paradigm.

A "New Globalism" finds companies searching worldwide for the best regional habitats for value-adding activities and creates unparalleled opportunities for subnational regions to participate in growing global industries. Information technologies decentralize organizations and decision making of all types, which stimulates horizontal networking among companies in regions. Political devolution shifts authority to local levels of government and also transfers responsibility from government to individuals, families, and other organizations in communities. Changing demographics move baby boomers to decision-making positions, as increasing diversity creates pressure and opportunity to open up community power structures.

Together, these forces are decentralizing economic leadership from countries and states to regions and communities. Together, these forces create the need for new collaborative relationships at the regional level between the economy and community. Where we once talked of a competitive advantage of nations, leading economic communities now speak of the collaborative advantage of regions.

Not since the end of the nineteenth century have economic, technological, demographic, and political shifts set in motion the development of a such a new worldview. The shift will be fundamental—from the centralized, vertically integrated model of business and government dominant in the New Deal and the Cold War eras toward a more decentralized, horizontal, and networked regional model. Although the nation and states will always have key support roles, as the millennium approaches, forces of change are making regions and their leaders the loci of action. Economic communities are figuring out how to thrive in a world shaped by these four forces (Figure 1.1).

NEW GLOBALISM: CREATING HABITAT FOR HIGH-VALUE BUSINESSES AND INDUSTRIES

Jim Morgan of Applied Materials knew firsthand that the global economy was changing his company and Silicon Valley. Even before global

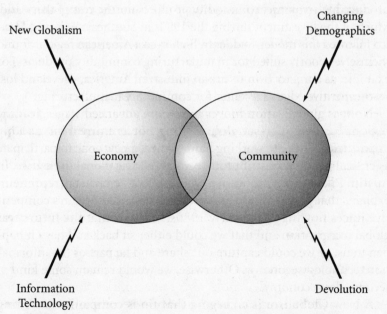

Figure 1.1. New Environment for Economic Community.

competition flattened the U.S. semiconductor business in the mid-1980s, Jim took his semiconductor equipment business into Asia to try to crack the Japanese market. His experience in Asia taught him that technology companies have to collaborate and that they have to be both global and local at the same time, that is, serving global markets but being connected to every region where they operate.

Global competition, global markets, global resources—America's regions have wrestled with the ultimate implications of globalization since the first serious challenge to the dominance of the Midwest's automotive and steel industries in the early 1980s. Regions have watched as globalization played itself out in step form: first, the integration of the world financial systems; next, the breaking down of trade barriers—the surge of high-quality foreign imports and the struggle to sell homemade products overseas; then, the expansion (or outright movement) of U.S. plants overseas and investment by foreign-controlled operations in American regions.

As William F. Miller of the Graduate School of Business at Stanford University has observed, the traditional Old Globalism paradigm was based on the search for low-factor costs (Miller, 1996). In their initial forays into international business, companies searched worldwide for regions with low-cost land and labor to serve as export platforms to produce high-volume, commodity products for the rest of the world. Much of the investment during the 1980s in Southeast Asia and Mexico followed this model. Suddenly, higher-cost American regions found themselves poorly suited for manufacturing commodity products. For example, as a microcosm of urban industrial America, Cleveland lost its competitive edge as a center for commodity manufacturing.

Now, as globalization moves into more advanced stages, leading regions have come to see globalization not as a threat but as a big opportunity. They are working hard to meet a new goal: to participate as critical regional contributors to value-adding global industries. In Austin, Pike Powers, an attorney and effective civic entrepreneur, explains that global opportunity was what started Austin's competitive juices flowing in the early 1980s. "We saw that the future was global competition and that we could either sit back and have it happen to us, or we could capture our share and be part of the information technology economy. Otherwise, we would remain some kind of second-class economy."

A New Globalism is emerging that finds companies searching worldwide for the best locations to host high-value, specialized, and innovation-related activities (Miller, 1996). Under this model, corporations invest in regions to gain access to specialized workforces, research and commercialization capacity, innovation networks, and unique business infrastructure. The focus is not just on low cost. Jack Welch, chairman of General Electric, described the way successful businesses will operate tomorrow. "The winners in these global games will be those who can put together the world's best in design, manufacturing, research, execution, and marketing on the largest scale. Rarely are all of these elements located in one country, or even on one continent" (Welch, 1987, p. 10).

Once companies invest, the goal increasingly is integration into the regional milieu. Under the Old Globalism, companies were footloose, often fleeing once they discovered a lower-cost location. Now, the recognition is increasing that healthy local roots are necessary to sustain global reach. Key drivers are access to local markets, workforce, technology, and suppliers. Lewis Platt, CEO of Hewlett-Packard, explains what global companies have to do to be successful in the regions where they do business. "To succeed globally, companies must be recognized as an asset to the local economy by providing good jobs, exporting, adding value to the community and above all, keeping promises. When you are seen as a local company you will enjoy a spurt in growth" ("Going for Growth in Global Markets," November 8, 1995, Global Breakfast Series). Increasingly, business strategy links global success to strong roots in multiple local habitats.

What is the implication of the New Globalism for economic community? Regions, even small ones, have the opportunity to participate in exciting global industries and host world-class companies. Explains Jim Morgan of Applied Materials, "We are entering an era driven by dramatic changes in information technology. The rapid mobility of people, capital, and knowledge have changed the world of business. This means that any region in the world is capable of participating in opportunities that are provided by the new rules of world commerce."

Regions participate in the New Globalism by creating specialized habitats that can grow high-value business. The goal is to be able to contribute something unique and different to global industries. From a company's viewpoint, it is easy to envision a worldwide network of regions, each playing a different role in the value chain. Some regions will position themselves as R&D wellsprings, others as high-value, quick turnaround manufacturing centers for a particular industry or collection of industries. With a lot of hard work, Cleveland, for example, has come back as a world-class center for advanced precision manufacturing. Some regions will leverage their geographic position or entrepreneurial bent. Still others will be conduits for information flows, goods and services flows, or financial flows. Just as successful companies develop and sustain core competencies, regions develop niches where they can sustain competitive advantage by investing in talent, technology, and specialized infrastructure. Often, this development means cultivating clusters of businesses in related fields as part of the region's milieu. At the same time, regions must offer a quality of life that will attract and retain knowledge workers essential to high-value activities.

William F. Miller explains this approach to fostering regional habitats: "What works? What is effective are 'people and places' policies. What does not diffuse away quickly are infrastructure and workforce. Although a few key people may be mobile, large numbers of the workforce are not mobile. Policies that support the education and training of the workforce, that support research combined with education, that support a modern infrastructure, and support the development of institutions that facilitate collaboration between business, government, and the independent sector will have lasting effects of building capacity that does not diffuse away. Develop the people and places—the habitat for living and working" (Miller, 1996, p. 15). Typically, these habitats span myriad political jurisdictions.

It is becoming common wisdom that globalization promotes regionalization. What is yet unclear is how well American regions will ultimately respond to their new role. American communities will either recognize and capture global opportunities or be cowed by global threats. Those that are succeeding place a premium on working across business, government, education, and community to position the economic region as a global contributor. Globalization is the first of four key factors driving the creation of such economic communities.

INFORMATION TECHNOLOGY: RISE OF THE NETWORKED ECONOMY

Lee Cooke, the former Texas Instruments executive who became president of the Austin Chamber and later mayor, understood the power of information technologies to change the economy and society. He saw a future for Austin in the center of the information revolution. What he learned was that the new economy is a fast-paced and relationship-based economy. To become a leader in information technology, Austin defined a new standard in networking a community and in preparing to participate in the information age.

The digital revolution is continuously creating new, empowering tools for business, government, and the community. Coming in waves, information technologies first gave us access to computing power, then connected computing and communications, and now are providing us with interactive multimedia. So far, the effect of these tools has been to flatten organizations, decentralize decision making, proliferate smaller players, and stimulate networking among organizations in regions. Although we do not yet know where the new information technologies will lead us, we know that the implications for economies and communities will be profound. What is clear is that the information revolution has a decentralizing power that make regions—and relationships that link players within a region—more and more important.

Birthed to propel the industrial age, the vertically integrated, centrally controlled organization is radically transforming into more focused, decentralized, nimble business units. Just as mainframe computers gave way to networked computing, centralized decision making is now giving way to more decentralized decision making, removed from the command of headquarters. This change is driven by the competitive need to be faster, better, and closer to customers and is enabled by information technologies. The result is companies and people operating in many different places under a corporate or team umbrella—people with more autonomy than ever before.

As big companies decentralize, the digital revolution also proliferates small company competitors and potential collaborators. As Don Tapscott explains in *The Digital Economy* (1996, p. 55), "The new technology networks enable small companies to overcome the main advantages of large companies—economies of scale and access to resources. At the same time, these smaller companies are not burdened with the main disadvantages of large firms—deadening bureaucracy, stifling hierarchy and the inability to change." These kinds of companies are growing in communities across America.

To remain competitive in fast-paced, high-value markets requires quality, speed, and innovation. Companies of all sizes are specializing in what they do best and contracting out or managing relationships to handle the rest. Companies focus on their core competencies and then look outside their corporate walls for the relationships and resources to help them compete. Silicon Graphics's Ed McCracken explains, "We are very focused. Everything we do, we have to do world class, so we can't do everything. We have to cooperate, to subcontract, to have partnerships with other companies that are world class. There is a business interconnection that is much more part of today's environment than twenty years ago." Traditional patterns of vertical integration to achieve economies of scale are giving way to new horizontal networks and alliances designed to achieve economies of scope.

The duo of decentralization and specialization is giving rise to the networked economy. The shift is from the individual firm as the business unit to networks of firms and other support players. Concentrations of people, companies, and organizations in a supportive habitat are creating wealth together. David Friedman, a research fellow in the MIT Japan program, describes the networked economy as "densely packed concentrations of entrepreneurs and companies in urbanized areas that generate virtually all the nation's globally competitive, high-wage industries. These highly specialized companies flourish because they can rapidly team up to manufacture products for world markets" (1996, p. 62).

Electronic networking happens on a global scale, and companies certainly have relationships with others throughout the world. Yet the networked business model achieves its propulsive power in the context of a particular geographic region. Geographic closeness accelerates time to market by reducing transaction costs, that is, the costs of finding the skilled worker, developing the specialized supplier, finding the right partner, or learning about a new technology. In her 1994 book, *Regional Advantage,* AnnaLee Saxenian of the University of California, Berkeley, documents the networked model as an unrecognized key to Silicon Valley's ongoing success. "By focusing on what they did best and purchasing the remainder from specialist suppliers, they (new generation of Valley firms) created a network system that spread the cost of developing new technologies, reduced product-development times and fostered reciprocal innovation" (1994, p. 141). Ed McCracken agrees. "Partnerships are much more effective if they are next door." As industries of all types, from semiconductors and software to apparel and wood products, become more dependent on speed, innovation, quality, and information, the more open, horizontal, relationship-based business model is proliferating.

Globalization finds companies and industries searching the world for distinct, value-adding habitats. The information age is spawning a new business model based on decentralization and specialization in regions. Together, both forces point to regions as centers of action and opportunity. The challenge for regions is to create habitats where fast-moving, innovation-based, networked companies can flourish.

CHANGING DEMOGRAPHICS: DISPERSING COMMUNITY POWER

Alan Hald, the cofounder of MicroAge, Inc., knew that a new kind of leadership was necessary to move Arizona into the twenty-first century. The Phoenix 40—the old club of developers and financiers—had come to the end of its era by the late 1980s. The real estate and savings and loan debacle decimated the ranks of the old leadership. Alan and his fellow baby boomers knew that the time had come for a leadership shift.

In communities across America, the locus of leadership is shifting from the hands of primarily male, primarily white, leaders of the World War II era to the hands of the much more diverse baby boomers. Every community in America can point to a small group of influential businessmen and politicians (the good old boys) who made the decisions and deals that shaped their communities. They worked wisely and sometimes selflessly to advance what they perceived to be the best interests of the community. Many left considerable legacies.

Along the way, a new generation started coming of age in a world that looked quite different, and they started operating quite differently. Many have had to learn to operate in ever-changing network relationships as opposed to a stable, hierarchical world. In this new world, women and minorities became active in business and community affairs. In this world, a host of new interests and organizations developed mature voices and influence. In many communities in the 1980s, these worlds existed in parallel. The good old boys retained a modicum of power and influence, yet their traditional, unilateral style prevented them from dealing with the complexity of the new problems and players. New power groups flexed their muscle and learned how to stop things, but they lacked the ability to advance the community forward.

David Chrislip and Carl Larson in their book *Collaborative Leadership* articulate this dilemma. "From one perspective, the dispersion of power caused by the empowerment of disenfranchised groups enhances democracy: more people affected by public policy decisions have a say in the outcome. But it also makes leadership more difficult. For one thing, there is, in communities, no prevailing hierarchy. There is no center to appeal to; no one group or organization has the authority to override other interests and act unilaterally. Yet there are many empowered interests that can say no. The result in many places is public policy 'gridlock' and an unfilled need for leadership that can act effectively in the broad interest of the community" (1994, p. 21).

In some communities, boomers have emerged to fill this void with a new, more collaborative style of leadership. From business, politics, education, and community, new leaders are starting to fill the void left by the waning of the old order, often by joining the best of the new with the best of the old. Sometimes, they are aided by traditional leaders who have learned new tricks. In Arizona, the alliance of up-and-coming technology entrepreneurs stepped forward after the final collapse of the Phoenix 40. They were guided by the head of the utility who finally found himself among the youngest of the old guard. What sets these new leaders apart from the previous generation is their value of inclusion as the means to action. They deliberately open up circles of influence to new people and new ideas. Whereas their fathers' focus was on unilaterally advancing their idea, these collaborative leaders manage consensus-building processes. Their position in the community stems from their ability to build trust and coalesce participation among a broad cross-section of peers rather than to impose hierarchical authority or heavy-handed power.

Al Ratner of Cleveland explains this shift. "There was a time in this community when four people could decide to do something big, and then just do it. This was also the time when systems were closed and when prejudice along racial, religious, or socioeconomic lines was very strong. Only when the system was opened up could we see opportunities and move forward." Cleveland and other communities warn that generational change can lead to a new-faces version of the good old boys unless community processes continually integrate new people and their ideas.

In some communities, increasing in-migration of new people adds to the transitional leadership challenge. One-third of residents have lived in Austin for less than five years. In Orlando, the share is 50 percent. In Silicon Valley, another relatively new community, the challenge is not to send the old boys packing but to create a broad cross-section of first-generation entrepreneurs in the civic arena. Explains Ed McCracken, "Silicon Valley has been a first-generation community, continuously. What we are trying to do is draft quickly a broader sense of community and shared values on the people that are first-generation in an area, that don't have roots and traditions. I think Silicon Valley is an example of how all communities will be eventually, with the most talented people moving around more often."

Communities can view shifting demographics, like globalization and information technologies, as a problem or an opportunity. What is inevitable is that demographic shifts will place a premium on collaboration and new leadership at the level of economic community. Those communities that can tap diverse talents and unleash a new generation of leaders will have a leg up.

Political Devolution: Taking Responsibility for Communities

"For Cleveland to survive, it had to become less dependent on Washington and more dependent on its own resources." Mayor George Voinovich explained his community's message of self-reliance for the 1987 Conference of the Council on Urban Economic Development. Voinovich and Cleveland's business leaders understood early in the 1980s that the era of federal support for cities would be over by the 1990s. Faced with the challenge of rebuilding their city using local resources, they pursued an aggressive model of public-private partnership in which Cleveland's public and private interests became joined.

When President Clinton declared in his 1996 State of the Union address that the era of big government was over, he was acknowledging a fact that most of America had recognized for many years. Public skepticism of the federal government's ability to solve our problems (a belief that prevailed from the New Deal through the Great Society) has never been higher. Although the Clinton administration has championed "reinventing government" to improve how the public sector does its business, the Republican Congress has sought to dismantle functions of the federal government. A fundamental rethinking of the role of government in our lives is sparking downsizing of government bureaucracy, privatization of public services, and budget cutting. The current wave of devolution raises the question: Who will take responsibility for dealing with the challenges that the federal government will no longer address?

Devolution will mean two things to America's regions. First, government will decentralize, shifting authority down to state and local levels of government. Second, governments at all levels will exit some arenas entirely, shifting responsibility to individuals, families, and other organizations. In both cases, the force of devolution clearly increases the importance of economic communities.

As David Osborne and Ted Gaebler point out in *Reinventing Government* (1992), this is not the first time that we have remodeled our governments to reflect changes in economy and society. "We last 'reinvented' our governments during the early decades of the twentieth century, roughly from 1900 through 1940. We did so, during the Progressive Era and New Deal, to cope with the emergence of a new industrial economy. . . . Today the world of government is once again in great flux. The emergence of a postindustrial, knowledge-based global economy has undermined old realities throughout the world. . . . Governments . . . have begun to respond" (p. xvi). Decentralization of government mirrors the decentralization of the new economy. Just as information technologies and global competition have flattened hierarchies in the corporate world and forced businesses to become more flexible and productive, government is adopting a more nimble, focused organization model as well. The hope is that more decentralized government institutions will deliver more limited but responsive services that keep pace with changing local needs.

The federal government may no longer be in a position to make major investments in regional infrastructure or industries. Silicon Valley lost thirty thousand jobs permanently to federal defense cutbacks. In the 1980s, Cleveland (one of the first cities to come to terms with this new federalism) lost millions in federal funds.

As the public sector decentralizes and shrinks and the private sector goes global, a major challenge for communities becomes managing the space in between—the civil society. The civil society (or the civil sector) is the arena of voluntary associations and networks that stands between the world of markets and business and the domain of government and politics. In this arena, voluntary relationships benefiting the long-term shared interests of business, government, and other community sectors can form. Consensus is growing that civil society is the next frontier, as Americans attempt to deal with continuous refocusing of their private and public sectors. It is to this arena, where multiple sectors can work together, that communities will increasingly turn.

This resurgence of interest stems not just from the third sector's ability to serve traditional social needs as government backs away but from its potential to serve as a critical intermediary linking long-term interests in a complex and fast-changing society. Out of necessity, Americans are creating new institutions to help people and communities adapt to a changed and changing world. These institutions help address challenges that cut across multiple sectors and communities (Dodge, 1996). Many are experimental in nature. John C. Anderson is the president and CEO of Enterprise Florida, a new privately led and publicly supported organization that replaced Florida's traditional, state Department of Commerce. Anderson observes, "Part of what we have going on is a very broad-based experiment in this country that will end up being evolutionary. We are modifying or creating new institutions that bring the public and private leaders together to deal with challenges and needs that our historic institutions, and ways of looking at things, just simply couldn't get done. Necessity truly is the mother of invention."

Peter Drucker, a long-time observer of economic trends, ties the importance of the third sector to the rise of the knowledge worker. He posits the development of the third sector as the major challenge for the twenty-first century. The knowledge society holds open the promise of heightened human satisfaction and achievement but requires a new third sector to achieve it. Drucker writes, "The knowledge society has to be a society of *three sectors*: a public sector, that is, government; a private sector, that is, business; and a social sector . . . it is in and through the social sector that a modern developed society can again create responsible and achieving citizenship, can again give individuals (and especially knowledge people) a sphere in which they can make a difference in society, and a sphere in which they re-create community." (Drucker, 1995, p. 258–259). Building this civil sector is the responsibility of both business and government leadership.

New thinking about the importance of the civil sector is coming from the right, as well as the left, of the political spectrum. Thinkers on both sides stress that civil society is not a replacement for government. They point out that the civil sector gets its identity precisely from standing between business and government. It absolutely depends on the unique strengths of both sectors; and often helps communities compensate for each sector's inherent weakness. William Eggers and John O'Leary, advocates of privatization at the Reason Foundation and authors of *Revolution at the Roots* (1995), are among a series of thinkers emphasizing the complementarity between business, government, and the civil sector. "According to popular mythology, Democrats are pro-government, Republicans pro-business. These alternatives are less than totally satisfying. The government is institutional, bureaucratic and predicated on the coercive power of the state. The free market is money-based, commercial and predicated on the interest of consumers and producers. . . . The false dichotomy of government and business ignores a crucial realm of human activity. This third pillar of society encompasses relationships that are voluntary but not for commercial gain such as associations and community groups. Variously referred to as 'mediating institutions,' 'civil society' or 'community' by addressing human concerns that cannot be satisfied either by government or business, this sphere enriches our lives not as consumers but as human beings" (p. 59). A mediating sector must have strong components to mediate.

On the opposite end of the political spectrum, Jeremy Rifkin, liberal social activist, also writes about the complementarity of the three sectors. "While politicians traditionally divide the United States into a polar spectrum running from the marketplace on one end, to government, on the other, it is more accurate to think of society as a three-legged stool made up of the market sector, the government sector, and the civil sector. The first leg creates market capital, the second leg creates public capital, and the third leg creates social capital" (Rifkin, 1995, p. 294). Although consensus is building on the need to revisit America's civil sector, the key question remains, What must its character and contribution be? America, with its long-standing tradition of community initiative, is poised to add to its traditional notion of the third sector—social services, arts and culture, philanthropy—some powerful new forums through which public, private, and individual actors can work together to build vital economies and communities.

Devolution will continue to push responsibility and accountability down to communities. This push is launching state and local government into an era of continuous restructuring and innovation—to date, largely the realm of the private sector. The result will be a government and social structure that more closely mirrors decentralizing business structures. Devolution heightens the need to build economic communities—places marked by strong collaborative relationships between economy and community that play themselves out through an active civil sector.

FORCES FLUX; NEW LEADERS EMERGE

Dramatic, related shifts in all four arenas—economics, technology, demographics, and government—are shaping a fundamentally different kind of environment from the one that dominated America during much of the twentieth century. A global economy rooted in regions worldwide is superseding a national economy dominated by national industries. Industrial technology and vertically integrated mass production are giving way to information technology and specialized production networks. World War II leaders struggle to remain relevant to boomers and increasingly diverse up-and-comers. And devolution tears at the big national government of the past and calls for renewed initiative at the community level. America is in the middle of a major transition.

This incidence is not the first time, however, that economic, technological, demographic, and political forces fluxed simultaneously. Periodically in American history, all four arenas change abruptly, and a new kind of leader emerges to move people and organizations toward their next plateau.

Industrial Revolution Produces the Philanthropist

A number of observers, including H. W. Brands (1995), have noted striking similarities between the 1990s and the 1890s, a decade of wrenching societal change as the economy and technology transitioned from an agrarian to an industrial base. Life in the nineteenth-century agrarian village—isolated, autonomous, self-sufficient—changed forever with the advent of mass production. In the agrarian village, the economy and the community were the same. The Jeffersonian view that the government that governs least governs best dominated. Families took care of themselves, augmented by voluntary associations and community self-government. Then, the birth of the mass-production industrial job sparked political and demographic responses that changed this way of life forever.

Industrial power, consolidated in the hands of large national corporations, built a national economy on the twin foundations of railroads and steel. Small-scale agricultural technologies gave way to manufacturing businesses, ever increasing in size and scope. Cities grew, as farmers left the land and immigrants flocked to America. Fear, anxiety, and backlash against rapid industrialization juxtaposed with promise for increased prosperity and a better life.

Out of this flux, a new kind of community and a new kind of leader emerged. The larger-than-life men who built the rails and factories also built communities. Carnegie, Rockefeller, Stanford, Crocker, Ford,

Morgan, DuPont—each invested his wealth to build new institutions. Libraries, universities, foundations, and civic centers helped people develop to a higher potential and transformed regional centers into great American cities.

Industrial Concentration Produces New Government Leaders

In response to the growing concentration of wealth came the Progressive Movement and a strong national government more appropriate for the new industrial economy. In 1909, Herbert Croly wrote *The Promise of American Life,* which reflected a new and increasingly popular public philosophy. Croly argued that the Jeffersonian civic tradition of dispersed governmental power had become a hindrance. Given the "increasing concentration of American industrial, political and social life," American government "demands more rather than less centralization" (Croly, [1909] 1965, pp. 272–275). Croly argued in favor of creating an active national government to tame the forces of the new industrial economy. In a masterful new formulation, he argued that Progressives should "pursue Jeffersonian ends using Hamiltonian means." What he meant was that traditional democratic goals of freedom and equality could be promoted by a strong and active government appropriate for the new economy. Although limited government may have been right for the agrarian era, big government was now necessary to counter the big business of the industrial age.

By the 1930s, the new paradigm emphasizing national economy and national government was firmly in place. Although Theodore Roosevelt adopted the new model in his New Nationalism, it reached full expression in Franklin Roosevelt's New Deal. From national industrial planning to trust busting, the Roosevelt government increasingly expanded its role in dealing with economic and social issues. Charismatic elected leaders like Fiorello La Guardia and Huey Long emerged as community builders or as populists fighting against concentrations of industrial power. The significance of the New Deal response was the understanding that big government was necessary to battle with big business, often in support of big labor. Under the new model of interest-group pluralism, large advocacy organizations acted as antagonistic forces in the forging of national policy. The overall effect was to amass action, power, and decision making in Washington.

"Wars" Lead to the Rise of the Technocrat

To activate this new model, a new kind of leader emerged in government and in business: the technocrat. Professional, well-trained managers of massive mobilizations won World War II and extended the reach of national government into the Cold War era and through the War on Poverty and the Vietnam War. In the private sector, new professional managers mobilized the "war" to invade and conquer global markets with mass-produced American products in the ashes of World War II.

Only professionally trained experts could analyze complex information, make decisions, and structure behemoth organizations. Dwight Eisenhower, Robert McNamara, the Harvard Business School class of 1949—all these leaders reflected the belief that professional expertise operating on a massive scale could take America into the future. The ultimate expression of this belief is John Kenneth Galbraith's *New Industrial State* (1967), where he declares the era of the entrepreneur as over and extols the leadership of business and government by the "technostructure."

The rise of the national economy dominated by vast corporations and checked by big government diminished the autonomy of local communities and undermined citizen initiative. As we approach the twenty-first century and look back, we see historians, philosophers, and politicians alike arguing this view persuasively. (Interestingly, this effect was anticipated by a core of dissenting thinkers at the turn of the twentieth century; chief among them was John Dewey [Ryan, 1995].) There was little room for civic initiative in a world where communities looked to national government to solve national problems and where informed deliberation was the domain of expert brain trusts. In fact, the best and the brightest of the 1960s saw local communities and ordinary citizens as provincial and backward at best and, at worst, parochial and bigoted. With the focus on scale, experts, and national primacy, for many people *community* became synonymous with *nation*.

New Forces Give Rise to the Civic Entrepreneur

Harvard scholar Michael Sandel argues in *Democracy's Discontent* (1996) that our increasing sense of losing control of the forces that govern our lives stems from the atrophy of our civic skills and the intermediary institutions of civil society as power centralized during the postwar period. We have shifted to a world of accelerating, never-ending change without the mechanisms for people to work together to deliberate about the changed environment and determine their collective fate.

Signs are everywhere that the old model, which focused on massification, experts, and business-government antagonism, simply does not work for the new environment. The answer is not replacement of Washington policies, programs, and institutions with new ones. Nor is it the wholesale dismantling of government and nation and returning to the agrarian village.

Rather, the answer will come from the "early adopter" communities across America that by necessity are shaping an entirely new business-government-community model for the future. Out of their experimentation and success will emerge the new model for the twenty-first century. What has become clear is that the changed environment creates a fundamentally different kind of relationship between regional economies and communities, and it requires fundamentally new leadership.

History has demonstrated that times of flux produce a new kind of leader. The requirement now is for leaders who can inspire and empower people to solve problems and take advantage of opportunities at the community level. The task is no less than to rebuild civil society (the institutions and the skill sets) from the bottom up. Joining the ranks of industrialist philanthropist, charismatic elected official, and technocrat as the leaders of their time will be the civic entrepreneur. The contrast between these leaders' creation and the model of antagonistic big business, big government, and big Washington-focused interest groups will be stark.

THREE FEATURES OF ECONOMIC COMMUNITY

We call these emerging communities *economic communities.* Economic communities are places with strong, responsive relationships between the economy and community that provide companies and communities with sustained advantage and resiliency. They are marked by mediating people and organizations that help interests come together to deal constructively with forces of change. We believe that communities that transform in this way will be where the action is. How do you know an economic community when you see one? Economic communities have three basic features (Figure 1.2):

- *Engaged clusters of specialization:* Concentrations of firms that create wealth in regions through export and are engaged by their communities to meet mutual needs
- *Connected community competencies:* The community assets and processes that create the foundations for competitive clusters and sustain a high quality of life
- *Civic entrepreneurs linking economy and community:* Leaders that connect economic clusters and community competencies to promote economic vitality and community quality of life

In economic communities, success is the product of continuous collaboration across the traditional domains of economy and community. Businesses rely on the community's assets—specialized suppliers, skilled workers, information networks, responsive government—for their competitive advantage. The community relies on businesses to invest in people and infrastructure and share responsibility for solving regional problems. Relationships forge links for continuous improvement. And civic entrepreneurs nurture these relationships.

Engaged Clusters of Specialization

"We have learned in Florida that regions, not states as a whole, compete globally. You have to allow local communities to compete on their

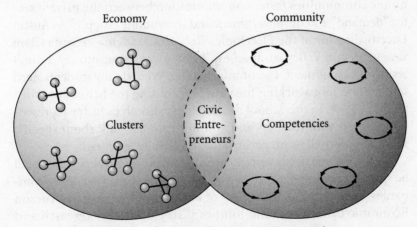

Figure 1.2.   Features of Economic Community.

own strengths. For example, we didn't realize we had a laser-electro optics cluster until we studied the economy. Now we think differently about our opportunities" (Mayor Glenda Hood, Orlando).

With the rise of the networked economy has come renewed interest in the clustering phenomenon. A networked economy is likely to have several clusters of specialization. Industry clusters are concentrations of competing, complementary, and interdependent firms and industries that create wealth in regions through export. Clusters are important for regions because they drive the vitality of support and local-serving industries. Economists from Marshall (1890) to Porter (1990) and Krugman (1991) point to several benefits to companies from participating in industry clusters:

- *Access to specialized workforce:* Companies in clusters can draw on large markets of people with specialized skills and experience working for related firms.

- *Access to specialized suppliers:* Companies in clusters have access to concentrations of specialized suppliers of inputs and services.

- *Access to networks:* Companies in clusters have access to information flows and technological spillovers that speed innovation.

A region with industry clusters can be a distinctive habitat because of the quality of its specialized resources and the ease by which those resources can be obtained.

The distinguishing feature of economic communities is not just that they have clusters but that they have mechanisms to engage their clusters and understand what they need from the community. Economic communities foster communication between the private sector "demand" and the government and community "supply." As Austin Lucero, director of the Electronics/Robotics Academy in Santa Clara says to Silicon Valley companies, "I don't want your money. I don't want your equipment. I want information. What do my students need to get good jobs working for you?" ("Building the School to Work Bridge,"1996). In this school district, every month industry representatives meet with teachers and administrators to talk about specific skills goals as well as preparing kids for lifelong learning.

Some of these needs will be common across all clusters; others will be specific to a single cluster. In Tucson, small and growing optics companies work with the University of Arizona and the Greater Tucson Economic Council to fund joint industry-university research and endow professorships for optics programs. Organized as the Arizona Optics Initiative, the cluster provides banks with technical help to improve their understanding of optics companies. Companies work with local K–12 and community college schools to prepare a pool of skilled optics technicians.

In economic communities, companies actively engage in articulating their needs and working with the community to meet them. In many communities, the opposite occurs. Community competencies tend to be dominated by supply-side rather than demand-side considerations. Governments and educators create programs to provide a service to business without a clear understanding of industry needs. Networks of providers talk mainly among themselves. Programs grow over time, becoming further and further removed from industry demand, creating costly bureaucracies that seek to perpetuate themselves. Or, communities take steps unintentionally that are detrimental to the industry clusters of their regions because of a lack of communication.

Economic communities view clusters as important customers. Just as companies increasingly ask customers to participate in interactive product development processes, so economic communities expect companies to engage in articulating and helping to meet their support needs. Explains Jim Morgan, "It's a process of discovering the need for a whole collection of core capabilities that a community comes together to build and continuously renew. Particularly in a high-cost region, only through this process of building shared capabilities together will existing industries be strengthened, new companies created, and new businesses attracted." In economic communities industry both benefits from and contributes to community competencies.

Connected Community Competencies

"A major area of conflict in Wichita was the educational process. Two teachers unions, diverse business and community leaders, a superintendent—all trying to determine whether a new look at schools was necessary. In forming BEST (Business Education Success Team), we had a leader who could 'walk between those raindrops' and bring everyone together. We signed a manifesto committing us all to educational reform. Not everyone was at peace; we had tensions. In most communities, there had been a distance between teachers and business. In this community, we broke down the walls" (Lionel Alford, former senior vice president, Boeing).

Economic communities understand the shift in thinking necessary to support a globally competitive, knowledge-based economy. The game used to be to provide a low-cost environment, including cheap and abundant labor. This effort made sense when the goal was a natural-resource-based or commodity manufacturing economy. Now, to foster the kind of economic activity that will sustain higher standards of living, communities need to create an environment that fosters speed, relationships, innovation, productivity, and global linkages, all while managing costs. It is not just a matter of eliminating the negatives but of cultivating the value-adding positives.

Economic communities develop a set of community competencies that are responsive to business needs. Every community has a core set of processes that, for better or worse, affect its economy. Some of these processes are driven primarily by government, such as K–12 education, whereas others, such as business financing, are driven primarily by the private sector. In economic communities, these processes are "attractors" because they are well linked to economic networks.

Some key community processes for the new economy are as follows:

- *Workforce education:* basic K–12 preparation, advanced preparation, renewal and retraining
- *Technology innovation:* research, information flows, technology dissemination
- *Business creation:* early-stage financing, entrepreneur support, culture and attitudes
- *Global trade:* specialized facilities and intermediary organizations, international networks, diversity
- *Physical infrastructure and planning:* transportation infrastructure, advanced communications, facilities development, housing
- *Regulation and taxation:* time-sensitive regulation, balance between taxation costs and value delivered
- *Quality of life:* recreation, culture, downtowns, neighborhoods

To date, the implicit assumption in the doing of economic development and in the writing about it has been that success comes from combining a familiar list of high-tech ingredients. AnnaLee Saxenian of the University of California, Berkeley, notes, "The secret, this thinking goes, is to combine a familiar list of resources: a research university, an industrial park, venture capital, public support for new technologies, and a desirable social environment. The assumption is that once these prerequisites are assembled, innovation and economic success will follow" (Saxenian, 1988, p. 67).

Economic communities, however, have discovered that how they use what they have is more important than just what they have. "Creating a dynamic high-tech region is not a matter of combining ingredients. It is one of building institutions and relationships—both locally and nationally—that support the development of innovative enterprises. . . . It is these relationships between the individuals, firms, institutions in the region that matter—not their simple presence" (1988, pp. 74–75). The important part is not just the ingredients; the important part is the recipe for how the ingredients fit together. Economic communities have responsive processes that leverage their assets to serve the economy.

Universities, for example, are often upheld as important for regional development. Yet the presence of a university does not guarantee an innovative economy nearby. Robert E. Leak, former president of the Research Triangle Foundation, explains, "It is not just the existence of advanced degree-granting institutions" that attracts high-tech firms. Rather, companies are impressed by "colleges and universities that express a willingness to provide an extra level of services to the industry—services such as making adjunct professorships available to the company's technical people—and a willingness to provide specially designed course work and library services to the industry's personnel" (Cummings, 1995, p. 115).

Cleveland and Austin provide rich examples of universities playing key roles in their region's education and innovation processes. In 1986, Cleveland Tomorrow began working with Cleveland State University and Case Western Reserve, both of which had strong engineering programs, to tailor these programs to the needs of the emerging advanced manufacturing economy. The result was the highly successful Cleveland Advanced Manufacturing Program, which became a model for the state and country. The University of Texas at Austin is one of the best examples of a world-class university that has shaped key competencies around the direction of the regional economy. Locally funded endowed chairs ensure high-quality research and fresh supplies of graduates and students. Since 1983, the university has taken an increasingly strong initiative in recruiting national research consortia, redefining its research parks, commercializing technology, and participating in Austin's regional development efforts (Engelking, 1989). The Austin Chamber president, Glenn West, contrasts this relationship with that faced by his counterparts in other communities. After receiving an invitation to a local Chamber of Commerce event, the head of a large midwestern university responded, "Our university is a world-class institute of higher education, and we should be just as interested in Nairobi as in our local community."

Economic communities know that quality of life has moved from the wings to center stage as condition for value-adding industries. Companies depend on highly skilled people, many of whom have multiple options about where to live and whom to work for. Economies based on the skills, experience, and creativity of people view quality of life as an economic asset. Austin's special quality of life was an explicit attractor, and the region is working hard to maintain quality as it grows in numbers. In Silicon Valley, the economic performance surged ahead as quality of life diminished, and the region is struggling to understand the interdependencies and bring economy and community into balance. Cleveland's quality of life was a people-retention tool, even as its economy sputtered in the 1980s.

Even traditional business-climate factors like regulation are viewed by economic communities as potential assets. Time-based competition means that product life cycles are now measured in months. The adage "time is money" has become "time is market," as failure to get new facilities up fast can shut companies out of markets. In the early 1990s, Silicon Valley's permit approval process—whether yes, no, or maybe—was incredibly slow. Explained Robert Perlman, vice president of Tax Licensing and Customs at Intel, "The eighteen months it took to get a building permit to expand an existing facility in Silicon Valley exceeded the time it took to design a new chip or to build a new facility elsewhere." With the help of private-sector total quality management experts, Valley cities have reengineered permit processes and slashed turnaround times to as little as one day. The city of Fremont seeks to turn the quality of its government services and interactions into a competitive advantage, becoming the San Francisco Bay Area's first Total Quality Community.

Civic Entrepreneurs Linking Economy and Community

Economic communities are rife with activity between the economy and the community. Economic networks and community networks bump up against each other and integrate. People from one sphere know and work with people from the other. People move back and forth between the two sectors, some more literally than others (Austin, for example, has Lee Cooke, the Texas Instruments executive turned Chamber president turned mayor turned technology entrepreneur.)

These relationships are the glue of strong economic communities. They link industry clusters with community competencies, creating a vital cycle in which community processes support the growth of the economy, and the economy creates wealth and experience that are invested in the community.

In economic communities, through ongoing interaction and working together, people come to know, trust, and like each other. Jim Biggar, chairman and CEO of Glencairn Corporation, explains the situation in Cleveland. "Most of the business people know each other and generally like each other. They like to do things together. There are a lot of cities where that is not true. People may know each other, but they don't like each other or they let competition get in the way of working for the city." Austin has turned these relationships into a selling point. Glenn West, head of the Greater Austin Chamber of Commerce, explains that when the SEMATECH site selection committee visited, "it was clear that we were a well-oiled team that you could count on to stand behind you. In [a competing region], the community leadership was meeting each other for the first time when they met with the selection committee." Orlando has dense networks of trusting relationships that extend across its public and private sectors. The community has evolved over the past fifteen years into "the most trusting civic environment in Florida" (White, 1995, p. 43). Talk to private and public leaders in Orlando, and it is clear they like and respect each other and that they have mastered the art of friendship building as an underpinning of economic strategy.

Strong relationships across sectors provide regions with the ability to respond to negative external shocks and to work proactively on opportunities. In effect, the web of personal networks in economic communities acts as a virtual system of governance. Distinct from government, governance in these communities means people, firms, and institutions working across sectoral, organizational, and jurisdictional boundaries to anticipate and meet the needs of their economy. Wichita's resilience—it has consistently enjoyed an unemployment rate below the national average despite its concentration in the cyclical aerospace industry—is rooted in strong relationships that enable it to act quickly when repeatedly challenged by global economic forces.

When Boeing laid off six thousand people in 1993—the kind of cutback that would launch any other economy or community into a tailspin—city, community, labor, and state leaders rallied together to coordinate an effective one-stop transition center. Strong prior relationships among educators, business, and government in Phoenix allowed them to create an initiative quickly to deal with skills shortages in the semiconductor industry. Explains Ioanna T. Morfessis, president and CEO of the Greater Phoenix Economic Council, "This type of collaborative, focused effort would not have occurred without the knowledge and relationships gained through the Arizona collaborative strategy process." By tapping private sector talent and building person-to-person, public-private relationships, Silicon Valley slashed permit processing times in local cities. Then, building on these relationships, twenty-nine jurisdictions in the region made uniform their complex building codes.

Yet how does a community build cross-sector relationships? Do they make a difference?

A number of credible researchers are concluding that regional economic performance is linked to community relationships. Robert Putnam of Harvard University describes networks as a key component of "social capital." According to Putnam, social capital is made up of the features of social life such as networks, norms, and trust that enable people to act together to pursue shared objectives. After extensive study of Italian regions and examination of others worldwide, he concludes that "social capital is coming to be seen as a vital ingredient in economic development around the world" (Putnam, *The American Prospect*, 1993, p. 38). Francis Fukuyama, the noted historian and social scientist, has reached a similar conclusion. Fukuyama believes that social capital, which he defines as a capability that arises from the prevalence of trust in a society, is an endowment determining comparative advantage just like the classic labor, capital, and natural resources. He concludes that "social capital is critical to prosperity and to what has come to be called competitiveness" (1995, p. 355).

Researchers have stopped short, though, of answering the question, Can social capital be created? The prevailing view is that it is an endowment that changes slowly over time, if at all. From our experience observing high-performance economic communities, however, the answer to the question is a definitive yes.

The catalyst for creating and connecting collaborative networks between business, government, education, and the community is a new type of leader—the civic entrepreneur. Civic entrepreneurs create social capital by creating opportunities for people to work together on specific projects to advance their economic community. In all of the places that this book highlights, civic entrepreneurs have consciously created mechanisms for purposeful, sustained collaboration by people across sectors. These communities believe that civic entrepreneur leadership has made a critical difference in their capacity for ongoing success.

Although it seems evident from practice that leadership makes a difference in economic development, the academic world is working to prove it. An interesting quantitative study of the impact of leadership and resource endowments on regional economic development found that leadership can amplify the impact of resource endowments on a region. The same study describes leadership for economic development as the "tendency of a community to collaborate across sectors in a sustained, purposeful manner to enhance the economic performance of its region" (DeSantis, 1993, p. 66).

The name *civic entrepreneur* combines two important American traditions: entrepreneurship (the spirit of enterprise) and civic virtue (the spirit of community). Entrepreneurs are change agents. Joseph Schumpeter was the first modern economist to focus on the special role of entrepreneurs as drivers of "creative destruction" in modern economies. The function of the entrepreneur, Schumpeter believed, was to reform or revolutionize the established patterns of production. So doing, the entrepreneur inevitably meets resistance. Schumpeter writes, "To act with confidence beyond the range of familiar beacons and to overcome that resistance . . . define[s] the entrepreneurial type" (Schumpeter, 1962, p. 132). Peter Drucker also views the entrepreneur as a unique agent of change. Drucker writes that "the entrepreneur always searches for change, responds to it, and exploits it as an opportunity" (Drucker, 1985, p. 28). He reminds us that J. B. Say, the French economist who coined the term *entrepreneur* around 1800, said that the entrepreneur "shifts economic resources out of an area of lower and into an area of higher productivity and greater yield" (Drucker, 1985, p. 21).

Like the business entrepreneur, the civic entrepreneur operates in a time of dramatic change, sees opportunity, and mobilizes others in the community to work toward their collective well-being. Jim Morgan's message of opportunity, of building, and of collaboration typifies the language and mind-set of the civic entrepreneur: "From my experience managing turnarounds and developing businesses, I've found three keys to success: recognizing opportunities, building consensus to capitalize on those opportunities, and building momentum. We believed it was possible to have a process in which the Silicon Valley community could establish goals and work together on a set of initiatives to support an array of competitive, global business capabilities." The task of the civic entrepreneur is to use the spirit of enterprise to restore the spirit of community.

CHAPTER TWO

Civic Entrepreneurs
Leaders at the Grass Roots

You cannot look to government or the political system alone to provide the leadership or the continuity. If you do, it is not going to happen. It happens because people step up. Civic entrepreneurship is more effective than politics.

—Susan Engelking, Senior Counselor, Staats, Faulkenberg & Partners, Austin, Texas

~~~

Born of fundamental economic, political, technological, and demographic shifts, a new kind of leader is emerging to help America's communities thrive as they enter an era of continuous change. Civic entrepreneurs are catalysts for building economic community. They forge the ties that bind economy and community for their mutual benefit. Civic entrepreneurs help communities collaborate to develop and organize their economic assets and to build strong, resilient networks between and among the public, private, and civil sectors.

Civic entrepreneurs have the personality traits commonly associated with entrepreneurial business leaders. They are risk takers. They are not afraid of failure. They possess courage born of strong convictions. They are people of vision. They are passionate and energetic. They bring out the best in other people and know how to encourage them along.

But civic entrepreneurs operate in a decidedly different and more complex arena: the interface between the economy and the community. Their task goes beyond re-engineering the corporation or reinventing government. They are doing nothing less than redefining a new type of business-government relationship, a new type of community.

Who are civic entrepreneurs? Where do they come from? How do they work? Why do they get involved? What obstacles do they face?

WHO ARE CIVIC ENTREPRENEURS?

Civic entrepreneurs are catalysts who help communities go through the change process. They build economic community—tight, resilient linkages between community and economic interests. Yet, how do you know a civic entrepreneur when you see one?

Civic entrepreneurs have five common traits. They:

- See opportunity in the new economy
- Possess an entrepreneurial personality
- Provide collaborative leadership to connect the economy and the community
- Are motivated by broad, enlightened, long-term interests
- Work in teams, playing complementary roles

Civic entrepreneurs can come from business or government, from education, or from other community sectors. They come from many segments of society and many walks of life. Anybody can be a civic entrepreneur—anyone who demonstrates these five traits.

They See Opportunity in the New Economy

Civic entrepreneurs understand the new economic realities and are compelled to act on an optimistic vision of how their community can be successful in the world of the next century. They believe that the new economy—global, complex, fast-changing—can provide unprecedented opportunity for people, places, and organizations. Civic entrepreneurs take their regional economy—its opportunities and needs—as a starting point and help communities make positive choices about their future, building the relationships and specialized resources for success.

They Possess an Entrepreneurial Personality

Civic entrepreneurs share some traits of the classic business entrepreneur. As people of vision, they see possibilities and work creatively and persistently to make possibilities real. In contrast to the bureaucrat, civic entrepreneurs always instinctively find reasons why things can happen, as opposed to focusing on reasons why they cannot. In contrast to the idealist, civic entrepreneurs are challenged by the how-to questions and delight in getting results. Mobilizing resources, persisting against all odds, driving toward tangible results—civic entrepreneurs bring their entrepreneurial mind-set and skills to the civic arena.

They Provide Credible, Collaborative Leadership

At the same time that civic entrepreneurs are entrepreneurial, they are collaborative. They know how to work with people to get results. Civic entrepreneurs believe that the benefits of a changed economic context can be realized only with more collaborative, resilient connections between the new economy and the community. They provide collaborative leadership to bring diverse parties to the table, identify common ground, and take joint action. They build bridges. More often than not, civic entrepreneurs lead with no formal power or authority—only their credibility. Civic entrepreneurs are worthy of people's trust.

They Are Motivated by Broad, Enlightened, Long-Term Interests

Civic entrepreneurs get involved in their community out of enlightened, long-term interest. Civic entrepreneurs believe that their personal long-term interests and those of their organization are tied to the health of the economy and the community. This motivation is in direct contrast to traditional roles that have been played by business and other community leaders—the philanthropist who contributes money, the lobbyist who advocates positions, the opportunist who seeks personal notoriety or pursues narrow economic interests.

They Work in Teams,
Each Playing Different Roles

Civic entrepreneurs work in teams to help their communities move forward. They are not lone eagles or solitary, charismatic leaders. Community change processes are complex undertakings that require multiple talents and a lot of teaming. Civic entrepreneurs play different roles on a team, each contributing their unique skills, experience, personalities, and connections. Only by combining roles and developing more and more new leaders are civic entrepreneurs effective.

WHAT IS NEW?

Civic entrepreneurs clearly build on a long American tradition of civic activism. Most communities can point to leaders from business and government who clearly made a difference in the past and who met many of these five civic entrepreneur criteria. In particular, the 1960s and 1970s proliferated new business and community organizations, especially focused on downtown or neighborhood development. But what differentiates civic entrepreneurs today from their counterparts in earlier decades?

The latest version of civic initiative is unique, because it is in response to factors that changed dramatically beginning in the early 1980s. The world is different economically, technologically, demographically, and politically, so the nature of effective community leadership has changed. Civic entrepreneurs, for example, value the entrepreneurial, export-engines of regional economies that need to compete globally; earlier business coalitions were dominated more by real estate and downtown business service interests. In fact, civic entrepreneurs typically preach interdependence, helping communities understand the economic link between export-oriented industries and local retailers, restaurateurs, construction, and service companies, as well as between downtowns and suburbs.

Civic entrepreneurs today practice collaborative leadership; in a world of decentralizing community power structures, they effectively bring people together. Earlier leadership was often far less inclusive. Effective organizations were often driven by and restricted to a handful of high-profile business leaders, wealthy individuals, or a mayor. Civic entrepreneurs today get involved in the hands-on implementation of change; earlier leadership tended to emphasize civic visioning

and making recommendations on what government should do. !
Because of the radically changed context, effective community leaders today think, look, and act quite differently than their counterparts
from previous decades.

GRASSROOTS LEADERS FOR THE NEW ECONOMY

Effective civic entrepreneurs come from many segments of the community and from many walks of life. The state's first wave of successful technology entrepreneurs initiated Arizona's collaborative strategy
effort. CEOs of *Fortune* 500 companies, midlevel professionals, small-
business people, city managers, and a labor union chief act as civic
entrepreneurs in Silicon Valley. And the team in Austin includes an
attorney, a Chamber director, a scientist, and an advertising executive.
Civic entrepreneurs come in both genders and all ages and from all
racial and ethnic backgrounds. What they have in common is their
interest in supporting economic vitality as a key component of
regional quality of life. Specifically, civic entrepreneurs come from *the
economy* (entrepreneurial businesses, business services and small businesses, global corporations, utilities, the media) and *the community*
(public office and public service, economic development, education,
unions, nonprofit and environmental organizations, foundations).

Community as Their Business

Although civic entrepreneurs come from many places, we have
observed that every civic entrepreneur team includes a core of leaders from the private sector. These business leaders view their future as
connected to their community—its ability to provide the kind of environment, commercial relationships, and amenities that support business vitality. Civic entrepreneurs tend to come from businesses that
believe in building and maintaining strong relationships between their
firm and suppliers, customers, and partners.

ENTREPRENEURS TURNED CIVIC. Not surprisingly, look for civic entrepreneurs in the entrepreneurial sector. Smaller and newer companies
that are locally based but globally oriented tend to spawn civic entrepreneurs. In many communities, a next generation of entrepreneurs
is building new companies in new industries operating under a new

business model. Many want to preserve a healthy habitat for their growing business. Seldom are these people part of their community's traditional leadership structure. Yet they are the future drivers of the economy and possess strong personal ties to their community. Many of them have come of age with a new networked business model, emphasizing relationships among diverse organizations and people as a key to success.

Alan Hald, the cofounder and vice chairman of Phoenix-based MicroAge, Inc., is an example of a classic entrepreneur-turned-civic entrepreneur. Hald has seen his company through explosive growth, near bankruptcy, and vigorous recovery. In the late 1980s, Hald emerged as leader of a new entrepreneurial sector in Phoenix. "My decision to found and grow a global business rooted here makes me care a great deal about the region's future. I found that other entrepreneurs of high-growth companies were by nature people who want to make a difference."

BUSINESS SERVICES. The business services sector is another breeding ground for civic entrepreneurs. Companies in this sector tend to view themselves as habitat-dependent because locally based companies are their main market. Printers, financiers, communications executives, attorneys, builders, and others understand that if the regional economy does well, they do well. In Silicon Valley, communications executive Brenna Bolger, printer John Kennett, and Chamber head Steve Tedesco were three of the initiators of the Joint Venture: Silicon Valley collaborative effort in 1992. They helped the downtown San Jose services community understand that their future was linked to the health of high-tech industry.

As place-dependent businesses, utilities traditionally have cared about community economic development as a means toward larger markets. As they move toward deregulation, civic entrepreneur activities that bring utilities closer to customers and community leadership may prove all the more important. District managers at Pacific Gas & Electric are encouraged to play leadership roles to help ensure the economic vitality of their regions, and now they receive training to increase their effectiveness.

GLOBAL THINKING, LOCAL ACTING. Private sector civic entrepreneurs also come from global companies that chose to locate in a particular region for its habitat. Some of these companies are truly practicing a

o Cliff Herald — Sun Micro⁻
o Bonnie Turner — Quzilk
o Level (3) — Kathy Satten

new globalism, believing that strong local roots are critical for global reach. To these companies, communities are resources that matter. Applied Materials, for example, adopted a unique global-local perspective early on. Jim Morgan said, "Some companies take their regions for granted. I think you have to maintain and take care of your regions, just like you have to take care of your roads, plants, and other infrastructure. My recommendation is that companies should have an ✗ executive in each region who's responsible for the company's relationships and efforts in the region." Although this strategic attention to managing corporate-region relationships is not yet widespread, more and more companies are learning from examples like Applied Materials, Motorola, and Hewlett-Packard.

CIVIC JOURNALISTS. An emerging private-sector springboard for civic entrepreneurs is the media, particularly community newspapers. Newspaper publishers, editors, and journalists are experimenting with new roles for journalism in building a sense of community, promoting public discussion about economic change, and prompting action. With its emphasis on community engagement, this orientation of "civic journalism" stands apart from the traditional role of the newspaper as solely a third-party observer. In 1986, *The Omaha World-Herald* became one of the first newspapers to act as a convening mechanism, bringing people from throughout Nebraska together to address economic issues affecting the state's future. During this time, the publisher of the *Austin American-Statesman* also emerged as a major player in developing and implementing Austin's economic strategy. More recently, civic entrepreneur Steve Ainsley, publisher of the *New York Times*-owned *Santa Barbara News-Press,* brought an outsider's perspective and the newspapers' credibility to help initiate the Santa Barbara Economic Community Project, which is building consensus to support the region's emerging technology economy. In these cases, newspaper leaders are moving beyond traditional roles of communicator and critic to new roles as credible convener, catalyst, and collaborator in public life.

Causal ?

For many communities, the rise of civic entrepreneurship coincides with a fundamental change in industry structure. Historically, executives from large, established businesses have provided a form of visible leadership in the community. Citizens could identify a stable handful of key executives from long-standing companies as business leaders. R. Scott Fosler, president of the National Academy of Public

Administration, has noted, "The structure of the private sector is changing. The CEOs of large corporations in a given city used to have enormous prestige and potential power if they chose to use it. That is less likely the case today, as large corporations have downsized, restructured, and in general have come under enormous competitive pressure. They are sharing the stage with a larger number of small- and medium-sized businesses whose owners are also likely to be seeking ways both to exercise their influence and address the problems that threaten their business base" (Frey Foundation, 1993, p. 21). A 1993 study by the Frey Foundation suggests that civic power has become more dispersed in communities in the past few decades. The money, clout, and authority once wielded by a few business leaders are now spread among many (Frey Foundation, 1993, p. 21). Demographic shifts mean that civic entrepreneurs from business will be younger, will be female as well as male, and will come from an increasing variety of racial and ethnic backgrounds.

Civic Entrepreneurs from Other Sectors

Business people do not have a lock on civic entrepreneurship. Although private sector leaders typically drive efforts to build economic community, they team with extraordinary individuals from government, the economic development profession, and other community sectors. Like their private-sector counterparts, these people become civic entrepreneurs when they reach beyond their traditional arena and provide leadership to build bridges and get results across sectors.

ELECTED OFFICIALS AND PUBLIC MANAGERS. An outstanding elected official can boost the power of civic entrepreneur teams. Mayor Susan Hammer of San Jose, encouraged by her chief aide Bob Brownstein and business executive Tom Hayes, accepted industry's call to play a leadership role in the broader Silicon Valley region—home to more than twenty municipalities that harbored long-standing suspicions of the dominant city. Her collaborative manner helped put other communities at ease and helped them buy into a new regional problem-solving effort. Mayor Glenda Hood of Orlando and Mayor (now Governor) George Voinovich of Cleveland represent a new breed of mayors who see their role as facilitating public-private collaboration, leading to results for the economy.

Public managers can serve as civic entrepreneurs when they reach out to help others understand and adopt new, more collaborative approaches. In the early 1990s, Tom Lewcock, city manager of Sunny-vale, spent a great deal of time telling other public managers about his experience collaborating with business leaders in a new effort to solve regional economic problems. "I saw something evolving here that was bigger than the sum of business and government together." What compelled him to act was his belief that reinventing government needed to be supplemented by new regional alliances to deal with radical economic change.

ECONOMIC DEVELOPMENT PRACTITIONERS. Thousands of people in the United States consider themselves economic development profession-als. From the 1950s through much of the 1980s, "recruiter" was the central role played by economic development practitioners; they wooed companies to locate in their community, often with local and state government subsidies and incentives. In many communities, recognition that more jobs are grown through expansion of existing businesses and start-up of new ones is dramatically changing the nature of the economic development professional's work. (See Luke and others, 1988, pp. 25–27.) Rather than focusing on bringing outsider businesses in, these leaders now focus on connecting insiders both inside and out. That is, this new breed of economic development professional delivers value to their community by connecting companies to local resources and by creating an environment in which local businesses can be globally competitive and linked. It is in this bridging capacity that some are emerging as true civic entrepreneurs.

John Anderson and Larry Pelton of Florida typify this new type of economic development professional—one who both acts as a civic entrepreneur and works with civic entrepreneurs. Both are radically transforming relationships and organizations to get results. Anderson, formerly a successful corporate recruiter, is now working with Florida's business and government leadership to affect the first large-scale privatization of a state economic agency. Pelton, of Palm Beach, views his economic development organization, the Business Development Board of Palm Beach County, as a "supplier" to local companies. He has developed an extensive personal and electronic infrastructure to help companies connect to local training and finance resources, and to each other. Both see tapping and developing business civic entrepreneur leadership as central to their new professional roles.

FROM THE COMMUNITY FOR THE ECONOMIC COMMUNITY. Some of the most effective civic entrepreneurs are longtime community advocates who decide to practice a new style to get results in the new economy. Unlike some of his counterparts, the labor movement's John Neece views working with business leaders, rather than advocating against them, as the best way to serve the long-term interests of his Building and Construction Trades Union. When Neece started working with business executives to implement a collaborative community effort, he challenged himself to focus on common interests: "If I shut my eyes and listen, it would sound like they [CEOs] were union organizers. They had the same ideas, and thoughts, and concerns about the community that we do." Neece has a keen understanding of the new competitive realities faced by his industry and others in his region, and he helps labor constituencies develop pragmatic and collaborative actions to get results.

Community-based foundations also can house civic entrepreneurs. For fifteen years, the Cleveland Foundation's Steve Minter has played on the team that has sparked some of Cleveland's success. At critical times in Cleveland's evolution, Minter networked talent and resources in the community and helped get the facts on the table and out to the public. Foundations across the country are demonstrating increasing interest in community collaboration and leadership in response to a changed economy. As they do, an important set of civic entrepreneurs may emerge from their ranks.

CIVIC ENTREPRENEURS IN TEAMS

Civic entrepreneurship is a team sport. Though the myth of the tinkerer in a garage still prevails, business entrepreneurs are seldom loners. Rather, they work with an extensive network of collaborators to bring an idea to the market. In a similar way, civic entrepreneurs work in teams. The days of Carnegie-type individuals single-handedly coming to the rescue of their communities are gone. Civic entrepreneurs bring the many faces of their community together in order to move forward—a massive undertaking that cannot be accomplished, or even sparked, by a single individual. Only by combining their skills, personalities, and connections and by bringing in new leaders have civic entrepreneurs proved effective.

Team Austin

During the 1980s, a remarkable team of civic entrepreneurs believed Austin could be more than an obscure government and university town. From his former perch at Texas Instruments, Lee Cooke saw how full of opportunity the Information Age could be. As the new director of the Austin Chamber, however, Cooke saw the constraints. The city was hostile to growth. The university, the state's flagship with fifty thousand students, was not a player in economic development. The nucleus of technology companies was small. Oil and gas were the Texas mind-set. Marshaling the leadership of the business community, Cooke undertook a strategy development effort that united business, city and state government, and the university around a vision of Austin as a quality information technology center.

A first leadership link was Pike Powers, an Austin attorney, then serving as executive assistant to Texas Governor Mark White. In 1983, Cooke and Powers rallied the community around an initial stretch target: landing the most prestigious economic development prize of the early 1980s—the Microelectronics Computer Technology Consortium (MCC), a national research consortium to further the U.S. competitive position in computing technology. To the community that won the national site competition, the consortium would mean research operations, laboratories, and skilled people and would be a magnet for attracting and growing technology-based companies. For months, an ever-expanding circle of interested people met every morning at 7:30 to develop the proposal, assess the competition, and practice presenting the pitch and answering questions. Explains Powers, "It was our first opportunity as a community to try to bring a consensus together. We were on a sense of mission, which helped us put our petty differences aside." Practice and teamwork paid off.

Success bred success, and the core team of civic entrepreneurs multiplied. The community next leveraged the relationships and experience it gained through MCC to win the SEMATECH competition in 1988, becoming host to a consortium of fourteen U.S. semiconductor manufacturers focused on new manufacturing methods. Led by William Cunningham, the young and aggressive business school dean turned University of Texas president, the university developed an advanced research park and created thirty-two $1 million chairs in engineering and natural sciences. When Pike left the governor's office, he became a key volunteer broker in future deals that helped put Austin on the map: Apple, Applied Materials, 3M.

Yet, according to Glenn West, current Chamber president, "These wins capture the most attention, but the really important work is hundreds of people involved in building Austin's 'product,' working on schools, transportation, leadership, downtown, the melding of environmental and business interests." Susan Engelking, a rising young star at the Chamber and now advertising executive, has been central to efforts to build the downtown, revitalize neighborhoods, and bring new talent into Austin's leadership circle. Neal Kocurek is an engineer, senior executive, and third-generation Austin resident. Rarely without a leadership project, recently Neal painstakingly brought factions together to create a convention center. His view of Austin's success: building the civic entrepreneur team. "Our success has come from leaders stepping up, training other leaders, and then passing the torch to them. We support each other."

In the past decade, Austin's leaders have propelled their community to a new plateau. In 1995, the Austin economy boasted a 3 percent unemployment rate, the lowest in the state and one of the lowest in the country. While healthy debates rage—How much development? How fast? How to spark homegrown businesses? How to maintain quality of life?—Austin's secret weapon, teamwork, remains razor sharp.

Team Arizona

Civic entrepreneur Alan Hald, of MicroAge, Inc., conceived and managed ASPED (the Arizona Strategic Planning for Economic Development) from 1988 to 1992. Frustrated by his home state's economic collapse and complacency toward knowledge-based industry, Hald sparked a revolutionary strategic planning process involving more than one thousand people statewide. The process involved engaging and supporting the state's new and transforming industries, such as optics, environmental technology, information services, and tourism. Hald's progressive management philosophy built on openness, accountability, and shared vision left its imprimatur all over the ASPED project. But although Hald served as the visible spokesperson, Hald was not alone.

The initial team included fifteen technology entrepreneurs who met every Sunday for two years to study the implications for Arizona of the industry cluster model of growth. The model suggested that the goal of economic development was not to chase smokestacks and develop property but to create a vital cycle of export-oriented, entrepreneurial industries and supportive economic foundations. Jack Pfister, general manager of the Salt River Project and the youngest of the old guard, gave the up-and-comers credibility with the established business leaders in Phoenix. Ioanna Morfessis, head of the Greater Phoenix Economic Council, worked across boundaries with business, governments, universities, and community groups to gain their participation in the new approach. Mary Jo Waits of the Morrison Institute for Public Policy at Arizona State University contributed extensive knowledge of Arizona's economy and state government workings. Enthusiastic entrepreneurs like Steven Zylstra of Simula and Robert Breault of Breault Research Organization rallied their industries to the cause.

Through the ASPED process, a core team of civic entrepreneurs with complementary skills mobilized thousands of people to work on a sustained basis to put Arizona's economy on a new growth path. Together, they have helped shift the state and its communities toward a more diversified, technology-based economy. Emerging sectors like optics and environmental technology developed mechanisms to work on joint projects, develop specialized human resources, and improve interactions with public agencies. Specific results include focusing state training resources on cluster industries and greater leverage of federal research institutions.

Team Cleveland

"We have never had a single person recognized as the leader; we've had hundreds. Every leader we've had has not only been anxious to share power but has gone out of the way to bring other people along," says Al Ratner, cochair of Forest City Enterprises, Inc., as he explains Cleveland's comeback key. "We have a collaborative mind-set that grew out of bad times."

In 1978, Cleveland became the first major city since the Great Depression legally to default on its fiscal obligations. Global competition pushed Cleveland's industrial economy into a tailspin. By 1983, unemployment had risen to 11.3 percent as more than seventy-five thousand manufacturing jobs vanished. Urban-suburban demographic fissures erupted. Federal resources were drying up. And the political system was falling apart. Mayor Dennis Kucinich proclaimed Cleveland's businesses "the archenemy of the people." Crisis propelled Cleveland's business leaders, who previously got together only for United Way or symphony fund raising, into action.

Leading the charge was a team of business people with a new-world twist. E. Mandell (Del) de Windt, then CEO of Eaton Corporation, called the first meeting. An early recruit was Richard Pogue, a leading attorney, who would become a key promoter of inclusion. Brock Weir, chairman of Ameritrust, had called the city's loan but then committed to solving the fundamental problems. Other early leaders included TRW chief Ruben Mettler; Mort Mandel, chairman of Premier Industrial Corporation; George Dively, CEO of Harris Corporation; and James Biggar, CEO of the international Glencairn Company, headquartered in Cleveland. Together, they rallied the business community around the new mayor George Voinovich by giving him their personal aid. Early steps aimed at stopping the fiscal bleeding. Almost one hundred corporate executives joined together to conduct a twelve-week assessment of city management, producing more than six hundred money-saving recommendations, most of which were implemented. Building on this initial team experience, they turned to tackling more fundamental problems in concert. A core team of business people committed to fight to rebuild Cleveland rather than give up and leave the city they loved.

In 1982, they carefully launched the process of forming Cleveland Tomorrow, a CEO leadership group. By definition exclusive, Cleveland Tomorrow provided an initial vehicle for CEOs of large corporations to focus new leadership efforts. From this base, civic entrepreneurs from business reached out to a broader base of community leaders to form new partnerships and coalitions. They helped form the Cleveland Roundtable, a biracial community leadership organization. Carole Hoover (business woman, civil rights activist, and former adviser to Martin Luther King, Jr.) played a key role in bridging business and community networks. Hoover is now chief executive of the Greater Cleveland Growth Association. Through Cleveland Tomorrow, the Cleveland Roundtable, and the affiliates they begat, this initial team of civic entrepreneurs leveraged the talents and resources of hundreds of established and new leaders. Cleveland's civic entrepreneurs are now being recognized for their powerful blend of process expertise, relationship focus, and results orientation. The results are impressive: transformed labor relations, reoriented education institutions, massive upgrades in physical infrastructure, a rejuvenated advanced manufacturing economic base, improved race relationships, and an economically vital downtown.

Team Silicon Valley

In the early 1990s, defense cuts and restructuring in high-tech manufacturing led to layoffs of forty thousand workers in manufacturing industries. The job engine that generated 7 percent annual growth for two decades stalled. Most disturbing: as homegrown high-tech companies retooled and positioned for growth, they increasingly looked elsewhere to expand. Companies needed world-class schools, time-sensitive government, and an environment that fosters communication and quick adaptation. Instead, what the region offered and the companies contributed to, was a culture of blame. A 1992 survey of business leaders showed confidence in the Valley's future at an all-time low.

As the local economy worsened, the San Jose Chamber of Commerce, prodded by Chamber Board Members Tom Hayes and Brenna Bolger, convened leaders from other business associations to begin meeting to organize a regional response. As both a member of the Chamber board and a high-tech executive, Hayes straddled both halves of the Silicon Valley, which was important to bringing all the players together. With the endorsement of Chamber Chair John Kennett, Tom Hayes, director of Global Corporate Affairs at semiconductor equipment giant Applied Materials, met weekly with an initial planning group of small business people, association heads, and mid-level technology executives. Within weeks, Hayes was chosen as chairman of the project, Joint Venture: Silicon Valley.

Encouraged by the momentum Joint Venture had from its start and by his connection to Hayes, Jim Morgan, Chairman and CEO of Applied Materials, became chief among a core of business and community leaders who helped propel the movement to its next stage. Recalls Morgan, "We had it all in the eyes of the world, but it wasn't working to our collective advantage." Morgan tapped his network of high-tech executives and joined forces with the business services, political, and labor communities to figure out how to use Valley talent to solve Valley problems. Through a top-down, bottom-up process, people from business, government, education, and community came together to reinvent Silicon Valley around the vision of a community collaborating to compete globally. Joint Venture: Silicon Valley Network, as the movement came to be known, mobilized more than one thousand leaders to create a *Blueprint for a 21st Century Community* and developed consensus to implement major change in eleven areas.

More than two hundred civic entrepreneurs are active in the implementation stage, from leading CEOs like John Young and Regis McKenna to ordinary citizens who contribute their time and talent. Teams are formed of people with complementary skills. Ed McCracken, CEO of Silicon Graphics, took the reins from Jim Morgan, as Joint

Venture moved from start-up to implementation phase. Explains McCracken, "I don't know if I would have been the Jim Morgan who got it started, but I thought I could help get it through the implementation process." Becky Morgan, a former state senator with a reputation for integrity, took over the executive reins as the movement evolved to new organization, which built broad credibility from its entrepreneurial beginnings. An innovative regulatory streamlining effort teams total quality engineers from the private sector with local government permit administrators. The idea was conceived by an innovative duo: Chris Greene, head of a local engineering company, and city manager Tom Lewcock, known for his re-engineering efforts on behalf of the Sunnyvale city government.

Four years later, more than $20 million in private investment is sparking reform in K–12 education. CEOs contribute one day a month and the time of senior executives to re-engineer schools. The Smart Valley initiative is developing an advanced information infrastructure and the collective ability to use it to solve regional problems. And companies, still courted by outside interests, have a local troubleshooter to call at the regional public-private Economic Development Team.

Team Florida:
Building State and Regional Alliances

One of the fastest-growing states in America, with booming tourism and real estate industries, Florida in the mid–1980s looked like a state that should not have a care in the world. At that time, Glenda Hood was a successful business owner. As the new chair of the Florida Chamber (the first from outside the development business and the first woman), Glenda brought a background and actions that embodied a departure from the past. "We realized that so many of the jobs in our state were in tourism and service industries, and we wanted to diversify our economy. Many other states and communities were competitive. We needed to develop a strategy to compete." Her words captured the mood of the business leaders of the Florida Chamber in 1987, when it launched Project Cornerstone, which would become a focal point for Florida's emerging business leaders to think about how to transition Florida to a new kind of high-quality economic development.

Released in 1989, the *Cornerstone* report provided a new way of looking at the Florida economy and its prospects for the future. For

Jim Gardner, the Mississippi-born, manager of ITT, along with other emerging business leaders, *Cornerstone* became a touchstone for the new way ahead. "*Cornerstone* pointed out the fundamental difference between 1980 and 1990. We had been talking about competing against Alabama and Georgia. Now we needed to look at competing globally." *Cornerstone* identified the key industry clusters that could generate high-paying jobs for Florida and the critical economic foundations necessary for attracting and growing those clusters. Florida was weak in several critical foundation areas, including human resources, technology, and capital. Florida's tax structure was also an obstacle to growing a high-value, knowledge-based economy.

A team of civic entrepreneurs, initially from the Chamber and later from Florida's regions, began to advocate for new state and regional economic strategies that were more attuned to the new realities of the Florida economy. At the state level, Jim Gardner and Glenda Hood advocated for an innovative public-private partnership (Enterprise Florida) to implement the *Cornerstone* strategy. Enterprise Florida would take over state-level economic development initiatives in training, high-technology, venture capital, and international trade from the Florida Department of Commerce. The goal was stronger orientation toward the needs of "customers"—Florida's regions and their industry clusters. In 1992, Governor Lawton Chiles endorsed the *Cornerstone* strategy and enlisted public and community support to legislate Enterprise Florida into being.

Leaders emerged to translate the vision of *Cornerstone* to action at the regional level. Larry Pelton, an economic development professional from Palm Beach County, worked with his business "customers" to implement a new approach using electronic networking for business-to-business and business-to-community communication. Terrell Sessums is a Tampa attorney who spent ten years in the Florida legislature, several as Speaker of the Assembly. Inspired by *Cornerstone*, Sessums has helped develop a regional approach to training and business attraction, connecting business leaders in Tampa to those in St. Petersburg. Architect and planner Henry Luke developed a team of leaders in Jacksonville who worked together to transform it from a paper-mill town to a high-end financial and health services center. And in 1992, Glenda Hood became mayor of Orlando, leading in the words of one observer, "the most trusting civic environment in Florida, enabling its political and business leaders to accomplish things that those in other cities cannot" (White,

1995, p. 42) Through this bottom-up community leadership, the statewide vision of a value-adding economy began to take hold.

Meanwhile, through persistence, state-level civic entrepreneurs were able to launch the new Enterprise Florida organization in 1996— the first state economic agency in America to transition so completely. In 1995, Enterprise Florida took over responsibility for high-technology and labor-training grant programs and a venture capital fund from the state. A fourth partnership focused on international trade development was added in 1996. Enterprise Florida recruited John Anderson, a Boeing executive and head of economic development in Oregon, Washington, Texas, and Miami, as the first CEO. The road to this point had been rocky, and plenty of hard work remained. Anderson explained, "Given the sea change in the economy, there was no easy way to get this started. No one had done this before." Yet the process of thinking collectively about the future has developed a cadre of leaders who have turned their passion about Florida's potential into actions to move Florida toward a quality future.

Team Wichita

The home of Cessna, Beechcraft, and Learjet, Wichita once again got caught in an aerospace downturn in the mid–1980s. At the same time, commodity agriculture and oil stagnated. As Wichita's employment and income growth lay stagnant, a new team of civic entrepreneurs emerged that was focused on diversifying Wichita's boom-bust economy. Ironically, the initial leader was the senior vice president of Boeing, Lionel Alford who said, "When the aircraft industry once again got soft, everyone worried about putting our eggs in one basket." Lionel, an outsider to Wichita, was the kind of World War II-era leader who would always get the job done and was groomed to manage big things. Alford linked with Jordan Haynes, who as chairman of Wichita's largest bank, Bank Four, was the consummate insider: connected and influential. Together, they recruited thirty other business and community leaders to create a strategy for Wichita's economic future.

One of their recruits was Hale Ritchie. The young entrepreneur, CEO of Ritchie Corporation, said: "Once we got together, we quickly agreed about what needed to happen: join the business community with political and educational communities to do economic development together rather than having economic development in each place." From the start, these civic entrepreneurs realized that the region would be repeatedly challenged by global economic forces and must have the capacity to act quickly and proactively. The team managed the process of consolidating economic development from the City, Sedgwick County, and the Chamber of Commerce into a new public-private organization: the Wichita/Sedgwick County (WI/SE) Partnership. With strong business support, WI/SE implemented an aggressive five-year action plan focused on education, technology, finance, biomedical research, downtown development, and transportation.

By 1990, the partnership reached all major objectives. Achievements in forging a new business-education partnership were especially noteworthy. In 1989, WI/SE won the Arthur D. Little Award for Excellence in Economic Development, which recognized the partnership as the most innovative economic development organization in the United States.

Alford and Haynes stepped forward again to lead the process of developing strategy for the next five years. Despite its strong leadership and success record, the team failed to implement the second five-year plan.

In the first five years, Wichita was successful because it had the support of top business leadership. As Lionel Alford said, "To have maximum impact, you need to have people who are business-focused and see the community as a unit that needs to be healthy." However, in the second five years, it proved difficult to maintain the high level of business leadership. As Hale Ritchie observed, "If we made a mistake back then, we did not go deep enough. We went deep enough to fund what we wanted to fund. We had a core group of companies that were partners. In retrospect, we should have gotten more people involved in the thought process."

In 1994, under prodding from local government, WISE began to reassess its broad vision on education and economic development. As Tim Witsman, president of the Chamber explains, "Two years ago, we began to lose vision. Business remained committed to the original vision, but it has been hard to sustain on the government side." The WI/SE experience shows what a team of civic entrepreneurs can accomplish together. It also, however, raises important questions about sustainability. As Lionel Alford comments, "We need to restructure every eight to ten years. You may find that circumstances are changing, and you may need to choose a new way."

WHY DO THEY DO WHAT THEY DO?

Civic entrepreneurs provide leadership for the long haul. They lead their communities through fundamental change and improvement processes that have no quick fixes. Sometimes, civic entrepreneurs make a significant but quick contribution and then exit the team. But most often, civic entrepreneurs persist over a long period, making exceptional commitments of time and energy. Explains Susan Engelking of Austin, "Achieving any significant community goal is going to be at least a four- or five-year effort." Says Seth Fearey of Hewlett-Packard, who has been championing a Smart Valley electronic community initiative since 1992, "It's a lot of work. You shouldn't expect this to be something where you can go to a few meetings, launch a process, turn over marching orders to other people, and it will just happen. You have to be prepared to commit a significant amount of time and resources to make these things happen." As Ronald Heifetz emphasizes in *Leadership Without Easy Answers*, "The long-term challenge of leadership is to develop people's adaptive capacity for tackling an ongoing stream of hard problems" (1995, p. 247). Our talks with civic entrepreneurs have unearthed countless stories of early-morning, late-night, and weekend meetings patiently trying to build consensus, to move from talk to action.

With all the competing time pressures facing leaders today and the inevitable challenges (and frustrations) of engaging in public activity, what motivates civic entrepreneurs? Why do they do what they do? And why do they keep their efforts up year after year after year? Most say their motivation is a blend of long-term economic interest, desire to make a difference in the community, and the challenge of it all.

Enlightened Economic Interest

Most civic entrepreneurs from the private sector believe that the leadership role they play outside their company benefits their company's long-term economic interests. Despite the commonly held belief that American executives focus chiefly on short-term earnings, in the ranks of large and small companies alike a growing cadre of executives takes a longer-term view. These leaders believe that, at some level, the long-term success of their company is tied to the long-term success of the communities in which they operate.

In places like Austin, Phoenix, Orlando, Cleveland, and Silicon Valley, civic entrepreneurs speak of the connectedness between the economy and the community. When asked why he has been a civic entrepreneur for well over a decade, Pike Powers, Austin attorney, sketches a diagram that is strikingly similar to those drawn by other regions, showing the vital cycle between business vitality, schools and universities, physical infrastructure, and tax base. Glenn West of the Austin Chamber believes, "Business understands this a lot better than they used to." Those business leaders that believe in this long-term interdependence provide role models for others.

Ed McCracken, chairman and CEO of Silicon Graphics, believes the economic importance of the community is heightened for highly specialized, Information Age companies. In particular, the need to attract and retain skilled, creative people is a powerful motivator for civic entrepreneurs. McCracken explains his corporate interest in the Silicon Valley community. "As an Information Age company, people are your greatest resource. And this resource goes home every night to the community, and they either will or will not come back the next morning. The most enlightened companies view all their employees as freelancers who are independent entrepreneurs. They just happen to work inside your boundaries and are on your payroll, but in fact they can choose to live and work anywhere. So the quality and vitality of the community matters a great deal—it affects employees' ideas, what they bring to the job, and their staying power with your company." Lionel Alford, formerly of Boeing, agrees. "The primary reason for large, export-oriented companies to get involved is for current and future employees. Unlike other local firms, we don't sell into the community. Our issues are the availability and quality of the workforce and the quality of life they will or will not enjoy in the community."

In an earlier age, physical resources mattered much more to business; workers were more fungible, and communities were primarily places to transform physical resources into commodity products at low cost. In the Information Age, human resources matter most, linking more tightly the destinies of business and community. Eric Benhamou, CEO of 3Com, a leading manufacturer of networking tools, believes that helping improve education in Silicon Valley is critical to recruiting future talent and ensuring a high quality of life for his employees. He is a civic entrepreneur in regional efforts to build a local information infrastructure and to bring technology into the local education system. He explained to a crowd of San Diego leaders his motivation. "My company needs to engage with the community because the community will be the basis for over 50 percent of our future workforce" (Speech to Smart San Diego, May, 1995).

Of course, leaders must decide at what point in their business's evolution civic entrepreneurship makes sense. This kind of leadership commitment must be made at the right time. Explains Alan Hald of MicroAge, Inc., "For our civic entrepreneur 'farm team' I'm targeting entrepreneurs of locally grown high-growth companies. But they must be over-the-hump from a development stage and positioned fundamentally to have a bright future here." McCracken makes a similar distinction. He points to a family line of Valley entrepreneurs, reared at Hewlett-Packard, who believe a core precept of the HP Way. Companies maximize the long-term value of their businesses by serving four constituencies: shareholders, customers, employees, and the community. But McCracken offers a warning. "These aren't all equal, but in the long run they are all necessary. You have to make enough money in the short term so your shareholders don't worry. That allows you to worry about customers, create growth opportunities for employees, and impact the community. The worst sin I've seen is in companies that make real contributions to the community, while their business is going downhill. They then have to lay off ten thousand people, which is the worse thing you can do for a community."

To Make a Unique Difference in the Community

"You increasingly have the presidents and CEOs of corporations today whose education, training, and background are much wider than their predecessors' may have been twenty-five, thirty, or fifty years ago. There is a much greater interest in community and how it works." John Anderson, president and CEO of Enterprise Florida, has spent his lifetime working with executives, and he believes he has spotted a new type.

Although economics matters, most civic entrepreneurs are motivated by more than economics. The other driver is the oldest civic virtue—the desire to create a better community. Most civic entrepreneurs say they do what they do because they want to make a difference in building economic community. Entrepreneurs, be they private entrepreneurs or civic entrepreneurs, are by nature people who want to make a difference. And, they want to apply their unique skills and experience to civic endeavors, not simply donate money or sit passively on a board.

Many civic entrepreneurs are people who have reached a point in their career where they have achieved considerable success and stature. They are ready to take on a new type of challenge that has broader, more lasting impact. As a civic entrepreneur with the Florida Chamber, Tom Keating was "motivated by the belief that I can make a difference in my community and industry, after having made a significant difference in my company and family. There are a lot of people who want to do good out there and don't want to wait until they retire. That was the old model." Often, civic entrepreneurs recruit others by recognizing the underlying need many successful people have to increase their circle of impact. Bob Breault, chairman of Breault Research Organization, responded to Alan Hald's call to organize Tucson's optics cluster, for a very basic, fundamental reason. "He made me feel like I could make a difference in Arizona's future."

The desire to make a difference is often linked to wanting to give back to a community that has provided a platform for the civic entrepreneur's personal and professional success. Pike Powers of Austin explains, "Finishing the job for me means putting a little bit back for what came my way. I have been enormously and generously provided for, and this is my attempt to stack the ledger up a little bit. This has been said a thousand times in a thousand ways by people more articulate than me, but this is part of what civic entrepreneurship is about."

Another powerful motivator is the idea: if we don't take the initiative, no one will. Like their business counterparts, civic entrepreneurs hate to see opportunities missed and challenges unmet. They have learned through experience the power of one person to make a difference by channeling the efforts of others. Think of a difficult but important challenge in Austin, and the surname Kocurek is sure to come up. Neal Kocurek and particularly his father Willie have championed every single school bond campaign in Austin for the past forty years—except for the one that failed. After others had tried to build a convention center for twenty-five years, Neal painstakingly over a five-year period built consensus among environmentalists and business leaders to get the job done. What motivates Neal? "If someone doesn't step forward and exercise the leadership, it's not going to get done. It only takes one person to make it happen."

Recognizing that civic entrepreneurs have something unique to offer can be a powerful motivator. Civic entrepreneurs have an invaluable store of contacts, skills, experience, and credibility that can unleash similar contributions from others. The desire to contribute themselves, not just their money, is a common and powerful motivator of civic entrepreneurs. Harry Saal, founder and chairman of Network General, admits that this desire was a compelling factor in his acceptance of the start-up position at Smart Valley, a new nonprofit to build electronic community in Silicon Valley. "I've always believed it important to give back to my community, and I've done that extensively through charities with money. But now I want to use my expertise and experience to provide a unique service to the community—one only I can do." Likewise, Keith Kennedy, CEO of Watkins-Johnson, plays an active role leading the Silicon Valley coalition. "I and the Valley's other civic entrepreneurs believed we could bring something different to problems where there was a perceived void."

The rise of civic entrepreneurship is linked to growing recognition by private sector chiefs that government and political leaders cannot provide sufficient continuity, initiative, or resources to affect fundamental change. Although Americans have always harbored a mistrust of government, equally deep in our consciousness is the belief that we elect politicians to lead our communities, so we don't have to. All the community leaders we interviewed for this book view government leadership as necessary but not sufficient for building strong economic communities. Explains Susan Engelking, "We elect these people and hope they'll provide real leadership, but it doesn't happen. Political leaders rarely get rewarded for taking initiative. Their world is special interests, divisiveness, and often paralysis." She and others in Austin have concluded that "civic entrepreneurship—picking up the ball outside the government system—is more effective than politics." Neal Kocurek jokes, "I have outlived several mayors, city councils, and heads of the Chamber of Commerce. Continuity, somewhere, is central to community success."

Even the most talented and visionary political leaders operate in an environment of real constraints and pressing demands. Florida's John Anderson says, "Government and business leaders are recognizing that the demands we place on government at all levels in this country are unrealistic. There is a finite and limited revenue base at all levels of government, and yet our aggregate demands and interests exceed the ability that we have to take care of those things. There is a necessity to look for other resources and revenue opportunities to help get these jobs done." Where others see government as the problem, civic entrepreneurs see themselves as part of the solution.

Personal Development

Enlightened economic interest and making a unique difference are the top two reasons civic entrepreneurs give for getting involved. However, when civic entrepreneurs talk about why they do what they do, personal development is a third underlying theme. They like the "stretch" of getting involved in a new and different arena; entrepreneurs in the civic arena get to face new challenges, develop new skills, and meet new people. Although this preference is seldom the reason to get involved initially, personal development appears a motivator for staying involved.

By nature, civic entrepreneurs are people who like to challenge and push themselves. Civic entrepreneurs enjoy the difficulty of solving problems, of persisting when everyone else has given up. For many, venturing into new territory and negotiating through new issues not only is a different kind of challenge but also is enjoyable. Steven Zylstra, an Arizona technology entrepreneur, says simply, "This is intellectually stimulating in a different way than business. And it is just a fun group of people. We enjoy what we are doing."

When civic entrepreneurs talk about their experiences, they value the new types of camaraderie they gain. Although none said that meeting others was the primary impetus to get involved initially, many pointed to satisfying relationships as a reason to stay involved. William F. Miller has spent his life in the bridge-building activities typical of civic entrepreneurs. As provost of Stanford University, president/CEO of SRI International, and professor at the Stanford Graduate School of Business, Miller has always sought to overcome the isolation of the executive office by working on projects with other executives. "Quite frankly, one of the reasons I'm so involved with Smart Valley and Joint Venture: Silicon Valley is that I get to know people I wouldn't ordinarily rub shoulders with—not just other CEOs, but executives from government, nonprofits, and education."

Keith Kennedy, CEO of Watkins-Johnson, believes that part of the power of the collaborative approach is that it creates opportunities to really talk and share with peers. He explains, "We all need that mentoring, even those of us in high places. We need to learn together." For some, civic entrepreneurship provides an unanticipated way to develop still more skills. Boeing's Lionel Alford, who came of age in the postwar period and was commander of huge manufacturing operations, evolved his style of leadership through his involvement in aiding Wichita's economy.

Despite all the ups and downs, one of the reasons Susan Engelking of Austin remains a civic entrepreneur is the entirely new kinds of personal connections. "What's satisfying? Running into a former gang member from East Austin who hugs me and tells me about his grandkids. We started out on the opposite sides of issues, and now we're friends, as different as we are." Relationships are what build community, even in big and growing places.

WHAT CIVIC ENTREPRENEURS ARE NOT

To understand what a civic entrepreneur is, it is important to understand what a civic entrepreneur is not. Civic entrepreneurs are not advocates or opportunists, nor are they philanthropists. Civic entrepreneurs become collaborative leaders in their community because they believe that their long-term interests, and those of their organization, are tied to the vitality of the economy and the community. They are not pursuing the short-term, specific rewards of the advocate or lobbyist, nor the financial or ego rewards of the opportunist. Likewise, they do not get involved out of strictly charitable impulses. And they contribute much more than money.

They Are Not Advocates or Opportunists

The media bombard us with examples of business people working the community to pursue narrow personal or corporate objectives. Some are perfectly legitimate influencing activities; some are clearly unethical, and others are in a gray area. The history of urban renewal and downtown redevelopment efforts over the past three decades is rife with examples of real estate developers and builders who got involved in civic affairs because they sought direct, bottom-line benefits from government-sponsored redevelopment projects. Development-oriented businesses seek positive relations with governments and communities so that permits get approved. Business leaders try to influence law, policy, and regulation to favor their direct business interests; some will support certain political candidates to gain influence.

But by definition, business leaders when acting in these capacities are not civic entrepreneurs. They are simply business people pursuing narrow, oftentimes perfectly legitimate, business interests. Civic entrepreneurs, by contrast, work collaboratively to strengthen linkages between the economy and the community in order to enhance the long-term viability of their business. This motivational factor is a crucial distinction.

A person who acts as a civic entrepreneur in order to advance a political career or otherwise to gain personally is also, by definition, not a civic entrepreneur. Experience demonstrates that communities ultimately sanction individuals who try to play this game.

People will question the motives of the civic entrepreneur. And all civic entrepreneurs spend a portion of their time encouraging others to suspend their disbelief that civic entrepreneurs are working to the overall benefit of the community. Explains Ed McCracken, "I don't know how many people have felt, whether they express it to me or not, that I'm doing this [cochairing Joint Venture: Silicon Valley Network, board leader of education reform initiative] so that I or other CEOs can set ourselves up for public office. I don't have any interest in this, and never will. I think this stems from people not being able to figure it out. We understand personal gain in Silicon Valley. The fact that my involvement is related to a broader objective that has longer feedback cycles and is still associated with maximizing shareholder value is not well understood."

Although leaders must be able to plow ahead when their motivations are in question, they must be honest with themselves and others about their true motivation. Collaboration is about melding the interests of multiple parties but depends on motivations being transparent. Community trust is damaged when individuals use the guise of civic entrepreneurship to build a personal political base, to position themselves for direct financial gain, or to lobby narrow interests. True civic entrepreneurs look at a situation, see opportunity, and mobilize others to take advantage of the opportunity for their collective benefit. This behavior is radically different from exploiting the community for personal advantage or profit.

They Are Not Philanthropists

Civic entrepreneurs are also not philanthropists. A philanthropist gives money to support humanitarian purposes. Civic entrepreneurs give their time, talent, personal networks, and money to support the long-term development of their economic community. After decades in which philanthropic activities funded the United Way and the orchestra, business leaders in Cleveland came together in a new way for a decidedly different purpose: to work on the region's fundamental economic problems. Recalls Al Ratner, "We had an ironic wake-up call. Even as our city government lay in default in 1978, Cleveland was number one in the United States, probably in the world, in philanthropy. But we had lost our way."

Ratner recalls the day he recognized the new role he and other Cleveland leaders needed to play. "I remember a conversation I had with a vice president of Marshall Field. I was trying to encourage them not to close the Halle Building in downtown Cleveland where they operated a department store. I was losing every bet—everything I told him, he deflected. I finally gave him the statistics that showed Cleveland had the highest per capita of any city in the country in giving to philanthropies. And, he looked at me and said, 'Al, that must be the answer. Everyone must be giving their money away, because nobody is spending it in this economy.' I was so mad, but a light bulb went on in my head. You know, the guy is right. We were spending all our time on the philanthropic stuff, busy going from one charitable event to another, and in the meantime we weren't paying a lot of attention to the city itself and what the economy needed. This distinction made a big difference in my life. What it said to me was that we were not going to have any charities left if we don't get more involved in the fundamental problems." Philanthropy, both old-fashioned and newfangled, has its role. In fact, many civic entrepreneurs are also involved in philanthropic activities. However, civic entrepreneurship is about cultivating leaders who can contribute their talent, experience, and networks in addition to financial resources to building strong economic communities.

OBSTACLES TO
CIVIC ENTREPRENEURSHIP

In the communities that this book profiles, and in others, civic entrepreneurs face many obstacles as they work to build collaborative communities. Many of these obstacles are the day-to-day cultural, political, financial, and personal challenges of being a leader across multiple sectors and constituencies. (Part Two describes how real civic entrepreneurs have overcome leadership challenges and what lessons they have learned.)

Yet certain characteristics of communities make civic entrepreneurship particularly difficult to spark. In every community where civic entrepreneurship is flourishing, an initial set of civic entrepreneurs broke through some fundamental barriers that were stifling the ability of talented people to lead and, in turn, holding the community and the economy back. The roots of these barriers often lie deep in the history, psychology, and culture of a community. Overcoming an initial set of barriers can unleash a broader group of civic entrepreneurs and lead to a more collaborative, competitive community.

Too Much Government

"The more you have politics get into this, the more you have business people go back to their offices saying, 'I don't need this.'" Hale Ritchie believes that politics has undermined Wichita's initial 1980s burst of civic entrepreneurship. Although elected officials and public sector professionals have important roles to play in economic development efforts, too much government undermines civic entrepreneurship.

In their desire to make a difference, elected officials often try to lead in the civic space between the economy and the community. Civic entrepreneurs have learned that being effective in this arena is about empowering others, persisting over the long term, and sharing credit. Politicians, like many other people, often have difficulty operating under this model. They feel pressure to demonstrate control, get results in the short term, and take credit for what happens. Communities where politicians insist on playing the lead role or on politicizing economic development often undermine their potential for civic entrepreneurship.

From a civic entrepreneur perspective, strong political leadership can be both a blessing and a curse. Indianapolis, for example, has benefited from the strong leadership of Mayors William Hudnut and Steven Goldsmith. This strong political leadership, however, may have allowed other leaders to take a sabbatical. Some local leaders confide that the community known worldwide for a successful privately initiated amateur sports strategy conceived in the late 1970s may now be suffering from complacency in its leadership structure.

City manager Tom Lewcock believes that the public sector should not drive collaborative initiatives. "To the extent that collaborative forums appear driven or manufactured by government, it is the kiss of death. The imperative of the world today is that the economy drives everything. If that's true, then representatives of the economy need to be in the leadership role." He adds, however, a warning. "If the business leaders don't bring others together, bad things will come." In successful communities, politicians know how to step aside and work with civic entrepreneurs. And civic entrepreneurs have learned how to share credit with politicians and to bring their constituencies along.

Government-initiated efforts to help the economy can lead to an alphabet soup of programs that go in search of businesses to help. Typically, these programs are developed at the initiation of well-meaning public servants but without real input from industry. They are dependent on public funding for their continuation. And at the margin, many have low impact.

Yet the economic development professionals who run these programs sometimes see themselves as the only civic entrepreneurs. Many do not see it in their interest or in their role to encourage new leadership from business or other sectors. Intramural competition among economic development offices and organizations can consume government's attention and breed cynicism in any businesses paying attention. Meanwhile, significant issues in the community that strike at the heart of its future go unattended.

In a variation on this theme, when government spending drives regional economies, civic entrepreneurship can be tough to stimulate. Communities dominated by large public sectors, public research facilities, ivory tower universities, military installations, and companies in government-serving industries like defense often feel isolated from competitive pressures. David Friedman, writer for *Inc.* magazine, coined the term "kluge economies" (1996, p. 62). These places are often dominated by special interest power politics, where government subsidy is viewed as the solution to a sagging real economy. The solution is always to use political power to bring in financial resources to solve a problem. The urgency of building collaborative networks across economy and community appears lost, because the government-driven "economy" in fact does not depend on the community or on strong business relationships. Although many people in these communities believe something should be done to leverage government-created resources, the government funding sedates the urgency to which real leaders rise.

Too Much Business

Just as efforts to stimulate civic entrepreneurship can suffer from "too much government," they can also suffer from "too much business." Civic entrepreneurs become collaborative leaders in their community because they believe that their long-term interests, and those of their organization, are tied to the vitality of the economy and the community.

In many communities, this way of thinking is met initially with strong skepticism. Here, civic entrepreneurs face a citizenry that fundamentally mistrust the motivation of business people. The perception is that business leaders step forward only out of narrow self-interest and want something specific in return. Often, these communities have become jaded by real experience with business self-interest. Deeply rooted belief systems hold that the only reason business people get involved in the community is to line their own pocket. In these communities, any initiative championed by business people or from a business-related organization is likely to be labeled automatically as "pro-growth" or "anti-environment." The space for talking about common interests is small.

Repairing trust is the central challenge facing civic entrepreneurs in communities marked by a history of enmeshed business interests or by community skepticism about leaders' motivations. Through actions and clear communication, civic entrepreneurs must distinguish themselves from predecessors perceived as similar. They must personally win acceptance from key community skeptics.

When business acts in a narrowly self-interested manner, there can be explosive community backlash. Whether business self-interest leads to unplanned urban sprawl, to destruction of the environment, or to a pay-off induced political scandal, reform constituencies often form to address the imbalance of power in the community. This reaction can turn into an outright backlash of misplaced retribution and unforeseen consequences.

Santa Barbara, California, illustrates how an irresponsible act by business can affect fundamentally the psychology of a community, the vitality of its economy, and its relations with all business leaders. Nationally, the Santa Barbara oil spill of 1969 helped stimulate the environmental movement. In Santa Barbara, the spill created a no-growth backlash that dramatically shut down the expansion of businesses in the community. The hostility the community felt toward the oil industry and anxiety about further environmental degradation was channeled into stopping the physical expansion of Santa Barbara businesses. Growth versus no-growth battles in the 1980s, waged with verbal attacks, media mudslinging, and lawsuits, tore the community apart. No-growthers effectively shut down approval of building permits from 1986 to 1990. Then the economy stagnated, and wages declined through the 1990s as defense companies cut back, and emerging technology companies left town embittered or grew elsewhere.

In 1995, leaders from business—technology-based companies and business services companies—invited community, education, and government leaders to come together through the Santa Barbara Region Economic Community Project. The Project's aim: to undertake collaborative actions to create a technology-based economy consistent with environmental preservation. At their helm was Steve Ainsley, publisher of the *Santa Barbara News-Press* and Bob Knight, former Xerox executive and successful technology entrepreneur. Both men, and the broad-based team they built, wanted to see Santa Barbara overcome the fragmentation that paralyzed it in the past. The focus of this collaborative effort is rebuilding relationships to create a community with a rising standard of living and quality of life.

A second form of "too much business" is a community that views business as a direct substitute for government or a business community that views its way as the reform cure for government. It has become fashionable to view business as a partial replacement for government. Politicians threaten and citizens believe that government spending can be slashed and the private sector can pick up the slack. Alternatively, in some communities it is common for businesses to claim that the solution to community challenges is to run government more like a business.

Both of these notions create a difficult climate for civic entrepreneurs. Civic entrepreneurs help forge strong links between business, government, and other community constituencies by working together in the civil sector. The civil sector resides between the private and public sectors and is predicated on having strong capacities in both sectors. An active civil sector can no doubt increase the effectiveness and efficiency of the public sector. But neither the private sector nor the civil sector can be a wholesale replacement for government. Communities that emaciate and demoralize their government lose a key leg of the civic stool.

Civic entrepreneurs have learned that solutions to community problems are not as simple as running government more like a business. Although this slogan has superficial appeal, what is needed is mutual exploration of what business can contribute uniquely to the civil and government sectors rather than arrogance that all business has to do is teach government to behave more like business. What civic entrepreneurs do is create and sustain working partnerships among business, government, and civic organizations that build on the strengths of each sector.

A final barrier to civic entrepreneurship associated with too much business is dependence on a single, larger-than-life business leader. Sometimes, a single charismatic business leader exerts tremendous influence in a community and appears single-handedly to make things happen (Luke, Ventriss, and others, 1988, p. 229.) With power based on personality and longevity, this person functions as a committee of one. People like this act as the community's thinker and doer, strategist and planner.

When a charismatic business leader passes, the community faces a tremendous vacuum. Almost by definition, the old-style charismatic leader did not mentor emerging leaders or challenge others to have meaningful community involvement. Although the traditional charismatic leader contributed greatly to communities, they seldom left a sustainable leadership base as a legacy. Stimulating civic entrepreneurship requires changing the very definition of leadership in these communities to one focused on the leader as a catalyst for collaboration.

Absentee Ownership

Communities whose economies are dominated by branch operations of companies headquartered elsewhere, or whose local companies have been bought out by outsiders, often view this situation as a barrier to civic entrepreneurship. They point to places with headquarters operations, locally controlled companies, and homegrown entrepreneurship and claim that leadership is easier there.

Stimulating civic entrepreneurship is more difficult for communities that have professional managers without a long-term stake in the community or without a short-term corporate directive to get involved. Jack Pfister, general manager of the Salt River Project and key civic entrepreneur in Phoenix, describes that community's evolution. "The first leadership group in Phoenix in the 1960s and 1970s was local entrepreneurs. As companies grew and were acquired, many of these people were replaced by professional managers from the outside. For many of these people, community leadership was a matter of personal discretion and style, not an executive requirement. Their goal was to get promoted up and out of Phoenix." Acquisition of local companies (particularly utilities, banks, and other financial services) changed the fabric of communities throughout the United States. To the civic entrepreneurs in Phoenix, this change makes it all the more essential that they identify and engage up-and-coming local entrepreneurs who are committed to growing their business in the community. And in fact, every community that this book profiles viewed executives of homegrown businesses as an increasingly important part of the civic entrepreneur farm team.

The counterpart strategy is to work even harder to engage managers new to the community. Austin's strategy has been to set high expectations and provide high support for community involvement from the day a company executive steps foot in town. Susan Engelking explains, "From the start, we tell them how much we need and value them. We set high expectations. We plan events and training to integrate new managers into our community. Most have responded very well." Cleveland's renaissance has been driven by local business leaders who refused to give up and leave, but they make a conscious effort to bring outside executives in. "When a new CEO comes into the job or into town, there is great interest in getting him or her involved. We want new people and go after them. It's about expectations," explains Richard Pogue of Cleveland. Glenda Hood, business woman and mayor of Orlando agrees. "Whenever a new business leader comes to town, I personally reach out and invite them to get involved. The key is communications." Like other Florida communities, Orlando is the classic outpost economy with no major corporate headquarters. The community's goal: to absorb new executives quickly to maximize their involvement during their tour of duty in Orlando.

Culture of Blame

"All we knew was that our community wasn't moving forward. We kept talking about the same problems, pointing the same fingers." Setting aside the economic analyses, John Kennett, owner of Pizazz Printing and chair of the San Jose Metropolitan Chamber, knew Silicon Valley's root problem.

Many communities develop over time a culture of blame, which paralyzes them from moving forward. Sometimes, at the other end of the pointed blame finger are outsiders. History demonstrates repeatedly the human tendency to find an outsider to blame for trouble. Communities experiencing economic anxiety blame all sorts of outside forces (Japanese competitors, the federal tax code, state cut-backs) before looking inside themselves. The Midwest in the early 1980s played this blame game well, before communities and industries began to take charge of their future.

In an equally insidious form, the targets of the blame game are entirely internal. Ask business people what the problem is, and they blame government. Ask government people, and they blame business. Ask community leaders, and they blame both government and business leaders. The blame game can be played forever, because no one will take responsibility for the economic community. Some communities marked by the culture of blame grew rapidly and increased in complexity; they lost the personal relationships, trust, and shared experience that characterized earlier times. Others cherished their decades-old way of earning a living and could not accept the need for change. The kind of process leadership provided by civic entrepreneurs is one way out of this conundrum.

In the early 1990s, Silicon Valley's culture of blame started bothering a few private and public executives so much that they decided to try to change it. The first step was to recognize that the blame game was in fact the "way things worked around here" and to name it publicly. The way out was to engage the community in specific collaborative efforts that bore fruit and thus demonstrate to one person at a time that working together can be better than pointing fingers. The process was slow and painful, but it has paid off. Explains Kennett, "How did Joint Venture overcome the culture of blame? Well, the answer to that is one step at a time."

Legacy of Poor Process

Some communities are haunted by past processes that failed to lead to action—otherwise known as the here-we-go-again syndrome. A legacy of poor process can make communities skeptical of new civic entrepreneurs. Often well-intentioned community visioning efforts leave people frustrated. A laundry list of ideas, unfiltered by reality and not acted upon, sours people to new initiatives. In a backlash, people reject all participatory processes as a waste of time. They make statements like, "We don't need any more meetings" or "Involving people slows things down." Yet process matters to civic entrepreneurs. Getting people involved in finding solutions to their own problems is the name of their game. So, by providing good process leadership, civic entrepreneurs help communities learn to manage constructive processes that lead to results.

Sometimes, unreasonable expectations undermine civic initiatives from the start. In these cases, high-profile regional efforts can become flashpoints for resentment instead of focal points for collaboration. Los Angeles has struggled to build consensus around strategies for economic and social renewal. These attempts have been plagued by overpromising, infighting, and inability to reach agreement on major strategy.

Yet the failure of previous efforts is not always a barrier to civic entrepreneurship. In fact, as with business entrepreneurship, successful communities often start, stop, and abandon efforts several times before they ultimately succeed. These experiences can be viewed as important learning and momentum-building opportunities. Alan Hald, vice chairman of MicroAge, Inc., credits the Phoenix Futures Forum, a community visioning effort, as an important training ground. In California, Santa Barbara launched several efforts to support and engage its new technology economy better before one finally took hold. But the knowledge and awareness created by the previous efforts accelerated the progress of the successful one.

Americans have always cared about their communities, and stepped up to improve them. Civic entrepreneurs are a new variation of American leader emerging in the last two decades of this century to help communities deal with a fundamentally changed economic context. As leaders, civic entrepreneurs are marked by apparent contrasts. Their style is entrepreneurial and collaborative. They are leaders, and they care about inclusion and process. Their perspective is economic, and they value the community. They tolerate ambiguity, and drive relentlessly toward results.

In their drive to build collaborative economies, what specifically do civic entrepreneurs do? What roles do they play? What practices have they found effective? To these questions, we turn next.

PART TWO

How Civic Entrepreneurs Build Community

C ivic entrepreneurs play specific roles in the process of building economic community. This process goes through a life cycle of four stages (initiation, incubation, implementation, and improvement and renewal). At each stage, certain roles of civic entrepreneurs become critical: those of motivator and networker in the initiation stage, convener and teacher in the incubation stage, integrator and driver during implementation, and mentor and agitator for community renewal. Part Two describes each stage of the collaborative process and how civic entrepreneurs help their communities progress to results. Practical advice is offered throughout for civic entrepreneurs trying to change their own communities.

CHAPTER THREE

The Four Stages in Building Community

I̶n communities across America—communities that are very different from one another in their populations, economies, and histories—civic entrepreneurs are at work. They work in remarkably similar ways. They build a new economic community by driving a collaborative process. This process typically moves through four stages: initiation, incubation, implementation, and improvement or renewal. The scope, timing, and success of each stage vary widely across economic communities. Some are more chaotic or informal than others; there is no one-size-fits-all approach. However, in every case, civic entrepreneurs are the catalysts that keep their communities moving through their change process.

A growing body of literature has focused attention on the nature of collaborative process in communities. However, as Scott London notes, "While the term collaboration (and its various offshoots—collaborative leadership, community alliances, participatory problem-solving, etc.) is bandied about a great deal today as an answer to politics-as-usual, surprisingly little substantive research has been done on the subject" (London, 1995, p. 1). Until such research is done, experience seems to be the best guide.

Much of the literature focuses on the dynamics and stages of the collaborative process, which often resembles an organizational strategic planning process. For example, Barbara Gray (1989) suggests a three-phase process that includes prenegotiation or problem setting, direction setting, and implementation. Our experience suggests that there are many process variations, from short, focused efforts to long, broad participatory processes. It also suggests that civic entrepreneurs are the key ingredient when community collaborative processes deliver tangible results.

Although civic entrepreneurship manifests itself uniquely in each economic community, these communities possess civic entrepreneurs who play distinct roles. The form and exercise of these roles have many subtleties, but strong similarities exist nonetheless among America's civic entrepreneurs. We have identified eight distinct roles across the four stages of the change process. For each role, we have observed specific practices pursued by civic entrepreneurs in communities across the country. While multiple roles are played across the change process, we have also found that certain roles and practices are intensified at certain stages.

CIVIC ENTREPRENEURS ACQUIRE AND USE SPECIFIC SKILLS

We are convinced that civic entrepreneurship is a learned behavior, not simply a genetic trait. Although individuals certainly have predispositions toward leadership, experience suggests that civic entrepreneurs develop in different ways. Some are naturals from the beginning. Others transform from combative or disengaged leaders to civic entrepreneurs over time, or in one galvanizing, defining moment.

What is the skill set necessary for civic entrepreneurship? Much has been written about leadership in business or government. Some people have talked about the emergence of a new kind of leader who can navigate both worlds. Some of these skills are critical to the successful practice of civic entrepreneurship.

John Gardner describes many skills common to civic entrepreneurs. According to Gardner, "Skill in the building and rebuilding of community is not just another of the innumerable requirements of contemporary leadership. It is one of the highest and most essential skills a leader can command."

Gardner goes on to say, "We need leaders who have some acquaintance with systems other than their own with which they must work. The day of the hard-shelled military leaders who never bothered to understand civilians is over, as is the day of the hard-nosed business executive who never bothered to understand government, and the day of the leader who never bothered to think internationally." He cites five specific skills as critically important for contemporary leadership (Gardner, 1990, pp. 118–120):

- *Agreement building*—having skills in conflict resolution, compromise, and coalition building; the capacity to build trust and the judgment and political skills to deal with multiple constituencies
- *Networking*—building linkages beyond traditional relationships, whatever it takes to get the job done
- *Exercising nonjurisdictional power*—exercising the power of ideas, the power of understanding how different systems work, the power of the media and public opinion
- *Institution building*—constructing new systems, building problem-solving capacity into them, and recruiting talent to operate them
- *Flexibility*—"steering a kayak through the perilous white water of the Salmon River" rather than "piloting a huge ocean liner"

David Chrislip and Carl Larson suggest other skills based on their assessment of collaborative leadership, as it is practiced in communities across the country. At its most basic, "collaborative leaders are sustained by their deeply democratic belief that people have the capacity to create their own visions and solve their own problems." Chrislip and Larson have derived four principles from the practice of collaborative leadership (1994, pp. 138–141, 146):

- *Inspire commitment and action*—Catalyze, convene, energize, and facilitate others to create visions and solve problems.
- *Lead as peer problem solver*—Do not do the work of the group; do not engage in command-and-control behavior; de-emphasize power and status differences among participants; invest energy in helping participants build relationships and own the process.

- *Build broad-based involvement*—Make a conscious and disciplined effort to identify and bring together stakeholders necessary for defining problems, creating solutions, and getting results.

- *Sustain hope and participation*—Help participants through inevitable frustrations; help them set and achieve incremental and attainable goals; encourage celebrations of achievement along the way; sustain commitment to the process when quick solutions are available or when power asserts itself.

Although these ingredients make up a good deal of the recipe for civic entrepreneurship, our experience suggests that building the skill base of civic entrepreneurs requires opportunities to experiment with the following:

- *Practice stretch thinking*—Budding civic entrepreneurs need to be challenged intellectually and behaviorally. They must be thrust into situations in which they can question their assumptions, connect seemingly disparate ideas in new ways, and jump the learning curve.

- *Practice breaking boundaries*—Civic entrepreneurship requires a true understanding of how problems cross traditional boundaries. It requires walking in another's shoes to understand truly the different vocabulary, symbols, and processes of their world—and to discover where values are shared and common ground can be found.

- *Practice exerting process leadership*—Civic entrepreneurs need opportunities to practice their role as process convener: working with multiple constituencies on complex issues, asking penetrating questions, ensuring that all voices are heard, creating process discipline to produce outcomes, and the like.

We have observed civic entrepreneurs at work in many communities. Many have acquired and use the aforementioned skills. Many pursue a number of other practices as well. More important, however, is that civic entrepreneurship appears in a recurring pattern. Across different communities, a similar pattern of behavior is evident: a collective of civic entrepreneurs plays certain roles and pursues certain practices that lead their communities through a process of change. This process is building the new economic community.

FOUR STAGES OF BUILDING THE NEW ECONOMIC COMMUNITY

The process of building economic community goes through four stages: initiation, incubation, implementation, and improvement or renewal. Civic entrepreneurs play distinctive roles and pursue specific practices that ensure that their community moves successfully through each stage of the process. At different stages, civic entrepreneurs assume certain roles (see Table 3.1). It is exceedingly rare that a single individual plays all eight roles. Many civic entrepreneurs are particularly skilled at one or more roles and seek out other civic entrepreneurs to form a team that can collectively play all eight roles effectively over time. Civic entrepreneurs never work alone.

The challenge is to find civic entrepreneurs who can play the most needed roles at different stages of their community's evolution. Some members of the civic entrepreneur team will know that a collaborative process is necessary to build momentum and secure commitments for significant change. Others will have learned not to rush the process by playing implementation roles too early. Others will know to ease off on initiation or process roles when implementation is critical. The best examples of civic entrepreneurs are those who have a sense of timing and sensitivity to the potential and limits of the roles that they can play.

Roles Played by Civic Entrepreneurs	Stage 1 Initiate	Stage 2 Incubate	Stage 3 Implement	Stage 4 Improve and Renew
#1 The Motivator	♦♦♦♦♦			
#2 The Networker	♦♦♦♦♦			
#3 The Teacher		♦♦♦♦♦		
#4 The Convener		♦♦♦♦♦		
#5 The Integrator			♦♦♦♦♦	
#6 The Driver			♦♦♦♦♦	
#7 The Mentor				♦♦♦♦♦
#8 The Agitator				♦♦♦♦♦

Table 3.1. Intensive Roles Played by Civic Entrepreneurs at Each Stage of Building Economic Community.

Initiation: Civic Entrepreneurs
as Motivators and Networkers

To get their communities moving, civic entrepreneurs motivate themselves and others to look at their community differently (Table 3.2). They personally demonstrate for others a new level of responsibility for the future direction of their community. They network among their friends and then move beyond their comfort zone to connect with other leaders in the community whom they do not know as well but who are critical to starting a process of change. They nail down the commitments of a core leadership team that can then catalyze and sponsor a process of change in their community.

Incubation: Civic Entrepreneurs
as Teachers and Conveners

Some civic entrepreneurs help educate their community, preparing it for participating effectively in a collaborative process of change. Such a process can be a broad, participatory effort (for example, Arizona, Silicon Valley) or efforts focused on more specific challenges or opportunities (for example, Austin, Cleveland). In either case, civic entrepreneurs make sure that the facts are on the table in ways that are meaningful to participants and that people are aware of the local implications of global forces. Some open minds to outside ideas and help build a framework for making sense of new and complex information. Once a foundation is built, some become conveners of a fair and effective decision-making or incubation process, ensuring that it involves a diverse cross-section of the community and operates according to clear rules and with a strong discipline that drives for results.

Implementation: Civic Entrepreneurs
as Integrators and Drivers

Some civic entrepreneurs play critical roles in supporting their communities as they move from the collaborative process of determining what to do about their situation to the collaborative actions that will actually change their communities. As integrators, some recruit expertise, locate resources, and otherwise help assemble the necessary ingredients for successful implementation of tangible initiatives. As drivers,

Civic Entrepreneur Roles and Practices	Stage 1 Initiate	Stage 2 Incubate	Stage 3 Implement	Stage 4 Improve and Renew
#1 The Motivator	♦♦♦♦♦			
Give the wake-up call	♦♦			
Take new responsibility	♦♦			
Declare interdependence	♦♦			
Raise the stakes	♦♦			
Create a sense of mission	♦♦			
#2 The Networker	♦♦♦♦♦			
Get friends to commit	♦♦			
Reach beyond the comfort zone	♦♦			
Buy time from skeptics	♦♦			
Recruit a complementary team	♦♦			
#3 The Teacher		♦♦♦♦♦		
Put the facts on the table		♦♦		
Localize global challenges and opportunities		♦♦		
Open minds to outside ideas		♦♦		
Build a shared framework		♦♦		
#4 The Convener		♦♦♦♦♦		
Create clear rules and discipline for results		♦♦		
Balance top-down influence and bottom-up innovation		♦♦		
Help people find the right fit		♦♦		
Persist through inevitable process attacks		♦♦		
#5 The Integrator			♦♦♦♦♦	
Manage leadership transitions			♦♦	
Forge deep commitments to change			♦♦	
Recruit a first-class support team			♦♦	
#6 The Driver			♦♦♦♦♦	
Press for measurement of outcomes			♦♦	
Discourage fragmentation and duplication			♦♦	
Keep the focus on challenging objectives			♦♦	
#7 The Mentor				♦♦♦♦♦
Build a platform for continuing collaboration				♦♦
Nurture a lasting culture of civic entrepreneurship				♦♦
Reach out and involve newcomers in the community				♦♦

Table 3.2. The Roles and Practices of Civic Entrepreneurs.

Civic Entrepreneur Roles and Practices	Stage 1 Initiate	Stage 2 Incubate	Stage 3 Implement	Stage 4 Improve and Renew
#8 The Agitator				♦♦♦♦♦
Push for a continuous process of change				♦♦
Constantly scan community issues and trends				♦♦
Keep talking about building a better community				♦♦

Table 3.2.   The Roles and Practices of Civic Entrepreneurs (cont'd).

some civic entrepreneurs ensure that measurable objectives are set and reached, that implementation efforts avoid fragmentation, duplication, or rigidity in approach, and that the focus remains on challenging objectives.

Improvement or Renewal: Civic Entrepreneurs as Mentors and Agitators

As communities try to turn short-term implementation successes into a culture that supports a sustainable, continuous capacity for change, civic entrepreneurs are once again at center stage. As mentors, some help establish organizational platforms for the community to continue working together on important issues. Some nurture a local culture for civic entrepreneurship. Some reach out and involve newcomers in the community. As agitators, some fight complacency. These civic entrepreneurs constantly remind people that change is a continuous process, that it is important to keep scanning the community for new issues and trends, and that an even better future is possible for the community.

The process of building economic community is continuous (see Figure 3.1). Roles are played over and over again. Practices change to fit a new situation—new people, issues, institutions, and obstacles. Although becoming a civic entrepreneur is not a science, the four chapters that follow show how people of very different backgrounds, occupations, and experience have practiced the art of civic entrepreneurship in their own communities.

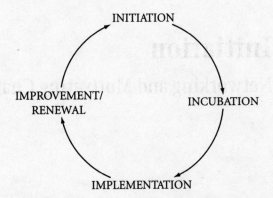

Figure 3.1. The Continuous Process of Building Economic Community.

CHAPTER FOUR

Initiation
Networking and Motivating Change

No one can do it better than people who live there. There is no answer outside.

—Al Ratner, Cleveland

Sure, a few of us could get together and develop a plan, but no one would believe in it.

—Jim Morgan, Silicon Valley

Civic entrepreneurs play two particularly important roles to get their communities moving. They act as *motivators* and *networkers*. They motivate themselves and others to look at their community differently and demonstrate a new level of responsibility for spurring change. They network among their friends and then move beyond their comfort zone to connect with other leaders in the community whom they do not know as well but who are critical to starting a process of change. They nail down the commitments of a core leadership team that can then catalyze and sponsor a process of change in their community. Specifically, civic entrepreneurs have accomplished the following during the initiation stage:

- Silicon Valley abandoned its culture of blame and initiated a process of change that involved more than one thousand people.

- Arizona refused to accept economic decline and bet on a group of entrepreneurs who initiated a statewide process.
- Cleveland's business leaders got back involved in their city and initiated a process of change that continues more than fifteen years later.
- A small group of Austin civic entrepreneurs met every morning for months to initiate a process that would win national competitions for MCC and SEMATECH and position Austin for future opportunities.

THE MOTIVATOR: CREATES A SENSE OF URGENCY

The first role a civic entrepreneur plays must be that of motivator. Civic entrepreneurs first motivate themselves, recognizing that they must take a greater responsibility for the direction of their community. Once self-motivated, civic entrepreneurs create a sense of urgency for improving their community, using their credibility to deliver a wake-up call to others. They also demonstrate a new level of commitment to the community through their personal investment of time and resources and the involvement of others. Civic entrepreneurs motivate by taking the following steps. They:

- Deliver a wake-up call to their community
- Take a new level of responsibility for their community
- Make a declaration of interdependence
- Raise the stakes about the future of their community
- Create a sense of mission about changing their community

They Deliver the Wake-Up Call

After decades of rapid growth, Silicon Valley got its own wake-up call in the late 1980s. It was not just a single-sector setback like the 1984–1987 commodity semiconductor slump but a broad-based, fundamental change. The job engine that had generated 7 percent annual employment growth since 1972 sputtered to 0.7 percent from 1986 on. Defense cuts and restructuring in high-tech manufacturing led to the layoff of forty thousand workers in manufacturing industries. New start-ups were forming at half the rate of 1987. As high-tech slowed, real estate and business services down the food chain suffered. Local business bankruptcies reached unprecedented levels. A 1992 survey of business leaders showed confidence about Silicon Valley's future to be at an all-time low.

Most troubling, headline after headline talked of mainstay Valley companies expanding elsewhere. Major companies announced expansions outside Silicon Valley. But this time, the corporate expansions were not labor-intensive manufacturing plants in far-off Third World countries but advanced manufacturing and R&D facilities in U.S. metropolitan areas like Austin, Portland, and Phoenix.

Recalls Tom Hayes, the director of global corporate affairs for Applied Materials, "In 1992, our company was growing so fast we were busting at the seams. To plan for our next major expansion, we pulled together a team to compare and contrast Silicon Valley, Austin, and other regions. We were looking both at cost and value parameters. Austin came out the clear winner. I was shocked. Jim [Morgan, Applied's chairman and CEO] was shocked. Being rational business people, we knew what we had to do." Applied Materials, now the world's largest semiconductor equipment manufacturer, announced plans to build a facility in Austin.

Yet Applied's decision troubled Hayes and Morgan. Both had grown to appreciate the Valley. They knew Applied had benefited tremendously from the relationships and diversity of the region. They did not want to accept that Silicon Valley was finished. Explains Hayes, "We decided to see what we could do." They had their wake-up call and now would see to it that other leaders in Silicon Valley would get theirs as well.

Many motivations spurred Silicon Valley's civic entrepreneurs into action. Jim Morgan was deeply affected by what he saw in other communities around the world. "I, and many other Valley leaders, had experienced how regions in Japan, Europe, and the United States simply worked better. We had seen the results in Austin, the strong coming together to make the community an attractive place to do business. A friend of mine, Alan Hald, the cofounder of MicroAge, Inc., had headed up a similar effort in Arizona led by entrepreneurial, next-generation leaders. While we knew Silicon Valley was different, clearly we had something to learn. I believed the time was right. We had to try."

Sometimes, civic entrepreneurs rediscover their community, which helps them motivate others to build on local strengths. Neil Bonke, CEO of Electroglas in Silicon Valley, recalls "sitting in my office worrying about all the problems facing the Valley. I looked out the window, and I saw what appeared to be an old bread truck. Well, on that truck was printed, 'Ion In-plant Services.' Then, it hit me. This was a delivery service for material that would be bombarded with high-energy ions—a very specialized service important to high-technology companies. It occurred to me that I had taken this kind of thing for granted. In reality, these are the kinds of things that make my community unique. I needed to start paying better attention."

In a period of pessimism in the early 1990s, Bonke delivered an upbeat wake-up call. He delivered the message that Silicon Valley should be proud of what it has and should work hard to maintain and build on those strengths as a region. Since that time, he has been one of the driving forces from the business sector promoting regional cooperation in economic development among Silicon Valley cities.

It was not just the high-technology CEOs who saw the need for change. John Neece, leader of the local building construction trade union and Joe Parisi, CEO of Therma, a firm that provides the air conditioning and related specialty services to high-technology companies, had a different kind of wake-up call. According to Neece, "I knew we had a bad attitude about business—and Oregon, Colorado, and Austin had a better attitude—but Joe Parisi and I knew we had to get involved when the governor of Texas came to Silicon Valley to steal our companies."

Like Silicon Valley, Cleveland received an economic wake-up call. Cleveland lost 24 percent of its population in the 1970s. The city was rocked by racial polarization and riots in the 1960s. Per capita income fell well below the national average. By the late 1970s, Cleveland became the first major city since the Great Depression to legally default on its fiscal obligations. This economic crisis propelled the business community, which had been relatively uninvolved up to that point, into action.

Civic entrepreneurs stepped forward and forced the community to face reality. Albert Ratner, civic entrepreneur and cochair of Forest City Enterprises, Inc., a nationally prominent development company based in Cleveland, recalls what happened. "The year 1979 was clearly the low point. [Then-Mayor Dennis] Kucinich was the portrait of

Dorian Gray, and voters saw that it was hopeless. The default had no reason to take place from a monetary standpoint; it was $28 million dollars. It was a banker at AmeriTrust, Brock Weir, who said we can't let the city go on this way, and so he called in the loan."

Despite the default, Ratner and others recognized that Cleveland was not finished. "What people tend to forget about Cleveland, while we were in default, Cleveland was the number one city in the United States, in the world, in philanthropy," explains Ratner. "But, I think it was a wake-up call to the community. Out of that came Cleveland Tomorrow (a group of leading Cleveland CEOs who stimulated a number of civic improvements). An interesting question is how bad things have to get before you change."

Richard Pogue, a civic entrepreneur and leading lawyer in Cleveland and now senior adviser with Dix & Eaton, Inc., adds that "by the 1970s, many executives were overseeing global operations and weren't paying much attention to what was going on in the local government arena. They were preoccupied with their own affairs. Default was totally unnecessary. But it was the wake-up call." Pogue describes a common situation, where business leaders naturally preoccupied with staying competitive in the fast-moving global economy lose touch with their communities and have to reconnect.

While Brock Weir delivered the difficult wake-up call by calling in the loan, another civic entrepreneur delivered a wake-up call of his own to his fellow business leaders. According to Pogue, "We had a de facto leader in Del de Windt in the business community who headed up Eaton Corporation, and he got a bunch of business leaders to sit down and say, 'Let's get back involved here.' So they worked out a series of agenda items to get things moving again, all built around working with government leaders. First, we had to get a mayor elected that understood economic development. That's how the public-private partnership began. Of course, in those days, we didn't call it a public-private partnership; we just did it."

In Cleveland's case, crisis was necessary as the backdrop for the wake-up call. "We would not have been able to accomplish the comeback without the trauma of default," observes Pogue. "We had to have so much adversity that we couldn't stand it anymore. Without default, the odds are that we probably would have just drifted along."

A crisis is not always necessary to create the conditions for a wake-up call. Civic entrepreneurs are adept at showing the gap between the current reality and a desired future. In the late 1980s, Nebraska's economy was comfortably drifting along, not growing significantly, but not falling apart either. Mike Yanney, CEO of an Omaha, Nebraska, financial institution, realized that his state would miss future economic opportunities if it kept riding on the economic momentum of the past.

He decided to deliver a wake-up call, not to crisis but to opportunity. He stood up at an annual state Chamber meeting and declared that "the future of Nebraska is not corn." Expecting to be booed, Yanney instead received an ovation. It was a message that people were ready to hear, delivered by someone who had a deep reservoir of personal and professional credibility. Yanney was asked to lead a statewide renewal initiative that later became the Nebraska Futures Project. After twenty town hall meetings, a new agenda for the state was adopted and launched—an agenda focused on shifting Nebraska to a more diversified economic base.

In Arizona, civic entrepreneurs appealed to both crisis and opportunity to get their state's attention. Like many other Sun Belt regions, the state had had success in attracting new jobs and population. At the same time, the per capita income of Arizona residents was stagnating. Arizona was not generating high-quality jobs. Civic entrepreneurs focused on both the limitations of the current economy and emerging opportunities for growth in electronics, optics, and other sectors.

Civic entrepreneurs in Arizona seized the moment. According to Ioanna Morfessis, president and CEO of the Greater Phoenix Economic Council, "It was timing and opportunity. Alan and his group [Alan Hald, vice chairman of MicroAge, Inc. and several other civic entrepreneurs] met together for a year. Then our state's economy began a rapid decline into recession, and our leaders were open to a new approach." Steve Zylstra, director of business development at Simula, who was one of the initial group of civic entrepreneurs driving change in Arizona, points out that "leaders help create a sense of urgency that physical crises can cause naturally. They can create urgency for opportunities."

Sometimes, a natural disaster can be the means by which civic entrepreneurs bring a community together. According to John Anderson of Enterprise Florida, "Hurricane Andrew had a major impact—more things changed in terms of how business and government worked together. It helped define economic development and the roles of public and private sectors, and identify new leaders." In all these cases, civic entrepreneurs stepped in and used the motivator with meaning to their community (economic crisis, opportunity, natural disaster) to spur change.

They Demonstrate a New Level of Responsibility for the Community

Civic entrepreneurs back up their wake-up calls by making tangible, personal commitments to change. They assume a new level of responsibility for their community, which sets a new standard for others. They do not engage in grandstanding but through action make it clear to other local leaders that a higher level of commitment will be necessary to improve the community. Civic entrepreneurs lead by example. They personally invest time away from their business or organization. They invest seed money. They assign top-notch talent to the cause.

They ask for little in return except that others rise to the leadership challenge. As Al Ratner of Cleveland has said, "The only thing that really matters is, are there committed people who are willing to step up to the plate either because they feel it's their responsibility or they think something good will come of it?" In fact, Cleveland is a good example of a community that has developed a recurring process that delivers new levels of responsibility. "When there is a task to be done, you go through a process and figure out here's how much money needs to be raised, and everybody says okay the process may take longer, but there is a strong inclination of the parties to do their fair share," according to Steven Minter, executive director of the Cleveland Foundation.

Civic entrepreneurs from the business world assume new levels of responsibility because they know the limitations of their government counterparts. In Orlando, Mayor Glenda Hood asserts that "government can be a facilitator and a partner, but it has to be the business community that takes the leadership for moving forward." Neal Kocurek of Austin concurs. "We don't have a political system where political leaders get rewarded to take initiative. Our system doesn't provide for sufficient continuity. So where is the leadership on new issues going to come from? It has to come from somewhere else in the community."

In Cleveland, Richard Pogue's experience is that "you have to look to the private sector to take the lead. Government has too many constraints. The private sector can accomplish a lot if they are willing to be partners, if they're willing to let the politicians take credit. Once in a while, you have a politician who is different. But, in the main, by the very nature of the political process, you're not going to get that kind of unselfish leadership from politicians. If I were to give advice to another city, the number one thing I would say is, see what kind of business leadership you have and get them organized and working together. You have to look to the business community as the catalysts."

Lionel Alford, former senior vice president of Boeing in Wichita, Kansas, believes that government can play more of a catalytic role in getting business leaders to take more responsibility for their community. "People in government with vision can help motivate business people to focus on a 'hot spot' in a community. If you have a visionary who understands what's going on in a community, they can be the means to get things focused. [Wichita Mayor] Bob Knight played that role in helping to motivate business leaders to get involved in WI/SE effort." While in each of these cases, business leaders generally stepped forward first, in latter stages civic entrepreneurs from government and nonprofit sectors became integral members of the team.

Civic entrepreneurs often spend time understanding the issues, considering many options for action, talking to many others, even experimenting with smaller-scale initiatives, before acting decisively. Successful civic entrepreneurs can see clearly their own value-added and where they need to recruit other civic entrepreneurs or specialized talent to complement their skills, experience, and social network. But, once they choose their best point of leverage, they are committed to seeing it through.

In Arizona, a group of civic entrepreneurs invested hundreds of hours of time to understand their state, the economic development field, and how they might help move their state forward. Alan Hald hosted the group at his home. "For about a year, at one point we were meeting virtually every Sunday, we tried to figure out what to do. We did future scenarios. We were reading [Harvard Professor Michael] Porter and talking about ideas of economic development. It became clear to us that entrepreneurship was closely coupled to economic development, that it wasn't just a city issue; it had to be a state and regional issue. Out of that evolved the vital cycle model." This model simply demonstrated how economic vitality helps fund economic and social infrastructure, which in turn supports economic vitality in a continuous cycle. It became a rallying cry for Arizona.

Hald and his group challenged other leaders and state government to invest their time and resources in the effort by putting their own resources on the table. "It was quite unusual and extraordinary that Alan and other leaders were willing to invest resources in this effort at a time when their companies could not have faced worse circumstances," observes Ioanna Morfessis. "For entrepreneurs to take that kind of time away from their companies—they don't have gargantuan staffs where they can say, director of public affairs do this or director of personnel you handle this for me—that they would actually do this is also extraordinary."

By raising their own level of responsibility for the future of their state, others followed suit. A town hall meeting was a key event at which others made commitments. According to Morfessis, "The town hall was a watershed. It was a mix of new and old leadership. Rich Kraemer [a then-president and chief operating officer of UDC Homes, a major homebuilder in several Sun Belt states and chairman of the two-year-old Greater Phoenix Economic Council] was skeptical but put his personal capital behind it ultimately and was able to convince others. A couple of people went to the mat, and the others fell into line."

The transformation was stunning. What began as a small study group of entrepreneurs had become a statewide effort. "What was interesting was that people were drawing on a model from a group of wacky entrepreneurs who met on Saturdays and Sundays—don't they have a life?—and were willing to put major dollars into it and take a major risk," according to Morfessis.

At the same time, Hald and his core team of civic entrepreneurs knew that without backing up their ideas with tangible commitments, they would have been written off as simply wacky entrepreneurs. It is typical for civic entrepreneurs to provide early seed money to demonstrate their confidence that the community can move forward. For example, in Silicon Valley Jim Morgan personally guaranteed the $75,000 consulting contract to get the initial study started. The results of the study provided the wake-up call that helped focus the Valley on the need for change.

Change in many communities begins with a relatively small core of civic entrepreneurs who become known for assuming a new level of responsibility. William Cunningham, chancellor of the University of Texas system, recalls that Austin won the MCC competition because "a few key people rose to the occasion and decided to meet the challenge. It comes down to a few individuals deciding to provide leadership, along with a good sense of timing and being fortunate to mesh the right personalities on a winning team." According to Neal Kocurek, executive vice president of Radian International in Austin, "You find that there are tremendous resources out there waiting to be tapped. But someone has to go forward and lead the process."

Tim Witsman, the executive director of the Wichita Chamber, knows how one person can make a difference. He recalls how "the downtown plan led by Jack DeBock energized the discussion and caused the city to commit $100 million and the county to commit additional resources to get something done. This was a defining moment in terms of business leadership."

In Cleveland, the default clearly provided a defining moment for many business leaders, after which civic entrepreneurs emerged to take greater responsibility for their city. Al Ratner's "real conversion" came when he realized that "what we were doing was spending all of our time on the philanthropic stuff, we were always busy going from one charitable thing to another, and in the meantime we weren't paying a lot of attention to the city itself and what it needed. It made a big difference in my life. What it said to me was we're not going to have any charities left if we don't get more involved." Al Ratner did more than get involved. He has consistently been one of Cleveland's most active civic entrepreneurs, stimulating new local development projects and investing his own time and resources working on important city issues.

Effective civic entrepreneurship requires focus and leverage. Civic entrepreneurs are strategic. They are busy running their own businesses or organizations and cannot afford the time to strike out in a lot of different directions. As to why he got involved in Joint Venture: Silicon Valley Network, Keith Kennedy, CEO of Watkins-Johnson Company, believes the organization focuses on areas where there is a perceived void. In the midst of the very difficult job of shifting his company from the defense business to a defense-commercial mix, Kennedy had no interest in recreating the wheel with Joint Venture: Silicon Valley.

Civic entrepreneurs are driven to be effective, to have a major impact, not to generate headlines or fleeting fame. They realize that there are many places to plug into the community. Like Al Ratner, they are often already making significant contributions of time and resources for charitable causes and community events.

Civic entrepreneurs can demonstrate that they are serious about assuming a new level of responsibility by directly confronting community stereotypes. Bob Keller, then-president of the Greater Baltimore Committee, a group of that region's top corporate executives, is a case in point. To demonstrate the need for fundamental change in K–12 education and his commitment to working together on solutions, he made a direct appeal. "Bob Keller agreed to come to Brown's Memorial Baptist Church, which is in a lower-income area of Park Heights, and talk to about fifteen hundred people. And he came. You know, you just don't see white people down there, and you certainly don't see white people of his stature. The fact that he came, I mean, it had an enormously emotional value and said something to people in a way they hadn't heard it before" (Chrislip and Larson, 1994, p. 83).

In Silicon Valley, T. J. Rogers, CEO of Cypress Semiconductor, delivering a keynote address at a major community event, spoke of his frustration in getting permit approvals to hoist a flagpole at his headquarters facility. What began as a familiar, belittling diatribe against bureaucratic bumbling ended very differently. This time, Rogers admitted that he was part of the problem. He had communicated through barbs in the local press. Not for a second had he thought of just picking up the phone and discussing the issue rationally with public officials. Rogers's speech was followed by testimonials from other Silicon Valley CEOs, talking about their love for the Valley and how they as individuals needed to change—to work collaboratively on problems and stop playing the blame game.

Silicon Valley's Neil Bonke overcame an admitted prejudice against bureaucracies and politicians by getting involved in Joint Venture. "I thought that they were just about preserving their jobs and that they didn't even understand Economics 101. But, I knew I had to work with them to get things done. And, when I started to peel away the onion, I found that there were capable and dedicated public servants who wanted change as much as I did. I gained great respect for them as we worked together. They were some good people." Bonke and other business and public sector civic entrepreneurs work together as Joint Venture: Silicon Valley's Economic Development Team, a regional effort to retain business in the region.

Civic entrepreneurs help their communities stop looking for scapegoats or waiting for saviors and take responsibility for their future. They discourage their communities from depending on outsiders to solve their problems. They help others understand that neither community problems nor solutions are the responsibility of the federal or state government.

In Silicon Valley, John Neece, the ex-Baptist minister turned chief of the Building and Construction Trades Union, provided just such leadership. With passion and pragmatism, Neece believed Silicon Valley leaders could and must determine the region's future. Clearly, the complexity of the region and the enormity of the issues it faced left the historical laissez-faire approach an impractical option; yet, Neece believed, the region should not fall prey to blaming outside competitors, the state, or the national government. A pragmatic, community-based course must be charted. As Neece is fond of saying, "Sacramento and Washington do not have the answer for Silicon Valley. Silicon Valley has the answer for Silicon Valley. The first thing that had to happen is we had to change; we had to take control."

Cleveland's Al Ratner echoes this belief. "The lesson is that no one can do it better than people who live there. There is no answer outside. There is no other place to look. Other people can give you some advice, but the bottom line is that unless you do it, forget it."

Al Ratner understands the importance of local responsibility well, because he and his fellow business leaders needed a stimulus to make the change. "Nothing happened until the default, even though many of us are in the same position (that is, job) we were in twenty years ago." But Cleveland civic entrepreneurs did take responsibility. "Key companies made the decision to fight not flee. What is it about Cleveland? It is a great community that lost its way, not a place that had not ever been a great community. Dick Jacobs was just a kid from Akron who wanted to own a baseball team. I always wanted to own a building downtown. It's a homegrown thing."

They Make a Declaration of Interdependence

Civic entrepreneurs challenge their community to stop assigning blame to the government, the global economy, other regions, or each other. In helping communities take responsibility, civic entrepreneurs not only discourage finger pointing, but they help people in the community understand their mutual dependence. By taking responsibility, an economic community can then develop a shared vision of future success. Silicon Valley's Mike Honda, a local county supervisor, recalls why he got involved in Joint Venture and how he describes its importance to others. "We're all in the same boat. If we're sitting in the back of the boat where there's no holes, we're still in the boat. We'll sink unless we all bale together."

John Kennett, the owner and president of Pizazz Printing, did not know much about Tom Hayes or his high-technology world. Looking north from San Jose, the mid-Peninsula, where most technology companies located, was a world of global jet-setters, electronics engineers, and MBAs—relative newcomers to the Valley from the Midwest, the East Coast, and around the world. Yet as the just-appointed chair of the San Jose Chamber, Kennett listened with interest as Hayes and Brenna Bolger explained their idea and plans for a project they called Joint Venture: Silicon Valley.

These initial discussions produced an implicit declaration of interdependence. As a printer for high-tech companies, Kennett understood the food chain—the delicate but powerful interdependencies among Valley companies. The economic collapse highlighted this interdependence dramatically. The parties agreed to work together to recruit others and launch an unprecedented collaboration to support the continued economic vitality of Silicon Valley. They brought together leaders of various trade associations, corporate leaders, and others from the community. According to Kennett, "The question that we put on the table was, 'Where do our circles of interest overlap; what common ground do we have?' And I want to tell you, that was a real small area at that point in time. A real small area. But, I think the circle has grown and grown, and that for me is really the evolution of collaboration."

In the beginning, they knew only one thing for certain: that a broad base of leaders representing many sectors of Valley economy and community must eventually come together to diagnose problems and take action. Nothing short of a grassroots community barn raising to develop a blueprint for Silicon Valley's future would do.

When Ed McCracken was approached to join the Joint Venture effort, he remembers thinking that Silicon Valley did not have an "understanding of the mutual interconnections required to have a successful place to live and work." Although McCracken was not sure where the effort was going, he believed strongly in the need to recognize and work on interdependencies in the region—between businesses and between the private and public sectors. He made his declaration personal and direct, agreeing to chair a working group on the future of the Valley's computer and communications industry. This group would help give birth to major initiatives supporting electronic community (Smart Valley) and educational reform (the 21st Century Education Initiative).

In Cleveland, civic entrepreneurs also stepped forward to forge a declaration of interdependence. Cleveland has made significant progress building bridges between the traditional leadership and the emerging minority leadership of the city. Recalls Carole Hoover, executive director of the Growth Association of Cleveland and one of Cleveland's prominent African American leaders, "When we saw an opportunity during that period of crisis to lift these issues up with the leadership, we did. People like Stan Pace, Del de Windt, Richard Pogue, Allan Holmes, a number of people were involved in the discussions. And, I was very impressed with George Voinovich [then mayor], who said he would lose before he played racial politics. He would have a unifying message for all the people."

After civic entrepreneurs made the stand, they followed through. According to Hoover, "We had an opportunity to bring together the community leadership, different disciplines, and talk about how to work together to move the community ahead. So, it was a very significant component of what happened during that period. The good relations we enjoy now emanate from the trust we were able to build then."

George Voinovich exemplified those unique individuals who as public officials can operate like a civic entrepreneur from the business community. Voinovich was instrumental in making it clear that Cleveland's many factions had to work together to rebuild the city. In fact, as Carole Hoover observes, "We were about the business of getting to the table and trying to make change. George Voinovich preached public-private partnership, and we started to win with it. And, those wins fueled the fire for more partnerships."

Richard Pogue remembers the transformation of a key member of the African American community, who also was the city council president. "George Forbes, like his predecessors, had been in the business of bashing business. He wanted to see what might be done to get better collaboration in the community. Along the way, as he has said several times, a light bulb went off in his mind. 'I realized that government can't create the jobs; it can create the conditions, but the private sector has to create the jobs.' And, he used to say, 'My people need the jobs.' So, he did an about-face and started cooperating with the business community and the mayor. It was a significant piece of the puzzle."

Al Ratner tells of a major turning point in which Mayor-elect Voinovich took a significant risk to demonstrate that a new era of cooperation and interdependence had begun. According to Ratner, "I came to him with a UDAG commitment that needed to be signed. He said, 'What's a UDAG? I don't know a thing about it; how can I sign it?' I explained and said if he didn't sign it now, we wouldn't be able to do the project. And, he said, 'Al I trust you, give it to me.' And, he signed it. Chances are if he hadn't signed it, we couldn't have fixed the bridges; we couldn't have done a lot of things. For me, that's how the public-private partnership started. He said, 'I trust you and go out and do it.'" Voinovich extended himself, expecting Ratner to deliver results in return. The tone of interdependence and mutual expectation had been set.

Civic entrepreneurs often point to a single event, interaction, or project that embodied a declaration of interdependence. Austin civic entrepreneur Pike Powers credits the MCC competition with helping leaders understand the nature of their interdependence. "People found a new way to work together better. The university found a new place in our community. From that time forward, we were able to do new things in new ways. It has permitted the university and the community and industry to be in a new relationship with each other. It's the ability to pick up the phone and call."

In California, who would have guessed the power of a single event in 1988 to accelerate the development of a set of shared collaborative values among a group of civic entrepreneurs? A sense of political gridlock had been growing in California through the 1980s, as critical problems were addressed poorly or neglected altogether. The governor's Office of Research and Planning asked a group of experts to help prepare a report—*California 2010*—that identified key challenges facing the state and outlined possible solutions. The leaders of this effort decided that the real problem was a lack of problem-solving capacity within the state.

This group joined with an emerging statewide leaders group called "California Leadership" to invite California leaders to a meeting in Monterey, California, to create a California Compact. The compact would be a set of principles and actions that would help address gridlock. The compact—a Declaration of Interdependence—outlined some key principles to guide California forward. The goal was to promote a more collaborative and inclusive style of leadership in addressing key issues such as education, water, and economic development on both a state and a regional level. The conclusion was that the *way* we were doing things was preventing us from doing the things that need to be done.

The impact of the California Compact was felt, as the signatories to the document began to bring those common values of collaboration and inclusiveness back to their organizations and communities. Becky Morgan, former state senator and now president and CEO of Joint Venture: Silicon Valley Network, applied those values to the revitalization of Silicon Valley. So did state assemblyman John Vasconcellos, one of the board members of Joint Venture and the author of legislation that created the California Economic Strategy Panel, which is helping to align state resources to collaborative regional initiatives.

The collaborative vision was implemented by Jane and Mark Pisano, who helped implement the Los Angeles Partnership and the Southern California Regional Economic Strategies Consortium. It was also carried out by Congressman Sam Farr, who helped create the Monterey Bay Region Futures Network, based on the principles of collaboration embodied in the compact. The inclusive and collaborative vision is driving the creation of the new California State University campus at Monterey Bay at Fort Ord, which was led by Congressman Farr with design support from Assemblyman John Vasconcellos's California Leadership organization. And the vision was followed by Nick Bollman of The James Irvine Foundation, who has been sponsoring collaborative regional economic development projects across the state.

All these leaders and others who came together to adopt a collaborative manifesto as the antidote to gridlock have been implementing those principles in their own way. Success so far has been limited to regional efforts. Building collaborative relationships is much easier for civic entrepreneurs to accomplish at the community level than statewide. What is interesting about this case is that the Monterey Conference appeared to accelerate the adoption of civic entrepreneurship in California at the region level.

They Raise the Stakes

Civic entrepreneurs also raise the stakes for their community, raising the ambitions, the expectations, the vision of their community beyond what currently exists. They help their communities ask the hard questions about where they want to go in the future. Most places know what they want to avoid. Portland knows it does not want to be Seattle; Santa Barbara knows it does not want to be Los Angeles, and so on. Jim Biggar, chairman and CEO of Glencairn Corporation in Cleveland, reflects on his own experience. "One of the most important things for us was having the business leaders focus on what kind of community they really wanted. This is going to be where your community is going to be. What kind of community do you want for employees, for yourselves?"

Often the biggest challenge is in helping a community break out of a cycle of pessimism. As Silicon Valley's Neil Bonke has said, "Don't just come to the opinion that your community can't compete. Look at your strengths. You can make change happen if you put people together. The individual problems are the easiest. It's hardest to strike out the defeatist attitudes. Waving flags and running to your congressman to save the economy is nonproductive energy. Put your energies into building on the unique qualities of your region."

Austin was a different story. National competitions for MCC and SEMATECH helped raise the community's sights. Victoria Koepsel, assistant director of development for corporate relations at the University of Texas in Austin, calls MCC in particular "a galvanizing event. Austin was not galvanized by threat but by national competition. We saw an opportunity to leverage our assets. It fueled our competitive juices. There was a lot of excitement about the future. Politically, the city seemed to gel for once. It happened because a few people like Pike Powers saw a role for Austin in technology. It was a very aggressive team that met every single morning at 7:30 A.M. for months."

Pike Powers recalls, "It was our first opportunity as a community to come together and work in big competition and to try to bring a consensus of our community together. It tested our community in ways we had never been tested before. These national competitions help foster a lot of legitimate community involvement in a way other things haven't or can't. It really helped us rally the troops. People were able to lay aside their petty differences."

Powers believed that Austin had to raise its sights, that more was at stake than just beating another city in a nationwide competition. "We have to compete with the Japanese. If we don't do that, then we will just be some sort of second-class citizen group." Adds Glenn West, the president of the Austin Chamber, "The value of MCC was that it gave the community a big victory. Success breeds success. It took us to a new level of conversation with our local manufacturing base. SEMATECH built on relationships and success of MCC. Ann Bowers [wife of Bob Noyce, cofounder of Intel, who later headed SEMATECH] said that 'Bob was impressed with Austin, because Austin wants it just a little bit more.'"

Whether it is through crisis or opportunity, civic entrepreneurs help their communities aspire to a higher standard of success than other regions. Many regions define economic success as job creation: the more jobs, the better. In Phoenix, with the urging of civic entrepreneurs like Alan Hald, the community began to recognize that more jobs do not necessarily mean a higher standard of living. Although Arizona as whole recorded strong annual employment growth from 1975 to 1990, it lagged behind the national average in per capita income and real wages. In the late 1980s, it actually ranked last among all the states in per capita income growth, while still expanding its job base by 3 percent per year.

Many regions led by more traditional business and community leaders have attracted new plants and jobs with an appeal as a low-cost location, only to see the plants and jobs leave. Places like South Carolina once sold themselves as low-cost regions, succeeding in attracting low-cost producers (for example, textile plants from Mass-achusetts). By the early 1980s, job growth was strong, but per capita income was only 75 percent of the national average, and factory wages ranked forty-seventh out of fifty states. And the state has since lost many of these jobs to even lower-cost regions in developing countries.

Today, however, South Carolina is a success story: government and business have come together to encourage investments in education and other infrastructure. The state now sells itself as a region that can do high-value-added work. The difference is striking: a recent attrac-tion of a BMW automobile plant was made possible by the value of the training package for prospective employees offered by the local community, in partnership with state government. This kind of change has enabled the state to enjoy one of the biggest jumps in liv-ing standards of any state in the past ten years.

Another traditional measure of success has been population growth—the more people, the more demand for construction, retail, and services, and the more jobs created. Florida has traditionally pur-sued this strategy by keeping taxes low to encourage continued pop-ulation migration. Only recently have Florida's regions felt the impact of a growing population without sufficient growth in infrastructure and services—including high crime rates and below-average schools.

With the help of civic entrepreneurs, economic communities look beyond these traditional visions of success. Although job growth is important, the quality of jobs is more of a concern. Civic entrepre-neurs encourage their communities to seek strong growth in value-added and productivity, which produces growth in real wages per worker. They advocate competing primarily on the basis of quality, not cost. They help others understand that competing primarily on the basis of cost is a no-win situation, because hundreds of regions in developing countries will always be lower-cost locations.

Advice for Civic Entrepreneurs Acting as Motivators

- *Do* use your experience with the global economy and other communities to dramatize the need for change locally.

- *Do* search for the right "motivation with meaning" for your community, be that crisis or opportunity.

- *Do* confront community stereotypes by reaching out to a group, taking a stand, or otherwise showing your desire for change.

- *Do* "put skin on the table," a tangible and visible demonstration of your personal commitment to community change.

- *Do* put pressure on others to raise their sights and challenge prevailing assumptions about what is possible for the community.

- *Don't* play the blame game about the past; instead, offer to take shared responsibility for the future with others.

- *Don't* ask government to lead, but make sure civic entrepreneurs from government and nonprofit sectors become part of the team.

- *Don't* let others look for scapegoats or wait for saviors to initiate the process of community change.

- *Don't* hesitate to start as the sole motivator, but quickly get others to share and spread the motivational message.

- *Don't* raise expectations unless you're at least willing to find the right people to take over the next stage of the process.

Alan Hald and other civic entrepreneurs in Arizona helped their state change its definition of economic success. In the early 1990s, the state shifted away from a reliance on population-driven job growth and from marketing its low-cost business climate to set a new course that focuses on quality jobs. And Hald and his partners made sure that the message went out far and wide, from bumper stickers to a newspaper insert that told the story of quality jobs, using cartoon characters and attractive graphics. The message was clear. They defined economic development as a process that raises the standard of living for people, creates opportunities for individuals and enterprises, and increases quality of life. It occurs as a result of actions by business, government, and the community that build strong economic foundations that attract, retain, and sustain dynamic clusters of manufacturing and service industries that add value and create comparative advantage in an increasingly competitive economy.

They Create a Sense of Mission

Civic entrepreneurs use such practices as delivering the wake-up call, demonstrating new levels of responsibility, making declarations of interdependence, and raising the stakes to get their communities moving. The final motivating technique they employ is to create a sense of mission, a fervor for change that many can share.

The feeling of shared euphoria is similar across communities that are successfully initiating the process to build economic community. In Austin, Pike Powers recalls how the initial core of civic entrepreneurs "had a sense of mission that was beyond any normal economic development effort. We created ways for people to contribute to a larger sense of mission or purpose. It was pretty magical."

Wichita's Hale Ritchie observes that "the biggest obstacle to the collaborative effort was the putting together of WI/SE in the first place. That we got that done, we thought we could do anything. It gave us momentum. Once we identified a problem, we got just the right people to solve the problem."

THE NETWORKER: LENDS CREDIBILITY AND LEVERAGES NETWORKS

The second most important role that civic entrepreneurs play during the initiation stage is that of networker. Civic entrepreneurs first network among their friends, getting them to commit to the change process. They then move outside their comfort zone and link with leaders in other sectors of their community who must be on board for any communitywide change process to succeed. They seek and receive the community's sanction or approval to move forward. Sometimes, this approval is nothing more than an agreement to withhold judgment on the fledgling change process, promising not to undermine it publicly or privately.

Civic entrepreneurs also elevate and challenge new leaders, giving them the opportunity to prove their readiness for community leadership, while at the same time making it clear that they must make a serious commitment to the process of change. They ensure that the core leadership team is composed of people with complementary skills, making up for one another's limitations of perspective, contacts, and resources. Civic entrepreneurs network by taking the following steps. They:

- Get friends to commit to the process by putting their personal credibility on the line
- Reach beyond their comfort zone to bring others into the process
- Buy time from skeptics, asking them to withhold judgment so the collaborative process can go forward
- Recruit a complementary team to design and launch the collaborative process

They Get Friends to Commit

Civic entrepreneurs almost always start working together as friends. It is a simple but important fact: the first step to growing civic entrepreneurship in any community is getting friends to commit to a new level of involvement. Arizona's Jack Pfister sees his role as a civic entrepreneur as "leveraging and linking. Leveraging and linking. That's mainly what I do."

Civic entrepreneurs are in the middle of leadership networks that, if activated, can create major change in a community. These are networks of trust and support. Civic entrepreneurs are those who risk making "the ask" of other leaders (usually playing off relationships built through prior business dealings) to get involved in a significant effort to build economic community. Lending one's network for community purposes separates the individual who is seeking personal glory from the civic entrepreneur who is willing go into debt with his or her social network (friends) by asking for commitment of time, expertise, and resources for a cause greater than any individual involved.

Often, this linking begins more informally than the convening of leaders around a solemn discussion of community affairs. Arizona's Steve Zylstra expresses it well when he speaks of the initial group of civic entrepreneurs that Alan Hald invited into his home for a year of Sunday sessions. "It was just a fun group of people. We enjoyed what we were doing. We brainstormed."

In Cleveland, competitors have found ways to work together for the good of their city. According to Jim Biggar, "They seem to come together for the city itself. It is a very important factor. We are a small enough city that we can pull together easily, and we're large enough that it makes a difference if we do."

Richard Pogue adds, "We have a diversity of major industry here. We have been to Detroit to tell our story. You have a situation where you have the Big 3 competing every minute of every day and dominating the business community of Detroit. Here, the business leadership is spread out, so you don't have the intensity of rivalry." Across communities, one of the biggest obstacles to collaboration is the competition of individual companies. In Cleveland, Silicon Valley, Wichita, and elsewhere, competitors have found ways to collaborate on some issues and compete on others—for the good of their companies and communities.

When David Rockefeller wanted to do something for New York City, he turned to his friends. In the early 1980s, he assembled a core team including Arthur Taylor (president of CBS), Richard Shinn (CEO of Metropolitan Life), Paul Lyet (CEO of Sperry-Rand), Ed Pratt (CEO of Pfizer), Virgil Conway (CEO of Seaman's Savings Bank), and John Whitehead (cochairman of Goldman-Sachs), among others. "The core team traveled all over the city for meetings with civic and community leaders in order to test the partnership's mission against the most pressing needs and interests of the day. They also attended an endless series of breakfasts sponsored by Rockefeller to solicit comments and criticism from executives of large and small businesses alike. They lobbied city, state, and federal officials. They explored the experiences of business groups in other cities. And, they continually tested, shaped, and argued among themselves over their purpose— help solve some of the city's key problems—and approach—prioritize problems for attack and then focus on a few" (Katzenbach and Smith, 1993, pp. 136–137).

Cleveland's resurgence in civic entrepreneurship in the late 1970s took a similar path. E. Mandell (Del) de Windt, CEO of Eaton Corporation, joined with Ruben Mettler (CEO of TRW), Mort Mandel (chairman of Premier Industrial Corporation), and George Dively (CEO of Harris Corporation) to create a vehicle to promote ongoing community partnerships. According to former executive director Richard Shatten, "When it was decided to create a permanently organized Cleveland Tomorrow, de Windt called thirty-six people on the phone and said, 'You're joining.' If they asked why, he said, 'Because this is the right thing to do, and I want you to do it.' " De Windt himself has said, "It was an extension of my role as CEO of a major corporation to recognize that we had to do something about the environment in which we lived" (Frey Foundation, 1993, p. 15).

Often, the individual who plays the role of networker is a leading lawyer or other business service leader who is well connected across the community. In Austin, it was Pike Powers. In Cleveland, it was Richard Pogue. In Seattle, a generation ago, it was attorney James Ellis. He was the consummate networker, and he cared deeply about the future of his Seattle community.

Recruiting his "friends," Ellis assembled a team of unparalleled expertise that conceived and won passage of a package of bond measures called Forward Thrust. "Ellis, in fact, had a small army of allies: altogether two hundred business people, lawyers, academicians, public servants, clergy, and conservationists. This extraordinary commitment of citizens who were not office holders literally transformed the face of the region. Forward Thrust's lasting legacy tells the story: generous open spaces and parks (including one atop a freeway), public waterfront use, storm-water control, community centers, an aquarium, and more" (Peirce, with Johnson and Hall, 1993, p. 102).

They Reach Beyond the Comfort Zone

Civic entrepreneurs understand that asking their friends to commit is a necessary but insufficient condition for success. It often takes a visionary leader to step beyond his or her own network and link to other social networks—building a bridge that others may cross, setting an example that others may follow. Some communities in the United States have a strong history of such catalytic leaders, be they from business or from government, who operate in the community or civic realm.

Civic entrepreneurs break down boundaries, make introductions, provide information, and inspire others to take risks and work together. They create openings for collaboration and opportunities for would-be leaders to emerge. They establish new communication channels that produce much more than anybody would have thought, including the civic entrepreneurs themselves. As Steve Minter of the Cleveland Foundation notes, "It makes a lot of difference when suddenly we could pick up the phone, and the conversations can go on easily, and we can begin to figure out how we can do these things jointly."

Ivan Allen, Jr., as president of the Atlanta Chamber in the 1960s, brought together the economy and the community (including minorities) around a long-term effort to build the image and infrastructure of Atlanta, including expressways and schools. While much of the South was in racial turmoil, Atlanta added 250,000 jobs. Atlanta's black community participated in this growth, and it now represents one of the nation's largest pools of black-owned businesses and capital.

Like George Voinovich, George Latimer as mayor of St. Paul, Minnesota, broke new ground in bringing all segments of the community together. When he became mayor, St. Paul was the weaker, blue-collar partner of Minnesota's Twin Cities. He could have followed the traditional economic development path of cities—that of attracting outside business. Instead, he rallied business, government, and community leaders around a vision of a homegrown, entrepreneurial economy. He garnered strong support from other civic entrepreneurs from banking and other corporations, foundations, and academic institutions to pursue a coordinated, comprehensive strategy supporting the local business creation process, including new partnerships, programs, and investments.

Lee Cooke, first as Chamber president and later as mayor, has developed strong linkages among business and government in Austin, leading to high-profile recruiting successes such as MCC, SEMATECH, and other research- and knowledge-based operations. Austin has proceeded to take steps to improve its university and public schools and has kept its regulatory processes attuned to the needs of its businesses.

In Silicon Valley, civic entrepreneurs quickly realized the need to move beyond their comfort zones. John Kennett explains, "Clearly, we could get one hundred smart people in a room, identify one hundred things we could do to help turn around the economy, and go do them. But this was not what Joint Venture was about. This was not what was needed." The original idea for Joint Venture was to bring individuals from throughout the Valley together. As Tom Hayes explains, "We created all kinds of avenues for their entry, including committees, events, weekly meetings and more. We wanted to hear from everyone and to have Joint Venture become dynamic as a result of the inputs from dozens of organizations, hundreds of companies, and thousands of individual people."

A handful of CEOs felt Silicon Valley's problems could be handled by just themselves. But this was not what Joint Venture was about. It was about process and involvement and collaboration. As Jim Morgan suggests, "Sure, a few of us could get together and develop a plan, but no one would believe in it. The world is full of examples where five or six executives got together and decided what was good for the community without any process, community buy-in, or mechanism for continuation, and therefore no impact."

Arizona's Jack Pfister came to the same conclusion in recounting the lengthy history of failed business efforts in Phoenix that did not involve the community. "All too frequently, a small group of businessmen got an idea, raised a lot of money, and never involved the community and the other business people that needed to be involved for the effort to be sustained. So they spent a lot of money, with few real results. The lesson is that if these processes are tightly controlled by just a few people, they will crash."

Not surprisingly, Silicon Valley's leaders found that working outside their comfort zone was difficult. Dealing with multiple constituencies is often more difficult than civic entrepreneurs initially believe. Ed McCracken has observed that "there can be a lot of arrogance involved when leaders from different environments start working across institutions, particularly when business people work with government. I learned a lot about dealing with multiple constituencies that I didn't know beforehand."

The first step in Silicon Valley was to create a project board representing the major businesses and industries of the region. The Valley had always had social networks—industry and trade associations, technical groups. The problem, from a community leadership perspective, was that these networks were not connected. One by one, the core team of John Kennett, Tom Hayes, and Brenna Bolger invited leaders to join the Joint Venture project board and meet bimonthly to design and manage the Joint Venture effort collectively.

While some were instantly committed and others exceptionally cautious, the group focused on what the first steps should be. Small-business people, realtors, builders, union leaders sat alongside corporate giants like Apple, Hewlett-Packard, IBM, Intel, Cypress, and Tandem. The board would grow to fifty and meet biweekly for fourteen months, overseeing a process that involved twelve hundred people, staying together until a strategy blueprint was done. Even arch-competitors joined this initial coalition for change. Recalls Hayes, "Enough pain was shared that people were motivated to come together. If we had tried to get this group together a year ago, it wouldn't have happened."

Nothing less than the personal touch is necessary to build these networks. The core Joint Venture leadership team made personal overtures to other leaders. Austin's Lee Cooke, Cleveland's George Voinovich, St. Paul's George Latimer—all took the time to make the personal connection.

One of the most important practices pursued by civic entrepreneurs at this stage of the change process is to make room for emerging leaders. In Arizona, Steve Zylstra recognized that Alan Hald's effort provided an opportunity for new, young leaders to emerge, himself included. At the same time, Jack Pfister helped elevate Alan Hald in more traditional leadership circles, saying in effect, "This guy is okay; hear him out." And, according to Ioanna Morfessis, the fact that "Alan was not part of the traditional corporate power structure was a plus," especially among those who felt shut out of that leadership circle.

Some civic entrepreneurs seize key moments of conflict to challenge an emerging leader to get involved and make a difference. Chris Greene, president of Greene Engineers, tells a story about just such an interaction early in Silicon Valley's process. "At the Joint Venture vision conference, I sat at a table with Greg Larsen [deputy city manager of San Jose] and Ko Nishimura [future CEO of Solectron]. Ko began a diatribe against the permit process in San Jose. Greg was not defensive but took it as a way to engage him. He challenged Ko to work with him to make it better." Larsen went on to cochair one of the Joint Venture initiatives (the Environmental Partnership); Nishimura later joined the Joint Venture board and lent several of his executives to assist cities in applying total quality management principles to improve public regulatory processes.

At the same time, the interaction hooked Greene as well. "I could see that this kind of interaction could have a good impact, so I thought there might actually be something to this Joint Venture thing. If it had been academic, I would have dropped out immediately. But, I saw real decision makers, so I stayed involved." Greene went on to chair the Joint Venture initiative on regulatory streamlining.

Many civic entrepreneurs have reached a point in their career where they have achieved considerable success and are ready to take on additional community challenges that have a broader, more lasting impact. They have unquestioned credibility and a reputation and a standing in the community that allows them to get a meeting with almost anybody, even those outside their comfort zone. They are an invaluable store of contacts, skills, experience, and credibility that can unleash similar contributions from others.

After an illustrious career as partner of a major West Coast consulting firm and Secretary of Finance in the gubernatorial administration of Ronald Reagan, Gordon Paul Smith retired to the Monterey, California, region. Some retirement. Now in his eighties, he has become one of the region's premier civic entrepreneurs. He has organized efforts to save two military installations and build a maritime museum, and he has helped establish a regional futures group to promote economic development. He taps his vast experience, network of business and community contacts, and sheer energy to encourage others and help spark a region that is otherwise short on corporate and other civic leadership.

In characteristic fashion, Smith turns the spotlight away from himself. "Being part of the [Monterey] Futures Network has expanded my vision even further to vast economic, educational, environmental, cultural, social, and other opportunities this remarkable area has to offer. The backbone of this Network and its successful programs is the pooling of a wide spectrum of professionals, so many of whom would not normally come in contact with one another."

They Buy Time from Skeptics

Civic entrepreneurs are careful to ensure that key constituencies have been consulted and obstacles removed before urging their communities on to the next stage of the change process. They buy the crucial time necessary to let a fledgling collaborative process get under way. They buy time from skeptics—often those who hold an influential position in the community and who have the power to stop new efforts.

In essence, they seek and secure broad community sanction or approval for undertaking the process of change. Such sanction does not necessarily equate to wholehearted endorsement. In fact, in most cases, many people and organizations are invested in old ways of doing things and see little need for a time-consuming process of change. However, civic entrepreneurs use their powers of persuasion to secure, at a minimum, approval to allow the effort to go forward—in effect to withhold judgment for a period of time.

This sometimes time-consuming process of securing approval from diverse segments of the community helps limit attempts to undermine the process. As Silicon Valley's John Neece said, "There weren't many people who could shoot at us, because they were all with us." Individuals who had community "veto power" were sought, as if to join a "security council" that required consensus to move forward. In Cleveland, echoes Al Ratner, "Our success has been the fact that we don't have a lot of people carping because they are inside the tent; we try not to leave them outside the tent. If you have everyone inside the tent, and everybody has the same objective, you're going to do it every time." Such consultations often result in unforeseen cooperation in return for an early invitation into the process.

In Arizona, this front-end work was critical. Alan Hald has remarked that in selling the concept of change to his state "luck met preparation. It really wasn't the money that was important but how to get the community sanction to move forward." Ioanna Morfessis echoes Hald's sentiments. "A few individuals made the case to more traditional corporate players and were finally able to convince them that this was important to Arizona." They didn't necessarily agree with all the ideas or the approach, but they were willing to give it a chance. In getting community sanction, that is all civic entrepreneurs need to move forward.

In Silicon Valley, initial work to buy time from skeptics was critical. Communications executive Brenna Bolger took a risk, tapping into the business network she had built over thirty years to ask key opinion leaders to give regional collaboration a chance. One of these leaders, Larry Jinks, publisher of the *San Jose Mercury News,* played an important role in helping the fledgling Joint Venture effort survive. According to labor leader John Neece, Jenks "courted individuals who carry big sticks and asked them to give this process a chance, to keep their sticks in the bag." For example, as a member of the executive committee of the Santa Clara County Manufacturing Group, he convinced its president to withhold judgment until the process had the opportunity to produce results.

Although some local elected officials were skeptical of her motives, the mayor of Silicon Valley's largest city, Susan Hammer of San Jose, made a concerted effort to reach out to bring other public officials into the coalition. She chaired a public sector roundtable, composed of elected officials from cities and counties, and the state and federal officials representing the region. It was important to have broad public sector representation, according to Hammer, because "the challenges in the Valley extend beyond city and county boundaries and require involvement by the greater community."

They Recruit a Complementary Team

Civic entrepreneurs realize early on that they need a close circle of team players with complementary skills to initiate the process of building economic community. Alex Plinio and Tom Hayes, in their positions as public affairs executive with Prudential Insurance and director of global corporate affairs with Applied Materials, respectively, knew they needed a lot of help from a core team of civic entrepreneurs if they were going to help their regions come together.

Both appealed to their CEOs to make a financial and personal commitment to a collaborative process. Plinio had his CEO David Sherwood and five other top leaders, including the mayor, to host a meeting of thirty-five key leaders, representing the core of the city's diverse leadership. "The meeting had a very simple agenda. We asked a couple of questions: What's good about Newark? What's bad about Newark? What, if anything, do you want to do about either of these things?" (Chrislip, and Larson, 1994, p. 133). It gave leaders who usually were in conflict with one another an opportunity to focus on the future and what they could do together. They were hooked.

Tom Hayes actually sat down with his CEO, Jim Morgan, one afternoon and worked with Morgan to make calls to Morgan's network of business colleagues, asking each one to work for a better Silicon Valley by chairing a working group. Hayes then worked on getting cochairs with complementary skills and perspectives to match with each corporate CEO, ensuring that by their interaction and collaboration, the chairs would demonstrate to working-group participants that the process was about constructive collaboration, not finger pointing or pushing one's private agenda. Hayes also asked a prominent consulting firm to join the team in order to give the community a reality check about its situation and prospects.

In Cleveland in 1979, business leaders were complaining about how the city was run. New mayor George Voinovich invited them to get directly involved to improve the situation. They responded to the challenge. Voinovich assembled a complementary team of almost one hundred corporate executives, who joined together to conduct a twelve–week assessment of city management, producing more than six hundred recommendations, most of which were implemented. Business leaders and other community leaders joined together to make the case for a major payroll tax increase to reinvest in Cleveland, which received more than 60 percent support from voters. This change fundamentally linked the destinies of the city and its suburbs, as suburbanites would pay about three-quarters of the new tax bill.

Although not hit as hard as other midwestern cities, Indianapolis entered the 1980s with a sluggish economy. It did not have a strong national economic identity. A small group of civic and business leaders stepped forward to stimulate the creation of a new economic sector for the region. The informally named "City Committee" developed a strategic vision and plan to make the region the amateur sports capital of America. The committee sparked a coordinated campaign, tapping companies, foundations, government, and an army of community volunteers to implement the strategy. The result: $11 billion of new investment and facilities in a decade.

Although the team was effective, in the late 1980s the City Committee approach became controversial because of its lack of inclusion. Rather than building a shared vision, the City Committee developed its vision and fanned out to sell it to the community. Though that approach worked in a late 1970s and early 1980s environment, the community has sent signals that a more collaborative process will be required to develop and execute Indianapolis's post amateur-sports strategy.

An important dimension of the recruitment process is to find talent outside of traditional leadership positions in the community. In Austin, Victoria Koepsel recalls the role Susan Engelking played in recruiting her. Engelking, accounting supervisor and senior counselor at Staats, Faulkenberg & Partners, taps people from her social-professional women's network and gets them involved at all levels. Koepsel was employed as coordinator of Industry Programs at Austin Community College's Business and Technology Center. In any other community, she would have been easy to overlook. Engelking invited her to join the Chamber Electronics Task Force. "She included me because I had something to offer. Because she had credibility, I was viewed as an equal in the process. Normally, I wouldn't have been around the table, because I wasn't a CEO or endowed university chair. I participate because I feel terribly included. I feel important, in the know. It is gratifying and fun. I get recognition for my accomplishments."

Wichita's Lionel Alford was a careful recruiter of talent to get his community moving forward. "Mayor Bob Knight asked me to become chair of the effort. I said I would do it if I could have Jordan Haynes [chairman of Bank Four] as vice chair. We then got thirty other community leaders involved. People got involved for two reasons. One, the mayor said do it. And, two, you turn up or else. Jordan Haynes knew everybody outside of my sphere." Together, Alford and Haynes, along with the mayor, complemented each other's personal networks and were able to get a community change process under way.

Advice for Civic Entrepreneurs Acting as Networkers

• *Do* go into debt with your friends and convince your competitors to set aside their differences for the good of the community.

• *Do* take the time to make the personal connection with leaders from other sectors, challenging them to join the team for change.

• *Do* identify those with veto power and secure their agreement to allow the collaborative process to proceed.

• *Do* take great care in assembling a core leadership team, filling out complementary roles that will be needed during both process and implementation.

• *Don't* let your friends get away with a cash contribution or passive support; insist they invest their time, expertise, and contacts.

• *Don't* leave the task of recruiting leaders outside your comfort zone to someone else, especially a subordinate; you make the ask.

• *Don't* assume that everyone will do the right thing; extensive front-end work to identify and neutralize opponents pays off.

• *Don't* involve only CEOs or a particular level of executive; mix levels, sectors, and established and emerging leaders.

CHAPTER FIVE

Incubation
Setting Shared Priorities

*It's the politics of inclusion. We need you all to make
this effort succeed.*

—*Pike Powers, Austin*

You need an action vehicle—tasks, deadlines, events.

—*Alan Hald, Arizona*

Civic entrepreneurs play two particularly important
roles in their communities as they go through the collaborative
process—helping people understand the situation and determine what
to do about it. They act as teacher and convener. As teacher, they educate their community, preparing people for participating effectively
in a collaborative process of change. As convener, they make sure that
the process involves a diverse cross-section of the community and
operates according to clear rules.

In any community, there is a constant need to set and pursue
shared priorities. An effective collaborative process meets this need. It
allows for the brainstorming of ideas, without producing "agenda
explosion." It produces priorities for action. An effective process balances top-down leadership, bottom-up participation, and strategic
expertise to help put the facts on the table, develop a new framework
for understanding information, or facilitate the process itself. And the

process can be widely participatory (for example, Arizona or Silicon Valley) or more focused on specific challenges or opportunities (for example, Austin or Cleveland). Civic entrepreneurs have achieved the following during the incubation stage:

- Silicon Valley's collaborative process produced eleven "business plans" for implementable initiatives, each supported by a core team of champions, in areas ranging from economic development to defense transition, new enterprise development, regulatory streamlining, and educational reform.

- Arizona's process fundamentally shifted the state's economic development strategy and programs (including training and other incentives), and spawned several industry cluster groups that continue to meet to work on joint projects and shape state policies.

- Wichita got a reality check with an independent analysis of its economic prospects, developed a detailed five-year plan for revitalizing the region, kept people involved to implement, and ultimately achieved every objective of the plan, investing millions to remake its urban core and receiving a national economic development award in the process.

THE TEACHER: CREATES A COMMON UNDERSTANDING

As a community moves from initiation to incubation, civic entrepreneurs play the critical role of teacher. They put the facts on the table in a form that is meaningful to process participants, helping people move away from decisions based on politics, anecdotes, or simply inaccurate information. They help people understand how global forces, challenges, and opportunities are relevant to the local community. They open up the community to ideas developed in other communities, overcoming the not-invented-here syndrome. And they help develop and promote a shared framework for organizing discussions about the future of the community. Civic entrepreneurs teach by taking the following steps. They:

- Put the facts about the local economic situation on the table
- Localize global challenges and opportunities
- Open minds to outside ideas, benchmarking other regions
- Build a shared framework to focus the collaborative process

They Put the Facts on the Table

Before they can make any real progress, people must have a shared understanding of the challenge before them, an objective assessment of their community's situation. The facts must be on the table for everyone to see. Civic entrepreneurs often have to help provide this foundation, while overcoming cynicism about past efforts. Many people will have sat through community processes rendered fruitless because the information about constraints, threats, and other realities was insufficient. Many will also know that expertise-filled studies often end up shelved and gathering dust, having failed either to educate or to influence.

Successful regional efforts start by taking stock of how the economy and community are doing. Through a diagnostic process, people in the region can learn how their community has performed over time. Civic entrepreneurs can use the facts from the diagnosis to rally the troops. At their core, regional strategy efforts attack complacency—the sense that we can continue doing things as we have always done them or that with time, our economic wounds will heal.

In Cleveland, the practice of civic entrepreneurs putting the facts on the table helped mobilize the community. According to Al Ratner, "Bringing the community together was not done emotionally. It was done putting together hard statistics so we could evaluate where we were, and that was very important." This step is often overlooked by communities rushing to implement something, turning what may be good initial ideas into solutions searching for a problem. Ratner, who has done work in many U.S. cities, concludes that "part of the problem in a lot of cities where I work is that they don't know where they are—they think they're good or they think they're bad—but there is no basis."

Civic entrepreneurs often insist on better information in the face of opposition—in effect, not allowing community processes to proceed without a better factual grounding. Recalls Cleveland's Steve Minter, "I remember a board meeting when Willis Wynn, who was then president of the Federal Reserve Bank, came in and chastised us for the fact that there was a lot of talk about the economics of this region, and there were a lot of anecdotes passing as science. What was needed was a database. And we ought to get about the business in Cleveland of building a database." Minter's foundation stepped forward and underwrote the work to get the facts on the table. Even then, as he recalls, "there were lots of naysayers, saying that was a tremendous waste of time and money; we can tell you what the answer is; why are you doing this?" In fact, it was not a waste of time, as the database was used to inform a number of subsequent community development efforts.

Other regions have learned the same lesson. Arizona's Alan Hald is convinced that without a factual foundation shared by all participants, the chances of coming up with poorly conceived solutions are high. "You need to have factual background and material that you can make reasonable judgments about. Otherwise, you go running off into the wild blue yonder with crazy ideas that aren't implementable." Wichita's Lionel Alford used the facts to call his community to action and ignite the kind of broad-based support necessary to design and implement a strategy. Alford called attention to the collapse of all three legs of Wichita's economic stool—aerospace, gas and oil, and agriculture—at the risk of turning people against his company. His effort to pinpoint the unstoppable, systemic changes taking place in the economy moved the community out of denial and into action.

Civic entrepreneurs acting as leaders of the Florida Chamber of Commerce commissioned a diagnosis of their state's economy to take a look at how Florida was positioned for the future. The central finding at first surprised everyone. Then, as it was discussed widely, few could disagree that residents' extreme dependence on passive, rather than earned, income grossly overstated the state's real economic vitality and was a source of long-run vulnerability.

Educating leaders about this distinction stimulated debate about what the state and its regions would have to do to be a national economic leader. It sparked a statewide shift in economic development strategy. In addition to the Chamber, local regions shifted to a focus on higher-value-added industry, and incoming governor Lawton Chiles embraced the work, translating it into new state government economic development priorities.

Perhaps the longest-running creation of civic entrepreneurs that continuously fosters education about community issues is the Minneapolis Citizens League. Established in the 1940s, the Citizens League logs three thousand individual and six hundred corporate members. Each year, members work together through subcommittees to develop consensus around a major policy issue. The process brings industry and community leaders together in living rooms across Minneapolis to discuss a single topic of community concern. Major policy innovations have sprung from this process: metropolitan government, school choice, managed health care.

They Localize Global Challenges
and Opportunities

Civic entrepreneurs like Silicon Valley's Jim Morgan have built their companies around a vision of success based on a shared understanding of the global competitive challenges and opportunities. They bring this perspective to the task of building economic community. In 1992, Jim Morgan and Tom Hayes of Applied Materials promoted the retention of an independent consulting firm that was then commissioned by the Joint Venture Board to assess the economic state of Silicon Valley. Recalls Tom Hayes, "From living rooms to board rooms, there was widespread belief that something was fundamentally wrong with the Silicon Valley economy." But at first, few agreed about the nature of the problem. Was this downturn cyclical? An effect of defense cutbacks? Something else?

The initial Joint Venture leadership group took an analytic look at the Valley's changing economy and competitive position. The leadership interviewed one hundred Valley leaders. It surveyed business leaders, public officials, and citizens. It pulled together the economic facts. Its work product, *An Economy At Risk,* documented the plunging performance of the Valley's economy after 1986.

What would capture the imagination of civic entrepreneurs and ordinary citizens alike was the finding that the Valley economy and community had grown apart. Explains Hayes, "What we found was this huge, fundamental disconnect between what Silicon Valley companies needed and what the Valley community was providing. It was like our companies had moved onto a whole new time dimension and global worldview and left the community in the dust."

Sunnyvale city manager Tom Lewcock was not surprised with the results. "The institution of government was not in the same age as the people or the industries of the community. The information age has changed fundamentally what government needs to do." Florida's John Anderson holds a similar view that economic changes require a new approach. "The dynamic global economy is a very complex piece of machinery. The truth of the matter is, it is not easy to understand how it works. And, it is even more difficult to understand how you could change its course to meet your broader social needs."

In the face of intense global competition, Silicon Valley companies had searched for new sources of competitive advantage and were fundamentally changing they way they do business. Leading-edge firms—large and small, high-tech, low-tech, and no-tech—were focusing on improving customer satisfaction, reducing time to market, enhancing productivity, controlling costs, and continuously improving product quality. To remain competitive in high-value markets requires speed, flexibility, and continuous innovation. These new sources of competitive advantage were helping Valley companies remain players and outright leaders in intensely competitive global industries—to survive and thrive where others had failed.

To focus on these new factors, the latest generation of Valley companies was specializing in what it does best and contracting out the rest. It was "unbundling" various company activities such as design, manufacturing, integration, testing, and marketing. Companies invested selectively to build world-class competencies; close relationships with suppliers, partners, and even customers formed to handle the rest. Ed McCracken of Silicon Graphics adds that "For a fast cycle-time company, these partners are much more effective if they're next door."

Flexible networks that link contractors, subcontractors, and customers in an elaborate web of relationships were becoming the dominant pattern. Although not all these external relationships were in the region, the focus on core competencies was making relationships with the Valley's supplier infrastructure all the more important.

For most companies, the importance of these external relationships extended to the community and its organizations. Local government, education institutions, and community organizations played either an additive or a subtractive role in each company's value chain, rush to market, and ability to attract and keep employees. This need to attract and retain quality employees provided a powerful motivator for companies to join the Joint Venture coalition. McCracken explains his corporate interest in the Silicon Valley community. "The quality and vitality of the community matters a big deal and affects employees' ideas, what they bring to the job, and their staying power with your company."

Valley companies were locating activities globally to take advantage of each region's unique offerings. They increasingly viewed themselves as knowledge brokers. By participating in many regional networks, the Valley's expanding firms transferred and tapped know-how and skills among different regions of the world. Sure, some companies for some types of business functions would locate in a region, draw on its resources, and take advantage of its cost structure until another location offered cheaper resources or financial incentives. But increasingly, firms depending on knowledge workers were engaging in new ways with the communities in which they operated. Successful companies linked closely with, and contributed to the development of, the assets base of each region. They have both local focus and global reach.

Although many Silicon Valley companies were competitive, the community was not. Corporate leaders began to realize that because they had not engaged with the community, the community had fallen behind. Companies needed adaptive and responsive community partners to provide the foundation for high-value-added work, including specialized workers. Silicon Valley's community infrastructure was nowhere near as quality-oriented in terms of customer (business) satisfaction, cycle-time reduction, and flexibility as the companies it was supposed to support. Yet the costs of operating in the Valley continued to rise.

The Valley's world-class companies, for example, need a world-class school system. Fewer than 10 percent of Silicon Valley schools were outstanding performers. Silicon Valley companies were reporting example after example of difficulty in attracting people—in part because of the reputation of Silicon Valley schools. Young professionals were reluctant to put their children in local public schools.

The Valley's world-class companies need time-sensitive government. Time-based competition meant that product life cycles were now measured in months. The adage "time is money" became "time is market" because failure to get new products out fast could shut companies out entirely.

World-class companies need a regional environment that facilitates communication. In some ways, Silicon Valley became a victim of its own success. The Valley had grown to such a size that the large number of institutions, jurisdictions, and individuals made it difficult to know whom to talk to and get things done quickly, much less implement fundamental change. The region had grown to more than two million people (more populated than eighteen states), spanning four counties and more than twenty municipalities. Just as companies were practicing flexibility in a fast-changing environment, the community's growth made it difficult. The community was not organized to deal flexibly with fast change.

Silicon Valley had grown into "a culture of blame." Explains Jim Morgan, "We seem, as a community, to have lost our consensus-building skills. Most of our problems are approached through confrontation and litigation rather than through negotiation, conciliation, and cooperation. We've reached total gridlock in our ability to set and meet common goals. This drains our ability to compete."

"The bottom line of our diagnosis: we had it all in the eyes of the world, but it wasn't working to our collective advantage," recalls Tom Hayes. Although the Valley had many of the ingredients for success— talented people, extensive industry networks, strong entrepreneurial culture—these resources had not been tapped to solve the festering problems undermining community competitiveness. The Valley community was feeling the effect of the economy's undergoing major, continuous transformation. The community's inability to respond to the changing needs of the economy was exacerbating the pain of that inevitable transformation.

In July 1992, Joint Venture released the diagnostic report, "An Economy at Risk," to the San Jose Metropolitan Chamber of Commerce annual event. Observes Jim Morgan, who became actively involved after the event, "The original plan was to do a study to get people thinking about the community, and then implement a few things. There was such a strong response to the luncheon that it quickly became apparent that the need was even greater than we imagined it would be. We thought maybe there'd be five hundred people there and that would be great. But there were eleven hundred people squeezed in, several hundred standing up, and a couple of hundred turned away. Executives, public managers, citizens. People got excited." More than one-third of the people turned in cards saying they would be willing to commit time to work on solutions. It was an extraordinary opportunity for a large number of people to learn together. Four years later, those who attended the event still speak of it as a key moment.

It was clear that the Valley economy was changing in response to global forces and that people felt the change widely. The key question was how to channel the swell of interest and concern into constructive action. The diagnostic report provoked the right questions but intentionally stopped short of providing solutions.

What the Joint Venture turnaround process had to do was build consensus. Explained Morgan at the time, "We believed it was possible to have a process in which this community could establish goals and work together on a set of initiatives to support an array of competitive, global business capabilities. Let me emphasize that this will not happen through simple 'hands-off' economic incentives or easy government subsidies. Instead, it's a process of discovering the need for a whole collection of core capabilities that a community comes together to build and continuously renew. Particularly in a high-cost region, only through this process of building shared capabilities together will existing industries be strengthened, new companies created, and new businesses attracted."

What Morgan and civic entrepreneurs from other communities have found is the power of connecting the challenges and opportunities of the new global economy to local concerns. It serves the purpose of waking people up to the realities of external forces, giving them hope that their region can find opportunities not just threats, and providing tangible examples of how local issues relate to the broader economic context.

They Open Minds to Outside Ideas

Although every community faces a different set of circumstances, much can be learned from the successes and failures of other places. Just understanding what others have tried can shape the thinking and action of local civic entrepreneurs. Generating options for action can stimulate innovation. Civic entrepreneurs are natural benchmarkers. They have a voracious appetite for learning about best practices and lessons learned.

Civic entrepreneurs often sponsor efforts to open up local leaders to new ideas developed outside their region. Even the best-intentioned local leaders, if not involved in enterprises that take them often to other U.S. and international destinations, will have a difficult time keeping pace with innovations developed elsewhere that might have some applicability locally. In some cases, leaders resist outside ideas, falling into a not-invented-here syndrome.

Whatever the predilection of their community, civic entrepreneurs take the time to provide the insights or sponsor discussions or trips so others in the community can be exposed to outside ideas and innovations. In some cases (for example, Wichita), they engage outside expertise to give their community a fresh perspective and a window on innovations from other communities. In other cases (for example, Cleveland), they engage local experts to take a fresh look at the challenges and opportunities.

Once benchmarking begins, communities can follow the thread of diffusion across multiple locations, learning an enormous amount along the way. Cleveland's Steve Minter recalls that "in 1980, we visited Baltimore, and we were inspired and thought if they can do it, we can do it. It turned out the Baltimore people were inspired by Pittsburgh. We also visited the waterfronts of Europe. Four or five groups went to St. Louis. The Roundtable was influenced by Detroit." In the past decade, this kind of benchmarking has helped Silicon Valley learn from Arizona and Austin, which learned from Cleveland, which learned from Baltimore, which learned from Pittsburgh, and so on.

At the same time, civic entrepreneurs are careful not to take benchmarking too far. They create opportunities to see what is happening without insisting that community leaders copy what is being done in other places or taking sides on which model is preferable. Cleveland's Carole Hoover emphasizes that "we didn't try to model from anyone. We looked at other communities and tried to use the best of what we learned to shape our own approach." And Al Ratner recommends that other communities need to "find out what everybody else is doing, then design your own program. Don't copy. If you do someone else's program, it doesn't work."

Active benchmarking in the form of on-site group visits is important. Civic entrepreneurs in Seattle have organized annual study tours of other regions in the United States and internationally to acquaint a large team of public and private sector leaders with the practices of other places. "It goes beyond just talking about it," according to Cleveland's Steve Minter. "You get a common experience, not that we'll copy them, but a feeling that we can do something like that."

Civic entrepreneurs personally join other community leaders to gather ideas from other community efforts and use them to build hope for improving their own community. According to James Gardner, president and CEO, ITT Community Development, "We looked at what was done in other states. We weren't hurting as bad as other states. We could choose the best parts of other efforts." In Cleveland, Richard Pogue remembers that "the leadership in the black community in the middle seventies felt out of the game, not part of community decision making. So Carole Hoover, Del de Windt, and some others went around the country to see what kind of urban coalition models there might be. In 1981, they formed the Roundtable. But even after that, it took time to build the trust to make partnerships work."

In Silicon Valley, the examination of other places was unavoidable, because some of the successes of other places like Austin were at the expense of Silicon Valley in terms of corporate relocations or expansions. Because the community was lagging so much, the health of Silicon Valley companies was not translating into the health of the region. Silicon Valley was capturing less and less of the value that the region's companies were generating. Investments in facilities, workers, and technology were being made elsewhere because the quality-cost balance of the region's infrastructure had not kept pace.

Looking beyond Silicon Valley, leaders could see that other regions with fewer amenities were consciously building them. Aggressive competition had set in from the likes of Austin, Portland, Phoenix, and Singapore. People wanted to know why Silicon Valley failed to attract federally funded consortia like SEMATECH and Microelectronics Computer Technology Corporation (MCC) that closely matched its industry base. Even the Earthquake Research Center went to New York. Looking at how other communities worked, local leaders could realistically assess how Silicon Valley did not work.

Much of the impetus behind the civic entrepreneurs in Silicon Valley, for instance, came from their firsthand experience with regions in Japan or Texas: they saw economic communities that operated much better than their own. They discovered what was possible with effective collaboration. And they helped others understand how effective communities functioned. Others, without firsthand experience, made the effort to learn. Early in the Joint Venture: Silicon Valley effort, a group of local business and community leaders traveled to Austin and returned convinced that they could work together, like Austin's leaders, to improve Silicon Valley.

Because they are often global players in business, civic entrepreneurs understand and appreciate the benchmarking of performance against that of other economic communities, regardless of the outcome. In their world, where you start matters less than where you are going and what progress you are making toward that goal. Companies learn about the most effective practices or methods of performing business processes, whether or not these practices exist in their own industry, and only then derive a quantifiable benchmark target. For leading companies, benchmarking has become an essential part of total quality management and is an ongoing process of seeking out and learning from world-class leaders.

Civic entrepreneurs apply the business concept of benchmarking best practices to their communities. As in industry, this type of benchmarking is a continuous process, not just a one-time effort. Also as in industry, learning and applying specific best practices are the focus of benchmarking efforts. Although it is unlikely that the entire economic development experience of a single community could or should be replicated in another region, specific best practices, including process improvements, can be incorporated into other regions.

Joint Venture: Silicon Valley's initial report—*An Economy At Risk* (1992)—in part benchmarked Silicon Valley's capacity to respond to change against four comparable regions: Austin, Phoenix, Portland, and Singapore. Most significant was the finding that Silicon Valley was suffering from a culture of blame, while these other regions had created a collaborative advantage based on cooperation among business, government, education, and the community.

Joint Venture designed a collaborative strategy process based on best practices from other regions. A widely participatory community process involving fourteen working groups and more than one thousand people produced an explosion of creative ideas from which emerged eleven specific recommendations for new initiatives. This process built on the experience of activating industry cluster working groups in Arizona and Oregon as a tool to engage industry leaders in regional strategy. Joint Venture established seven industry cluster groups that identified common issues and developed action plans. These groups included semiconductors, computer-communications, software, bioscience, defense, environmental technology, and business services.

Joint Venture learned from the experiences of Arizona and Florida in developing infrastructure working groups to help promote collaborative strategies. In fact, the leaders of this effort watched videotapes on the Arizona and Florida experience and studied the Arizona Strategic Planning for Economic Development (ASPED) and the *Florida Cornerstone* and *Enterprise Florida* reports prepared by the Florida Chamber and the Florida Department of Commerce. Joint Venture created infrastructure working groups focused on education-workforce, technology, regulatory process, tax policy, and the physical environment. In preparing their regional education improvement initiative, participants studied what had worked and not worked in other regional education improvement efforts across the nation.

Joint Venture also built on the experiences of Austin in creating a collaborative business, government, and education leadership group to guide regional economic initiatives. This collaboration helped Joint Venture and the city of San Jose successfully recruit the U.S. Display Consortium to San Jose in 1993, whereas prior efforts of this type had failed, including the loss of SEMATECH to Austin in 1988.

In 1989, a group of business and civic leaders came together to take responsibility for Arizona's economic future. Joining together with the Arizona Department of Commerce, these leaders created ASPED, which began by searching for best practices in other states and creating a state-of-the-art economic development model for Arizona. This effort was begun by the leaders of ASPED themselves, aided by the help of a consulting team.

The first ASPED document prepared in 1990 was "Redefining Economic Development for the 1990s." By reviewing best practices across the nation, this document created a new model of economic development for Arizona. It started by defining economic development not as industry attraction but as "a process of creating quality jobs through public and private investment in the economic foundations that sustain high-value-added industry clusters." The document described how economic development can assist a "vital cycle," in which a strong community supports a dynamic economy, and vice versa.

This benchmarking document was based on research that identified the best practices in other states and regions in supporting industry clusters and building strong economic foundations. It identified best practices in states such as Pennsylvania with its Ben Franklin Partnership and Industrial Resource Centers, Oregon with the *Oregon Shines* Strategy and its key industry networks; North Carolina with its apparel and wood products networks; and Florida with its *Enterprise Florida* industry cluster strategy. In addition, it identified specific best practices within economic foundations such as technology, capital, and human resources.

During the ASPED process, researchers at the Morrison Institute at Arizona State University (ASU) held a seminar involving leaders from other states to focus on lessons from the new economic development model. State leaders from Florida, Oregon, Texas, Kansas, Indiana, Minnesota, and Pennsylvania attended the ASU seminar. The ASU researchers published a seminal article in the *Public Administration Review* in 1991 highlighting the major lessons from the Arizona experience and making the best practices available to other regions.

In 1995, ASPED's successor, the Governor's Strategic Partnership for Economic Development (GSPED), was host to a national meeting on industry clusters, supported by the Economic Development Administration of the U.S. Department of Commerce. Arizona continues to be on the leading edge of states promoting cluster-based economic development strategies. Continued benchmarking by GSPED helps to upgrade Arizona's efforts. For example, one of the major initiatives launched by GSPED is an Arizona Information Infrastructure Initiative (AIII). Recently, leaders from Smart Valley spoke to the AIII about best practices in Silicon Valley.

They Build a Shared Framework

Building economic community requires good, well-packaged information and broad participation. Broad, meaningful participation requires a shared vocabulary and commitment to action. In any community, people will have a wide range of knowledge about economic issues and global competitiveness. They will possess very diverse experiences tackling issues at the interface between the private and the public sectors.

Civic entrepreneurs understand that to participate fully in a strategic planning or problem-solving process, people need relevant information and ways to make sense of it. The most successful collaborative forums provide all participants with basic information about the topic at hand. They either provide or develop with participants a framework for making sense of facts and for thinking and talking about complex issues. They create a unique vocabulary for their economic community.

Expertise always exists in communities, yet too seldom is it harnessed in a way that people can use it to solve problems. Civic entrepreneurs are talent scouts seeking people with expertise who can translate specific information into frameworks for decision making.

Arizona represents one of the best examples of the use of a new framework by civic entrepreneurs to give their region a way to organize facts, issues, ideas, and themselves to move forward. As Bob Breault, chairman of Breault Research Organization Inc., points out, "Alan Hald came through with a new concept, and people were ready for a new concept." According to Hald, "A network of informal groups were talking; people had also gone through the Phoenix Futures process, and many learned from that that it was important to have a framework going into the process. The core of the vision was the vital cycle. A vital economy creates high-quality jobs; it does improve the quality of life of the community; it does involve everybody, brings everybody into the economy."

Of course, it was not just Hald, and it was not a new framework quickly assembled. As he does in his business, Hald followed a typical product development cycle. He tinkered with the design (that is, held weekly brainstorming sessions), assembled a prototype (that is, published a report on redefining economic development for the 1990s), tested the prototype with customers (that is, shared the document and personally consulted with dozens of stakeholders), and refined the product (that is, refined the document), before taking the product to market (that is, used it in the collaborative process).

Austin adopted a similar framework, although by very different means. Through collaboration on the Microelectronics Computer Technology Corporation and SEMATECH national competitions, they learned their own version of the "vital cycle" framework, a circle of interdependency between the community and economy. As Pike Powers notes, "If you don't have that circle in place, you can't be competitive to do the things you want to do with your company. We have a sense of the circle in Austin. We don't want it to fly off, be lopsided; we want to drive it into the future."

Civic entrepreneurs instinctively understand the importance of a vital cycle of mutual support between the economy and the community. They know that a thriving economy can support community investment and vice versa. They are skilled at helping people understand how their actions have consequences on others in the community. They are good at making the case that the fates of business, government, and community institutions are intertwined.

In Florida, the Cornerstone project provided a framework that helped shift thinking fundamentally about the economy and the community. Jim Gardner explains the shift that took place. "Residential property could not carry the tax base; we needed an industrial base that creates high-paying jobs. Financing was hard for new enterprise but fine for the fern business—they understood agriculture but not industry. Cornerstone pointed out the difference between 1980 and 1990—we had been talking about competing against Alabama and Georgia; now we need to look at competing globally."

Creating broad and deep understanding of a shared framework is difficult and takes significant time. Civic entrepreneurs seize every opportunity to introduce and reinforce new frameworks for thinking about economic community. According to Hald, "We hammered that [the vital cycle framework] over and over and over again as part of the process. The hardest part is that people interpret it differently than what you meant. You learn about a fire over here and there and have to put them out."

In Austin, as Glenn West recalls, "SEMATECH built on relationships and success of MCC. For [the SEMATECH competition], we had rehearsals and a training session. We thought everyone knew this and were surprised to learn it wasn't so. We practiced answering questions. Eventually, the rehearsals went away, and we became articulate. The network had been built. When they came here [to evaluate our proposal], it was clear that we were a well-oiled team that you could count on to stand behind you."

Civic entrepreneurs also understand how important it is to share a new approach with more than just the top leadership elite. According to Neal Kocurek of Austin, "You have to identify who the players are: who is for it and who is against it. You need to come to know all the players. And then you have to educate everybody, and you have to educate them at the same time. And if you stick with them, they finally begin to trust you, and you have credibility. They are willing to spend the time, if you arrange so the time can be spent on their terms."

Civic entrepreneurs realize that the process of creating and sharing a new framework for thinking about one's economic community cannot be rushed or shortchanged. Mayor Glenda Hood of Orlando found that "people tend to simplify. They want to solve it box by box, but you can't do it like that. You can't solve one piece at a time. You have to deal with the whole ball of wax." Hood's view is echoed by John Anderson of Enterprise Florida. "There is a tendency to underestimate how tough economic development is. People have a short-term orientation—like fixing potholes. We have got to get beyond that. Historically, development programs are simplistic." Wichita's Lionel Alford believes his community should have done more. "Not only did we not think deep enough, we did not think long enough."

Civic entrepreneurs can help people challenge their assumptions, their internal mental frameworks, sometimes radically. The shift in Cleveland's focus to the unlikely target of tourism was the work of a civic entrepreneur. Richard Pogue recalls, "As we lost manufacturing, we tried to figure out which areas to emphasize. The idea that Jim Biggar [chairman and CEO of Glencairn Corporation] promoted was tourism. Today, everybody in this country wants to go for tourism, but this was ten to fifteen years ago. We began to understand that this was a way out for us. So, we began on various projects to fit them into this concept of a destination city, despite our horrible reputation at that time. Out of that general philosophy, that by gosh there is something here, came a whole series of projects. That was a very important revelation and one that never occurred to me: when you come from a manufacturing town, you do not ordinarily think of yourself as a potential destination center."

As newspaper publisher and new chairman of the Governor's Job Training Coordinating Council, Philip Power engineered a major shift in thinking in Michigan. "I kept asking people who was the expert? Who was the genius who could come in and tell us how the system worked . . . and the governor's staff would say, 'there isn't any.' So then we went to lots of conferences, but we didn't find anything there either." Power took an inventory of existing programs that, in his words, "tore my head off." Some seventy categorical pots of money in a nonsystem costing $800 million, with virtually no way of telling what kind of impact they were having. "We all thought we had a money problem—but we didn't have a money problem; we had a management problem."

Power knew the process was flawed and set out to change the paradigm by which Michigan invested in its people. He and fellow civic entrepreneurs dove in and designed a new framework, a new way of thinking about human resource investment in Michigan. It took the form of a coherent "human investment system," which included common intake forms, performance measures for the system, and an Opportunity Card—a "smart" card with a computer chip for all working adults to keep track of their interaction with the system. In the end, however, Power had not built enough "economic community" around the vision, and when the governor who appointed him lost the 1990 election, the effort lost steam. Nevertheless, the paradigm breakthrough did have an impact, because several other states began to look at these and other innovative ways to create cohesive human resource development systems (Osborne and Gaebler, 1992, pp. 188–192).

Building a shared framework for decision making is an important piece of the puzzle, but it has to be positioned just right. Too much information poorly presented can overload participants and be counterproductive, leading to confusion and debates about the finer points of the data. Too little new information or a rehashing of what is generally known also gives participants the wrong signal—that the effort is not really breaking new ground, which will produce a quick exit by civic entrepreneurs. The key is to give process participants a tangible feel for the regional situation, trends, and issues, put in terms that are directly related to their own personal situation.

Another common pitfall is that communities will invest too much importance in the information, pouring thousands of dollars into

Advice for Civic Entrepreneurs Acting as Teachers

• *Do* spend time to ensure that the facts you put on the table are concise, understandable, revealing, and widely shared.

• *Do* articulate tangible examples from your experience that connect new global realities with local issues and concerns.

• *Do* sponsor multiple ways of giving other leaders exposure to the experiences of other communities.

• *Do* spearhead the development of a shared framework by treating the process like a product development cycle (design-prototype-test-refine-take to market) involving the "customers" (that is, your community) all along the way.

• *Don't* allow perceptions, predictions, or personal opinions to be put on the table as facts, or the whole exercise could be written off by critics as thinly veiled, self-serving advocacy.

• *Don't* oversell your first-hand experience with the global economy, or local leaders may feel patronized and label you "out of touch" with the everyday concerns of the community; always follow up by asking local leaders to provide insights about the community and point out how it all connects.

• *Don't* take sides or push your favorite model (even if it may clearly be the best approach); expose community opinion leaders to the benchmarking process and a variety of examples, challenging them to relate the examples back to your community.

• *Don't* offer a neat, well-packaged framework, but make it a developmental, even somewhat messy, process to build ownership and find the right vocabulary that fits your community.

cutting the data from many angles. The most effective civic entrepreneurs know when to stop teaching and start acting on what has
been learned. Arizona's Alan Hald puts the role of information and
a shared framework in perspective. "You have to have a framework, a
sanction by community leadership, and a core of people who will be
drivers that will keep it moving and involve large numbers of people."

THE CONVENER: PROTECTS AND ENRICHES THE PROCESS

Civic entrepreneurs protect and enrich the process in several ways.
Playing the traditional role of convener, they enforce clear rules for
conducting the process, which include a discipline for turning ideas
into actionable initiatives. However, they go beyond running good
meetings. Civic entrepreneurs work to achieve a balanced process,
which includes a mix of top-level leaders and grassroots innovators.
They are always opening up new pathways for process participants,
helping them find where they can contribute or benefit most. And,
most important, they persist in the face of inevitable criticism and
impatience with the process. Civic entrepreneurs convene by taking
the following steps. They:

- Set clear process rules and create a discipline for results.
- Balance top-down influence and bottom-up innovation.
- Help people find the right fit.
- Persist through inevitable attacks on the process.

They Set Clear Process Rules and Create a Discipline for Results

Civic entrepreneurs provide a level playing field for community problem-solving processes, while also exercising a strong discipline that
drives for results. The rules are clear for participation in the process.
The expectation is also clear that the process is about moving to
action, not about producing a position paper. The process is a vehicle
for people serious about working together to change their community, not an open forum for grandstanding on polarizing issues.

Civic entrepreneurs know that successful implementation requires widespread participation in the process of designing new strategic directions. They also know that broad-based participation must ultimately connect to community leaders for good ideas to get implemented. Under the traditional paradigm of urban and regional planning, as with that of business planning, there were two ways to chart a strategy. The classic method was for several people with some combination of power, influence, and expertise to meet behind closed doors, put pen to paper, and publish the "strategic plan." The other method, of course, was to do nothing but follow a de facto strategy. Implementation and real change in either case were either difficult or unimportant.

The civic entrepreneurs who conceived Joint Venture: Silicon Valley wanted action. Yet they resisted the urge to "ready, fire, aim" and exerted process leadership, pioneering the most participatory strategic planning process ever attempted by the region. The process provided a structured way for people from government and industry, education and community, to talk, work interactively, break down barriers, and address together some troubling impediments to Silicon Valley's economic well-being. "We gave each other permission to ask questions we normally wouldn't ask because of the roles that we play or the geopolitical areas that we belong to," remembers county supervisor Mike Honda. "But those melt away as we get to know each other and realize that we have the same goals in mind."

The process was open but disciplined, and it inspired people to take action. "To get something like this off the ground, you need to get the chips off your shoulder," according to former Cupertino mayor Barbara Koppel. "Break down all the barriers, like the Marines break them down, and build things back up as a unit." Labor leader John Neece remembers, "After I left those meetings, I had a different attitude about where I lived and how I felt about my community. I felt proud." Printer John Kennett believes that the process produced the best of both worlds. "We had fourteen places for people to go to express themselves, and out of that process came a sense of hope and a sense of focus."

The process achieved a blend of mass participation and leadership at the highest levels. This combination ensured that the resulting action initiatives would be implemented. By the end of the nine-month process, more than one thousand people would contribute to development of *Blueprint for a 21st Century Community.* "People felt as if they went through boot camp together—worked hard, made new friends, new contacts, and felt real pride in participating," according to John Neece. This set the stage for the commitment necessary in implementation.

The civic entrepreneur creates a "process environment" that is attractive to serious participants. It is efficient, fair, demanding, and outcome-driven. It is efficient in that time lines are clear, process roles are well articulated, and staff and administrative support is available. Steve Zylstra recalls the approach Arizona took: "It is important to get law firms, accounting firms, PR firms on a pro bono basis to provide administration, meeting notices, mundane stuff like letterheads. It's absolutely critical."

Civic entrepreneurs steer the process as clear of politics as possible. Steve Zylstra worked hard to make Arizona's process nonpolitical. "People want a way to participate and make a difference without having to deal with the political games. You can make a contribution and see changes that will improve the environment that your business operates in, make changes that will be positive for your children." Zylstra believes, "It must be a private sector driven process, with government quietly supporting the process." Wichita's Hale Ritchie puts it simply. "The more you have politics get into this, the more you have business people going back to their offices saying, 'I don't need this.'"

Richard Pogue asserts that Cleveland's nonpartisan processes have been a key to their success. "In March 1989, *Fortune Magazine* wrote an article entitled 'How Business Bosses Saved a Sick City.' The guy who did the story came out here for a week and interviewed everybody, and as he was leaving he said to me, 'You know, there's a unique thing about your city. When people focus on a project, they park their ideology at the door.' He was so right. You look at our meetings. We got people way off on the left and way off on the right, people with all kinds of strong convictions and backgrounds, but they focus on the project and forget all the other stuff." Of course, such an environment does not come naturally. It has been the work of civic entrepreneurs like Richard Pogue that has set the standard and protected the process.

While steering clear of partisanship, civic entrepreneurs must also be careful to exercise process leadership instead of advocating a particular solution. Process leadership means first talking about the importance of following the right process. Jim Morgan set the tone when he said, "I think one of the biggest failings in our country and here in our Valley is that we've become so legalistic and confrontational in our decision-making processes that we have reached total gridlock in our ability to meet common goals. We hope that Joint Venture can be a meaningful process with the potential for creating an enduring legacy." In this sense, Morgan did not dictate the outcomes of the process, only that the process be effective. He knew that a good process is the best insurance for producing good outcomes.

Civic entrepreneurs avoid getting too invested themselves in any particular outcome. Alan Hald demonstrates the true spirit of the civic entrepreneur when he reflects on his most satisfying moment. "The highlight was that Saturday morning when we came to consensus on top collaborative initiatives. We had such diversity, but we came together and said let's do these things. People left that meeting with a changed view of what economic development was in Arizona. The process had stuck, regardless of the specific initiatives. And that was the most rewarding moment for me."

By 1984, Prudential Insurance executive Alex Plinio did not know what the answers were, but he knew that Newark better start working together to find them. A crumbling infrastructure, dramatic population loss, a hemorrhaging economy, and "very little trust, very little hope, no vision, and [a] governing sector [that] on its own could not manage the city effectively" (Chrislip and Larson, 1994, p. 43) provided the troubling backdrop for Plinio's exercise in process leadership. He interviewed a large cross-section of local leaders, asking them if "there was enough leadership to address the major issues and to find out if people would be willing to work together" (Chrislip and Larson, 1994, p. 132).

He did not push one solution or another but rather sought commitment to a process for developing answers. His relentless efforts resulted in the creation of a forum called the Newark Collaboration Group, which implemented a process of "issue discernment" to identify the most important issues facing the region. (Chrislip and Larson, 1994, p. 43).

Civic entrepreneurs like Alan Hald, Jim Morgan, and Alex Plinio set the standard for others. Silicon Valley labor leader John Neece admits to his conversion as the process began to unfold. "At first, I had selfish motives—get to know these business guys and get more work for my people. That changed after the first meeting. The CEOs didn't pretend to have the answers but wanted to work together to get something done. There were things I wanted in the worst way that I didn't get. And, you know what? That's fine, because the impact of overall effort has been far beyond what I could have imagined."

Lionel Alford set the tone in Wichita. "When we got started, we said we are not trying to protect turf here. We had some of the smartest people in our group who had been through the trials and tribulations and understood that diversification had inherent benefits. One of the biggest questions is how broad the group should focus. I had complained about the education; others complained about transportation. We included these things in our view of economic development along with diversification." Alford knew that a good process would evaluate the whole range of issues, and if education was important, it would surface in the process as a priority. Education did emerge, as did other priorities. Today, Wichita has a major educational improvement initiative that has been under way for several years.

In creating an environment for process success, civic entrepreneurs exert a strong discipline that drives relentlessly to outcomes. Arizona's Alan Hald may be America's foremost practitioner of process discipline. "We needed to have structure, a process, and to be inclusive, and to have broad diversity. We created almost a weekly communication fax to keep people informed." Hald insists that any effective process needs an "action vehicle—tasks, deadlines, events."

Hald conceived and managed ASPED from 1988 to 1992. Inspired by Alvin Toffler's call for anticipatory democracy and frustrated by his home state's complacency toward knowledge-based industry, Hald sparked a revolutionary strategic planning process involving more than one thousand people statewide. Hald believed, and still does, that the potential of the information revolution can only be realized with organizational and societal revolution.

Hald's progressive management philosophy built on openness, accountability, and shared vision left its imprimatur on the ASPED process. As CEO of a fast-growing, highly networked company, Hald had learned that the primary role of an effective leader is to develop a shared mind-set and action orientation. He created opportunities for Arizona's citizens to develop a common language for talking about how the economy works and what their shared economic goals should be. Just as employees of MicroAge knew early on the power of networking and the importance of total quality management, citizens of Arizona now know the value of inclusive process.

Hald pioneered new process techniques for his "community." After four regional forums across the state brainstorming economic goals, ASPED produced thousands of bumper stickers dissecting the goals to their essence: QUALITY JOBS. Hald pioneered three distinct types of meetings to develop and test economic strategy ideas. He designed public forums to secure widespread public input, town hall meetings to make decisions, and focus groups on specific industries and infrastructure areas to develop action items and implementation plans. The resulting comprehensive strategy was distributed in easy-to-read newspaper format, which included a cartoon explaining why "Arizona's economy is everybody's business."

Mary Jo Waits of Arizona State University describes how the discipline worked. "There was an overarching structure. Alan was a master of process where we would have public show-and-tells. Group chairs were all very busy people, but when they knew they had to make a public statement and all the other clusters were going to be there, they put tremendous resources into making cluster meetings go. They didn't want to stand up there with a blank piece of paper and report out."

This approach weaved through all aspects of the process. Phoenix attorney Bob Moya describes how he, as a working-group chairman, "would identify someone who was a very effective person who I knew could get things done either in community or business. That person would be given a title and a charge, so there would be a certain amount of ego involved. So they would not only have something that would be a little negative if they didn't deliver, but there would also be something very positive as their own deliverable product. And that is ultimately in our group what motivated people to bring back actual conclusions for the full group."

Leaders in Arizona have seen the results of Hald's process discipline. Bob Breault remembers that "someone would step up to volunteer but would then have to deliver. Alan asked several of us in Tucson to pull together the optics industry. He encouraged us to organize, look at the vital cycle [framework], and deliver results in three weeks! He made us feel like we were making a difference." The discipline continues to this day. According to Breault, "I still ask for outrageous schedules."

Silicon Valley's widely participatory community process involving fourteen working groups and more than one thousand people produced dozens of creative ideas, which winnowed to forty-three specific recommendations for new initiatives. Process discipline was exercised to set priorities and gain focus. A leadership group considered for support only initiatives that could best demonstrate the following:

- The collaborative initiative and its major components
- Reasons why this initiative is necessary and how it will benefit Silicon Valley
- Specific actions and resources necessary to implement the initiative
- The implementation champion and partners of the initiative
- Specific implementation objectives and milestones
- A target date for achieving success
- Issues that remain unresolved

This approach set up a fair system for selecting priorities. The criteria were explicit and widely communicated, keeping political favoritism to a minimum. A Darwinian process ensued in which some initiatives were championed, some combined with others to create a critical mass of support, and most withered away for lack of commitment to action or an inability to articulate the purposes and outcomes of their proposed effort. The discipline of this process clarified the thinking and approach of the survivors, in some cases sparked creative collaboration, and forced others to recognize that some ideas were not worth pursuing.

The practical result was the formation of fourteen initiatives (which further reduced to eleven over the next year). Each of the surviving initiatives agreed to a memorandum of understanding (MOU) with the leadership group (which evolved into the board of a new nonprofit organization). At the heart of the MOU is described an explicit set of measurable objectives for implementation.

They Balance Top-Down Influence with Bottom-Up Innovation

Civic entrepreneurs practice the delicate art of mixing top-level leaders with grassroots innovators to achieve a whole that is greater than the sum of its parts. They understand that we are in an era when problems and opportunities are increasingly complex and interdisciplinary. To avoid gridlock and to enrich the mix of ideas for addressing community issues, civic entrepreneurs seek talent and support outside of existing leadership circles.

At the same time, achieving the right balance is extremely difficult, because a bias in either direction can undermine the effectiveness of the process. If top leadership is too heavy-handed, community buy-in will be minimal and community opposition can become significant. If the grassroots involvement is wide and unfocused, top leaders will lose interest. Becky Morgan, president and CEO of Joint Venture: Silicon Valley Network, explains why the balancing act can be both difficult and essential. "Unlike a business, Joint Venture conducted its R&D in public. The creative process was inherently messy. It did, however, build commitment for implementation top-down and bottom-up" (*Joint Venture Way,* 1995, p. iii/1).

In Silicon Valley, the core leaders understood that what was needed was a collaborative, communitywide effort combining the most innovative thinkers from industry, government, education, and the community. They designed a regional strategy process that was top-down and bottom-up, was inclusive of all sectors, and was action-oriented. They knew that the process required individuals at all levels to take ownership of results. It must be open enough that anyone who wanted to participate could. They knew also the necessity of having high-quality, high-level participants who are willing to participate in the process and champion its outcomes.

What Silicon Valley's civic entrepreneurs did was give people from many levels their first forum to work together. Gil Amelio, chairman and CEO of Apple Computer, said, "Don't underestimate the power of a neutral forum. The rate of learning grows exponentially due to new linkages that create real value." Researcher Michael Schrage (1990) notes that "collaborations rely on a shared space. It may be a blackboard, a napkin, a piano keyboard, a rehearsal room, a prototype, or a model. . . . Shared space is essential as a technique to manage conversational ambiguity. In effect, these shared spaces are the collaborative tools that people wield to make sure that the whole of the relationship is greater than the sum of the individuals' expertise" (pp. 153–154). Civic entrepreneurs design and manage processes that create this shared space for community collaboration.

Sensitive to the needs and interests of top leadership, civic entrepreneurs ensure that the shared space is substantive and meaningful. Too often, volunteer leaders are asked to make financial contributions and support staff-driven decisions but not to apply their expertise to real challenges. As Richard Shatten, former executive director of Cleveland Tomorrow, has remarked, "The real secret to Cleveland Tomorrow's effectiveness is not the staff but the organization's members. Staff rarely meets alone with elected officials. Instead, staff supports board members in those discussions. Everything we do provides opportunities for member involvement and participation. . . . If they are not involved, the organization quickly degrades into just another volunteer board hiring staff to do a job" (Frey Foundation, 1993, p. 26).

Recruiting the right top-level leadership to assume important positions in the process is one of the most important tasks for a civic entrepreneur. Arizona's Alan Hald notes that "recruiting cluster chairs was a challenge. They had to be entrepreneurs and willing to put in time and energy, and have the ability to recruit others." According to Richard Pogue, "*Cleveland Tomorrow* allows no substitutes, only CEOs. Do they all show up at every meeting? No, but a good number do. In the more traditional model, if the CEO sends a vice president, well maybe the person will report back or not, and maybe the CEO will look at a stack of reports, but it's not the same. If you as the CEO are there, you're part of it. I think that mechanical rule is extremely important." Wichita's Lionel Alford concurs. "You must have the top leadership of companies involved or it dribbles off."

Civic entrepreneurs often act as go-betweens, convincing natural competitors in business or government to try working together. Recalls Phoenix attorney Bob Moya, "The greatest accomplishment is to get people from different areas who usually compete with one another to come together and work toward a common goal." Wichita's Lionel Alford also found that "competitors were willing to work together. This community is different than other communities where I have worked. In other communities, competitors were standoffish. Here, they work together. Jordan and other leaders were on the Bank Four Board and knew each other. While competitors, they were willing to work on community issues. They had a sense of community interest that went beyond their business."

Civic entrepreneurs often bridge the gulf between business and government. Mayor Susan Hammer recalls that the Valley's leading business leaders, after organizing themselves, reached out to include her and others in the public-private initiative. Since establishing Joint Venture, "many of the Valley's companies have become more engaged in community programs and government affairs," according to Hammer. Hammer's aide Bob Brownstein adds that "one of the real benefits of Joint Venture is that it has helped demolish stereotypes about how public and private sectors look at each other."

Civic entrepreneurs often have to convince two very different groups to get involved simultaneously—a reluctant leadership cadre and those at the grass roots who have traditionally had little say about the direction of their community. Arizona's Alan Hald sums up the challenge. "Most of the people don't care. Most of the people that 'count' are against it, that is, the people with the money. And then there are a few of the revolutionaries that say this is wonderful. So, they tap into the latent emotional energy of a crisis. So, the people in power say this is probably the only way we're going to get out of this. The people who didn't care are excited because they have been under stress. And, the people who think it's the right thing become hyper-charged and push to make it happen."

Civic entrepreneurs make personal appeals that clearly communicate the commonality of interest between different segments of the community. For Silicon Valley union leader John Neece, it is a moment he will never forget. "I remember listening to McCracken and Morgan talking about the importance of education and minorities. They weren't talking money; they were talking about people and about the kind of workforce they needed. I realized that we think 95 percent alike. I have a lot of allies out there."

Morgan and McCracken gave Neece the opportunity to challenge his own assumptions about management. Neece responded and remains an active member of Joint Venture: Silicon Valley Network. He continues to interact constructively with the CEOs of the region on important community issues, without titles or history getting in the way. "They have accepted me as an individual, and I accept them the same way."

Civic entrepreneurs protect the process by diligently practicing inclusion. Arizona's Bob Breault recalls, "I could get involved, because they threw away the rule book. I'm in the grass roots, and I can learn and communicate and make a difference." The key to the success of Austin, according to Pike Powers, is "the politics of inclusion rather than exclusion. You have to work very hard. Include as many disparate groups as you can. Have a sense of openness, of taking down barriers. There is no ticket, no price of admission, except personal interests. Whoever you are, you're welcome and we need all of you to make this effort succeed. That is what happened with MCC, SEMATECH, the convention center. Then you can convert that inclusion into a sense of mission and purpose that permits people to set aside their petty differences and go on to the greater community good."

One of the most difficult challenges for the civic entrepreneur is to resist attempts to shortcut the process by rushing to implementation or purposely leaving organizations that "just don't get it" behind. Cleveland's Al Ratner observes, "We finally understood that you have to do it through a process and, of necessity, a process will have thousands of pitfalls. You're talking to a whole bunch of people that you wouldn't want to talk to if you wanted to get it through quickly."

Silicon Valley's Neil Bonke recalls "sitting with Jim Morgan in his office one day. I was thinking that we might have to work around some established organizations because they were uncooperative or ineffective. But Jim said no. These organizations may have differing degrees of effectiveness, but all serve legitimate interests. Let's not work around them because that would lead to back stabbing. Let's embrace them and bring them in. Of course, now these organizations are involved heavily in Joint Venture."

By practicing inclusion, civic entrepreneurs give people the opportunity to earn their place in the leadership of their community. They act as intermediaries, bringing different levels of the community together. They do not act in the interest of equity. Civic entrepreneurs are not interested in ensuring that every organization is represented, that all political figures are given their due, or that people pushing their "solution" are given a soapbox to espouse their views. Rather, they are after meaningful inclusion that produces shared ownership for tangible outcomes.

An example from Denver demonstrates the power of meaningful inclusion. Tim Sandos and Harry Lewis were an unusual pair of civic entrepreneurs. Sandos was a young neighborhood activist, viewed by some as a political boss, a grocery store manager, and a Democrat. Lewis was an older Republican and corporate executive. The mayor and city council of Denver convened a diverse ninety-two–person committee called Citizens for Denver's Future and picked the two to cochair the effort. The committee had to do the hard work of identifying and prioritizing a package of infrastructure improvements for voter approval. With complementary skills and experiences but a shared interest in collaborative solutions, Sandos and Lewis set the tone for the committee, asking members not to take narrow, parochial stands or submit to special interests. Thanks to their efforts, the process was fair and effective. In the end, ten bond issues totaling more than $200 million were passed by the region's voters (Chrislip and Larson, 1994, p. 43).

Civic entrepreneurs create and protect a process that rewards people from the grass roots who have compelling ideas, drive, and willingness to work for the community good (not just their own self-interest). They are given the opportunity to interact with the existing community leadership. In an effort to launch a new convention center, recalls Austin's Neal Kocurek, "We would come together at 7:30 and work until 11:00 twice a week for five months. People learned that everyone can contribute. We had people from the environmental community and the business community, and generally they don't communicate. Somebody has to be an intermediary that both parties can feel comfortable with, so they will talk, really, instead of through the newspaper." As Cleveland's Jim Biggar observes, "It's about earned mutual respect and trust. Trust can't be demanded. Respect can't be demanded. They have to be earned. I think if you look back, that's what kept it together [in Cleveland]. If someone calls a meeting, you trust the person that it's the right issue and that we have to address it."

If anything, civic entrepreneurs lament not working hard enough to bring about and sustain the balance of top-down influence and bottom-up innovation. Wichita's Hale Ritchie observes, "If we made a mistake back then, we didn't go deep enough. We went deep enough to fund what we wanted to fund. We had a core group of companies that were the partners. In retrospect, we should have gotten a lot more people involved in the thought process." In Florida, Jim Gardner believed that they missed involving perhaps the most likely opponents. "Selling to the business community was too limited. The business community is not the biggest block of support. The people have to be behind it. People generally view growth and development as bad, especially retirees. We should have sold our program to the citizens at large."

Civic entrepreneurs have also learned from experience that working for that balance is important from a very practical standpoint: burnout. If a relatively small group of leaders is involved in every civic activity, the leaders will be unable to do any of them well or will try to be conscientious and neglect their business to the detriment of the community. Wichita's Hale Ritchie laments, "One of the problems that this community had is that we burned out all those people. I am afraid we won the battle and lost the war. We lost [the leaders from] Pizza Hut, Coleman, Cessna, and others. How much did that have to do with not keeping them plugged in the community, because if you're really plugged in the community, it is hard to leave. You need to have a broad base. If you try to do it with thirty people, you will wear them out. The more people you can get involved, and can sell the passion to, the better."

The role of civic entrepreneurs shifting their community to the practice of inclusion is one of the most important reasons Cleveland has experienced success in the past fifteen years. "In 1968, I went through a process of meeting with a group of people," remembers Al Ratner. "At the end of the process, someone said I should meet with a particular person. But, another person we were meeting with said, don't waste your time, he really won't want to deal with you because you're Jewish. There was a time in this community when prejudice was very strong."

The prevailing culture changed. "What changed was enlightened leaders who understood that for Cleveland to work everybody had to be involved," according to Ratner. "The system had to open up, and that's very, very important, and once the system opened up and once the opportunities were there, then you could move forward. While no community will admit it's prejudiced, every one of us is prejudiced against something or somebody. The question is how to open up that window. Whether it's allowing the poor people who live in the neighborhoods to have their voice, or whether it's racial, or religious, that is something you need to get done and be serious about changing." Cleveland has opened its process and has one of the best environments for collaborative problem solving of any large American city.

They Help People Find the Right Fit

One of the most important practices of civic entrepreneurs as conveners of the process is to find the right fit for individual participants. Often, the first point of participation is not the optimum point of participation. It takes time for people to explore the process, work with others, and practice their civic skills.

Civic entrepreneurs help participants find their best point of leverage. Sometimes, they do it by suggesting they move from one working group (or civic group) to another. Sometimes, they even create new working groups, as new issues crystallize with a core of champions behind them. In short, civic entrepreneurs are always looking for opportunities as the process unfolds, to clear new pathways that give individuals the best chance of working together and developing collaborative initiatives that will make a difference for the community.

Civic entrepreneurs guiding Silicon Valley's Joint Venture process used this practice extensively. For example, based on their knowledge of the changing economy and research on the region's environmental companies, they gave the region's fledgling environmental industry its first seat at the table. Companies in fields as diverse as clean-up, instrumentation, engineering, and pollution prevention for the first time began thinking of themselves as an industry. They researched the size of their industry and discussed common problems. They involved other organizations that could help or hinder their industry's development: universities, national laboratories, environmental groups, and regulators.

Led by civic entrepreneurs Rich Morrison of Bank of America and Gene Herson of EMCON, participants contributed time to develop the region's capacity to support and grow environmental companies, which would benefit all of them. Over a two-year period, they worked jointly to create the nation's first incubator for environmental start-ups, to promote state regulations that reduce barriers to new technology, and to develop specialized curricula for environmental health and safety managers with local universities and community colleges.

Joint Venture's collaborative process was dynamic and nonlinear. It continually evolved to link related ideas to each other and good ideas to people who could help develop them. Many of the cochairs from the collaborative process continued to provide leadership, as their working group ideas transformed to become initiatives and then moved into implementation (see Figure 5.1).

One of the best examples of helping someone find the right fit is the story of Chris Greene. Greene was the president of a small engineering services company in Silicon Valley. Although a graduate of Harvard Business School and a McKinsey alumnus, he was not among the leadership elite of the community. Nonetheless, the quality of his contribution was recognized, and a civic entrepreneur cleared a path for him. According to Greene, "Jane Shaw [then-COO of ALZA Corporation] was a real champion for me in this process. I was a member of the bioscience working group, which she cochaired. At our second meeting, we broke into subcommittees. I joined the committee on the interaction between universities and industry, which interested me. Jane came over and yanked me into her subcommittee on permitting issues."

Shaw spotted Greene's skills and potential and found a better place for him to work. Greene "suggested the idea of a regulatory forum

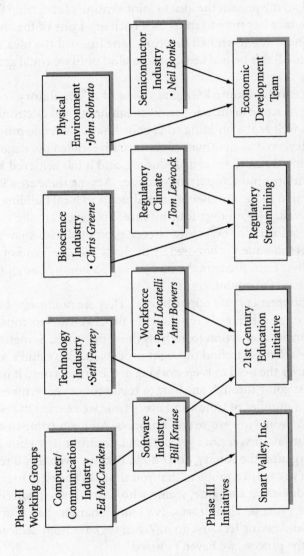

Figure 5.1. Creating Pathways for Civic Entrepreneurs in Silicon Valley.

between government and industry that would allow both sides to develop common ground on building codes and other issues. Jane then sent me over to the regulatory affairs working group. They were suspicious of my involvement and rejected the idea. But Jane came back and had me present the idea to Joint Venture's Leadership Group, having me take her time to speak as a cochair of one of the working groups. Then, at a town hall meeting, Jane insisted the idea be put forth again. All this helped keep the idea alive until we could get more support."

Joint Venture adopted Greene's idea of a "regulatory forum," expanding its scope to include permit streamlining and electronic permitting as well as the building code coordination Greene proposed. Greene has served as chairman of the initiative, called the Regulatory Streamlining Council, since its founding, and it has achieved several of Joint Venture's most important successes. Among these are a 95 percent reduction in the number of amendments to local building codes in Silicon Valley (from over four hundred to eleven among twenty-nine jurisdictions), the exact idea Greene promoted with Shaw's help. Greene was subsequently honored by the Joint Venture board of directors as a Civic Entrepreneur, the first person so honored among their many hundreds of volunteers.

Civic entrepreneurs are opportunistic. They are not invested in one approach or another, only in whatever process leads to consensus about priorities and action to address those priorities. Sometimes, it takes a few attempts to find the right process fit. Cleveland's Al Ratner recognizes the need to keep working at the process until it is right. "We are just going through an effort to revise county government. We have tried a number of times, and every time we've tried to revise it, we've never won. Now we've got a process. And you come to a conclusion that says if you can't get the black community to buy into a way to reorganize the county, don't do it. Because even if you reorganize it, you've caused a problem that you shouldn't cause. That comes about by looking at the issue, seeing who hasn't been involved, and designing a process. That process is so much harder than four of us sitting around saying let's just do it. When we have been dedicated to following the process, we haven't missed."

Bob Keller, former president of a business group called the Greater Baltimore Committee (GBC), discovered the importance of taking time to find the right fit, working with a local community group on education and training issues. BUILD "wanted a major commitment around job training and jobs. So we danced with them on it for a long time. . . . We were making no ostensible progress. What we were doing, however, was establishing some credibility with one another. . . . And there was a meeting; and the Boston Compact idea was put on the table; and so we had switched from job training to education. Here was a place where GBC had a commitment, BUILD had a commitment, and we began to see some real possibility. That started the negotiating process" (Chrislip, and Larson, 1994, p. 92).

They Persist Through Inevitable Attacks on the Process

Despite all the preparations of civic entrepreneurs, complex community processes are often messy. Perhaps the greatest contribution that civic entrepreneurs make to the process is patience. They have the credibility and influence to ward off challenges to the process. They are willing to absorb criticism, use their own political capital, and provide cover to those in the process. It is one practice that Austin's Neal Kocurek knows well. "You have to understand leadership, and you have to take the heat. Inevitably, there are more activists that are against things than are for it. You need patience." Silicon Valley's John Neece echoes Kocurek. "I have really learned to have patience and the value of process."

In Cleveland, the process of bringing together the business and minority communities required inordinate persistence. Richard Pogue remembers that "there was a latent lack of trust. We had an executive committee of ten to twelve [black people and white business people] who met behind closed doors and really went at it—really telling each other how they felt about things. Gradually, a trust developed in that little leadership group, and that rippled out into the broader group. But, if we hadn't had those closed-door sessions, I'm not sure we ever would have reached that sense of trust."

The civic entrepreneur is the convener of a process that inevitably some people try to seize for their own purposes. Silicon Valley's John Kennett offers a blunt assessment. "The process is ugly. You find things out about your community that you don't want to know. You gotta realize that some people will be out for their own self-interest and learn how to deal with it."

Newark's Alex Plinio had to exert his influence to keep the process on track. Early in the process, "people would come to the meetings and try to railroad an agenda through. We had to dismantle that immediately." A series of task forces and public meetings ultimately produced a future vision and strategic plan for Newark. Subsequent implementation has led to "significant improvements in housing, education, and economic development. In 1991, Newark received the National Civic League's coveted All-America City Award for its collaborative revitalization efforts" (Chrislip and Larson, 1994, p. 44).

Civic entrepreneurs resist inevitable pressure to undermine the integrity of the process when quick solutions come up or power asserts itself. Harry Lewis and Tim Sandos, a corporate executive and a neighborhood organizer and cochairs of Citizens for Denver's Future, had to exercise this kind of process persistence. "All Tim and I did was steer the boat to try to keep from running up on a sandbar. We just tried to keep the process going and shepherd that process so that the committee could decide what they wanted to do" (Chrislip and Larson, 1994, p. 93). After some special-interest pressures attempted to compromise the process, Lewis stepped forward in a defining moment. "We've been committed to this process all along that's inclusive and relies on consensus. We're not going to let this whole thing go up in smoke. We agreed on how we would do things, and we're going to hold to the integrity of the process" (Chrislip and Larson, 1994, p. 98).

Sometimes, civic entrepreneurs must forcefully put criticism to rest, and do so convincingly. In a speech early in the Joint Venture process, Jim Morgan gave critics a reality check. "There have been some, including a few economists, who have criticized the Joint Venture: Silicon Valley effort. They argue that our problems are simply the result of a long recession. But most of them don't run companies, most of them don't travel on a global basis, and most of them don't have to deal with the reality of the local regulatory environment."

Morgan then shared how he was persuaded to take action—all but silencing the criticism that the process was a waste of time. "What crystallized it for me was a twenty-seven-year-old who stood up at our visioning conference and declared, 'I think you people don't really understand the urgency of what must be done. Do you know what we discuss with our friends? Almost 80 percent of our conversations are about how we can get out of Silicon Valley.'" Morgan had captured the essence of the Joint Venture process: it was not about a short-term correction but about the long-term future of Silicon Valley.

For Phoenix, Austin, Silicon Valley, Cleveland, and other communities that have had some success, process persistence has been the difference. Steve Minter of the Cleveland Foundation looks beyond the

Advice for Civic Entrepreneurs Acting as Conveners

- *Do* significant up-front work to assemble the group, personally inviting key participants to ensure high-quality discussion and the involvement of people who have the capacity to implement.

- *Do* insist that process participants link problems or opportunities with specific ideas for solutions, which sets the tone for constructive problem solving.

- *Do* create an explicit screening mechanism that rewards solutions with a strong rationale (that is, tied to high-priority issues or opportunities), credible champions, and growing support from the group.

- *Do* work behind the scenes to encourage participants to pursue their ideas, recruit allies, and find the right fit in the process (for example, join another working group, team up with someone else, and create a new group).

- *Don't* eliminate unpredictability from the process; be open to ideas and emerging leaders from the grass roots; be ready to nurture unforeseen but compelling solutions that may appear.

- *Don't* let process participants get prematurely preoccupied with prepackaged solutions (for example, "My organization is already doing that" or "There is a neat program from this community that would fit perfectly here"); give them time to think through options.

- *Don't* let people off the hook for half-baked proposals; use Socratic questioning to help them refine their ideas, link them to others, and build a core of champions to take them forward.

- *Don't* expect many ideas to survive the final cut; the whole point is to brainstorm possibilities then systematically winnow them down to the few that meet a two-part test: (1) they address the high-priority challenges or opportunities facing your economic community, and (2) they are implementable (that is, have clear objectives and committed champions).

headlines. "The thing I've learned is that when you don't succeed, there are one hundred persons pointing fingers, and when you do succeed, there are one hundred persons claiming credit. One way you can tell something is really a success: get all the annual reports of all the organizations involved in it, and they all have the wonderful story in it about how they leveraged this great project. I think what doesn't get written out is that along the way, boy, it took a long time, there were a lot of issues, and a lot of disappointments. The pieces really have to come together from a lot of different places. We had a sense that these are all components that will make us a very different kind of city. So let's go the extra mile. Let's not quit."

CHAPTER SIX

Implementation

Mobilizing Resources
to Get Things Done

Implementation is the hard part—it requires focus, perse-
verance, and flexibility.

—Becky Morgan, Silicon Valley

It's important to create structures that allow people to feel
accountable for results.

—Alan Hald, Arizona

Civic entrepreneurs intensify their focus on two roles to support their communities as they move from the collaborative process to implementation—helping participants move beyond what to do about their situation to the collaborative actions that will actually change their communities. To achieve this transition, some act as integrators and others as drivers. Those who act as integrators recruit expertise, locate resources, and otherwise help assemble the necessary ingredients for successful implementation. Those civic entrepreneurs who act as drivers ensure that measurable objectives are set and reached, that implementation efforts avoid fragmentation, duplication, or rigidity in approach and that the focus remains on challenging objectives. Civic entrepreneurs have achieved the following during the implementation stage:

- After three years of implementation, Joint Venture: Silicon Valley's eleven collaborative initiatives have leveraged more than $35 million in cash and in-kind resources for implementation; the regulatory climate has measurably improved, including documented reductions in permitting times in local cities and a unified building code across twenty-nine jurisdictions.

- In five years of implementation, Arizona has created a Small Business Innovation Research program and the Arizona Technology Development Authority; $10 million in funding has been generated to improve math and science curriculum, a new job training fund, and new export development activities; and numerous projects have been pursued by the state's industry clusters (which continue to meet regularly).

- Over the last thirteen years, Austin's approach has secured two national R&D consortia (MCC and SEMATECH), built a new convention center, attracted millions in new investment in the University of Texas, and recorded the largest increase in manufacturing jobs of any region of the country.

- Cleveland has invested $5 billion to remake its downtown urban core over the last fifteen years, stemmed its population decline, raised millions in venture funding for new high-tech start-ups, expanded the capacities of local higher education institutions, and improved the competitiveness of its precision manufacturing sectors.

THE INTEGRATOR: OPERATES
LIKE A CIVIC VENTURE CAPITALIST

As a community moves from process to implementation, some civic entrepreneurs will play the critical role of integrator. In a sense, they play the role that venture capitalists play, but in the civic realm. Venture capitalists are widely recognized for the funds they invest in new ideas or enterprises. However, to people in the business, venture capital is a contact sport. Venture capitalists work directly with new enterprises to help them gain access to specialized business, technical, and other talent to make the venture a better candidate for success. They often sit on the boards of new enterprises, staying active in strategic decisions. And, with their involvement, they give the company greater credibility with other companies and investors.

Civic entrepreneurs operate much the same way to nurture new, collaborative community initiatives through their start-up period. Al Ratner focuses on the key role he and others play in Cleveland. "So many of these things take on their own life. Do leaders have to do everything? No, we need to ensure that the environment is in place that will allow the right things to happen. That's the biggest single thing we can do. And whatever it takes to make that environment, we must do it."

Civic entrepreneurs integrate pieces that are important for implementation by taking the following steps. They:

- Manage leadership transitions
- Forge deep commitments to change
- Recruit a first-class support team

They Manage Leadership Transitions

At the point of transition between incubation and implementation, many community efforts collapse. In many cases, the initial leaders of the process are worn out; new champions are just emerging. There is delay, with loss of momentum and the sense of urgency. People who actively participated in the idea-generation process do not hear from the process leaders about next steps and go on to something else. In the management of the leadership transition, civic entrepreneurs first make their mark in the implementation phase.

"The Smart Valley board recognized that a full-time commitment was needed to make Smart Valley really happen. Volunteerism only gets you so far," says Seth Fearey, Internet Solutions marketing manager at Hewlett-Packard. "We had to hire a strong manager, pay him appropriately, and give him a lot of latitude to execute." Tom Lewcock, the city manager of Sunnyvale, agrees. "It takes a lot of time, and it requires some real guru-type steering, or things can blow early; [Joint Venture] certainly required the steadying hand of Becky Morgan." Morgan left the California State Senate to join Joint Venture as president and CEO during the transition from process to implementation. She helped create a stable implementation organization and recruited other leaders to ensure an effective transition.

In the Joint Venture process, new leaders emerged from the working-group process who were willing to champion certain initiatives and work with influential community leaders to implement them. A kind of civic venture capital process allowed the best ideas—those that stood the rigors of the process and became linked with competent "champions"—access to resources that could be leveraged by senior community leaders. The relationships and momentum that developed through the working-group process became a foundation for ongoing problem solving within the region.

At the same time, civic entrepreneurs handed off leadership at the highest level. Knowing that he had to give others an opportunity or run the risk of the effort being seen as "a Jim Morgan thing," Morgan voluntarily stepped down as cochair once Ed McCracken had agreed to assume that responsibility. According to McCracken, "I don't know if I would have been the 'Jim Morgan' who got it started, but when we got to the transition point, I knew we couldn't let the interest, involvement, and excitement about Joint Venture die. I really believed Silicon Valley needed a long-term feeling of family."

McCracken believed that the opportunity might not come again. "If we let Joint Venture die at implementation, people would have used this as a 'see I told you so' forever and set back the interdependence theme twenty years. Once you get started, it is really important to make it work. I thought I could help it through the implementation process. I felt somebody needed to. I'm glad I did it."

To facilitate the transition, civic entrepreneurs simultaneously give up control, secure the commitment of other civic entrepreneurs to follow through, and remain involved in a new capacity. Although Jim Morgan stepped down as chairman, he has remained on the board and active in fund raising. Al Ratner reveals that the key to Cleveland's sustainable success is that there "has never been a single person who was recognized as *the* business leader." Over time, many business leaders have contributed, recruited others, and then either remained involved or transitioned.

At the same time, Wichita's Hale Ritchie warns of a common pitfall. "Instead of getting the best people to do the job, we were filling chairs." Ritchie and others believe that they did not work hard enough to find the diverse leadership talent that could carry through in implementation. A good process will produce some implementation champions, though additions and corrections are inevitably necessary.

Perhaps the most critical ingredient to civic entrepreneurship is the willingness to give it away. The most effective civic entrepreneurs practice *enlightened selflessness*. Like many of the best corporate leaders, they personally value helping others succeed. They must sometimes, in effect, relish the role of the unsung hero. In writing about Seattle's past civic entrepreneurs—including James Ellis, the attorney who inspired a major package of bond measures that transformed the region, and Joseph Grandy, the car dealer who stimulated the successful effort to make Seattle's 1962 World Fair happen—Neal Peirce has suggested that sometimes there is "leadership so 'big' that it doesn't seek its own reward" (Peirce, with Johnson and Hall, 1993, p. 102).

Alex Plinio, Prudential Insurance executive and civic entrepreneur who founded the Newark Collaborative Group, understood the importance of enlightened selflessness to keep collaboration progressing. He knew well enough to "put as many people 'up front' as possible—not the leadership of the collaboration but the leadership of the city. We were not to become a shadow government, for example, but to give credit to council persons, mayors, heads of colleges, neighborhood groups, and so on. This is the exact opposite of what most organizations do early on; they try to attract credit for themselves. You should do just the opposite. Give it away. Don't claim credit. Be sure that someone else gets it, whoever is working on it or is at the center of it" (Chrislip and Larson, 1994, p. 95).

George McLean, newspaper publisher and civic entrepreneur in Tupelo, Mississippi, learned as a newcomer to the community the necessity of building trust. McLean spent a lot of time listening to current leaders and acting as a "servant leader" to help them help themselves. And he gave away credit for achievements readily. Although he would receive more national than local acclaim for his innovative economic development ideas, he was effective in moving his community forward.

Florida's Larry Pelton emphasizes the importance of securing implementation commitments, believing that "it's not something you can just hand off and expect to happen. We need champions, both corporate and community leaders, committed to long-term leadership. It's gonna rain, so you have to look beyond the short term." Mayor Glenda Hood of Orlando adds that "the easy part is the visioning exercise. The hard part is the implementation. Too many times those plans end up on the shelf. You need to make sure you have your champions identified."

In Austin, project after project has been launched and populated with leaders who could see them through to implementation. Civic entrepreneur Neal Kocurek describes how the transition to implementation is made. "It all boils down to leadership. One person someplace needs to get capable people to take on projects. And those capable people will make those projects succeed. And then a series of successes will attract other people to take them on."

Kocurek also recognizes the need and difficulty of securing long-term commitments to implementation. "You can't decide I'm going to give it a year. You can find lots of people who will help you with some aspect of something for a short period of time. But it's very difficult to find someone who will undertake projects where you start and you work at it for years to make it happen, but that's what it takes to make significant projects happen in our community today. People are used to watching TV and seeing things happen in thirty minutes, and they think that's what it takes. And they become discouraged when they spend a year at it and they don't seem to be any closer than they were. But when you work on a project for five years, and then you begin to make progress, you become even more determined that you are going to make it happen. That's the leadership that you need to develop."

Cleveland offers a specific example of transition from design to implementation—the Rock & Roll Hall of Fame and Museum. One of the city's more senior civic entrepreneurs, Al Ratner, describes the transition. "A lot of us were major players, as unlikely as that may seem, since a lot of us aren't exactly the biggest rock 'n' roll fans. So, we knew that we could help build it but that a whole new group of people would have to take it over to make something of it. What we have done is make a conscious effort to find these people. We have found a terrific young accountant, found key people in the minority community; we called up Keycorp and said, give us one of your top three executives at the bank, and he joined the board. We are cognizant that there has to be this continuity, and it has to come from a diverse pool of people, and therefore it is our responsibility to see that there is someone in place to carry on."

Civic entrepreneurs are realistic. They know that major transitions are messy. Steve Minter puts to rest the notion that it has come easy for Cleveland. "It's important to understand that there are plans and visions, and sometimes when you look at the finished product, it looks so wonderful and seems like a straight line. The reality is that we could take every single major thing that we point to in this city where there has been some accomplishment and say, 'But if you only knew all the pieces.' Let's take Playhouse Square. It wasn't the business community that first stepped up and said we ought to save the theaters. It was the Junior League of Cleveland many years ago. Foundations then came in, the business community then came in, state and county government then came in—it was a messy affair, a lot of pain, a lot of blood on the floor."

Civic entrepreneurs have the persistence to keep searching for the right combination. According to Cleveland's Richard Pogue, "We have a collaborative mind-set that grew out of that terrible pre–1980 time in our community. It became a way of looking at problems. Take the Gateway Project. I mean my god, the twists and turns in that thing, the obstacles, and the headlines that today it's dead. Then, someone would come up with some other way to solve the problem. Same way with the Rock & Roll Hall of Fame and Museum. That thing died at least nine times. Each time, someone would say, How about this, or How about that? You automatically think that there must be another way to solve it, and we've been through this now enough times so we know that somebody out there will help put the collaboration together to get over that particular obstacle. When you run into a problem, you find somebody else to come in and supply what's needed." Or as CEO Jim Biggar sums up Cleveland's approach when faced with implementation obstacles, "If it's third down and twenty-seven, you better find a way."

It is difficult for communities to have the staying power to find a way through the transition to implementation. Florida's Jim Gardner recognizes the need for strong continuing of leadership from concept to implementation but also believes, "We made a mistake—more thought should have been put into the organizational phase. It took much longer than anticipated to implement." Good organization and process make implementation less difficult, though hardly easy. Silicon Valley's Becky Morgan emphasizes that effective implementation "requires attention to the dailies—the people, the implementation plan, the fund raising."

There are moments when civic entrepreneurs have to provide the continuity. Wichita's Hale Ritchie remembers that at one point, they had "a room full of people with everyone worried about everyone else pulling out." Arizona's Alan Hald found that people naturally shifted roles as the process moved to implementation. "Going from planning to implementation, people go from cooperation to competition. That, or many people go back to their jobs."

They Forge Deep Commitments to Change

Although managing the leadership transition is essential, civic entrepreneurs focus a lot of effort on ways to deepen the commitment of
existing and new parties. For example, securing the involvement of a
company's CEO is only the first step. Deepening the commitment to
other members of the management team and ultimately to other
employees makes implementation everyone's concern. It also unleashes
an enormous reservoir of talent to carry out collaborative community
initiatives.

Silicon Valley's Glen Toney, group vice president of Global Human
Resources at Applied Materials, and chairman of Joint Venture: Silicon Valley's 21st Century Education Initiative, observes that forging
an implementation partnership with other companies can have big
payoffs. "Joining a broader community effort enables individual companies to fit the scope of their participation or their particular interest
within a larger framework for success. The key is leverage. You can't
do it alone, but working collaboratively, almost anything is possible."

The typical scenario is that implementation remains with a small
group of champions and the staff support they assemble. Most groups
are wary of the time and resources that are necessary to deepen partnerships. Successful groups view these costs as investments in an
implementation network that will be able to achieve far more than
small-scale programs. Austin's Neal Kocurek believes that "the leader
has to bring about that sense of inclusion" to ensure continuity of
people from process to implementation. Instead, what usually happens, Kocurek argues, is that "a political body will often set up a blue
ribbon committee to address an issue. And the blue ribbon committee spends an awful lot of time addressing the issue, and they come up
with some good points. And then they prepare their report, give it to
the political body, and they disband, and the report sits there. What
is the missing ingredient? There wasn't the individual that will stay
with the project and make sure that the inclusion remains and the
project moves forward."

Civic entrepreneurs are always looking for creative ways to deepen
community commitments. Like a broken record, Wells Fargo Bank
president Bill Zeundt keeps asking those involved in Joint Venture: Silicon Valley's education reform initiative exactly what skin they will
put on the table as their commitment to change. Austin's William
Cunningham points to the ever-growing commitment of the Univer-

sity of Texas to the region's economic development. "With SEMATECH, the university went beyond anything it had done before, helping to put together a winning formula that included providing land and a facility for the consortium, and helping to secure legislative financing on the basis of a handshake deal. . . . In the beginning, the university's involvement was based on a rather small number of dedicated individuals, but now our willingness to be supportive has become institutionalized."

In Cleveland, Jim Biggar and others assembled an innovative approach that enabled local companies to make much deeper investments in new city development projects with some expectation of return. "Companies invested with the idea that their financial return would be half of what they would expect in their own business. The other half of the reason to justify it would be that by having that kind of a city, we would be able to attract and maintain key people who were competitively better than the people on teams in other cities. It would be hard to quantify, but you felt you would have a better company. We put together model units, proved their viability, then let the private market take over."

In Silicon Valley, Glen Toney has used his experience in the Joint Venture process to rethink his own company's community involvement. He discovered that "recent research has identified more than seventy thousand business-education partnerships in our country. Many of these last less than a year. Most are 'helping hand' relationships—with business providing resources to schools. Few really involve a true partnership where business people and educators are working shoulder-to-shoulder to improve student performance in measurable, sustainable ways."

Toney recognized the kind of deep commitment and partnership that was necessary. "What I have learned is that my involvement as an individual (and as a representative of my company) needed to be more strategic. I was feeling frustrated that our corporate contributions weren't having more impact. But, I shouldn't have been surprised. We were not really engaging with educators as true partners, nor were we injecting ourselves and our resources into situations where there was a comprehensive strategy and commitment to change. I have learned the importance of positioning our efforts within a broader educational reform initiative, making a long-term commitment, and coordinating our efforts with those of other companies and organizations working on educational improvement."

Joint Venture: Silicon Valley Network has used the venture capital model impressively in several of its implementation initiatives—

particularly in K–12 educational improvement, in the development of a catalyst to stimulate use of the information superhighway, and in local regulatory streamlining.

The citizens of Silicon Valley can now take a free test drive on the Internet, one lane of the information superhighway. At sites throughout Silicon Valley, Public Access Network provide free, high-speed Internet access to information on education, employment, community, government, and other resources. Soon also, city planners, property developers, and ordinary citizens will find at their fingertips an Internet-accessible geographic visualization system for the Bay Area. Through the Bay Area Digital GeoResource (BADGER), people will manage vegetation, track ground water contaminant flows, manage storm water discharge, and predict fire hazard risks, among other uses. Through CommerceNet, companies gear up to buy and sell billions of dollars worth of business products electronically. And more than thirty other projects are applying information and communications technologies to benefit key areas of the community—changing the way people work, live, and learn in Silicon Valley.

It is fall 1992. Hundreds of Valley leaders challenge each other to develop new initiatives to improve the Valley's ailing business infrastructure and to envision the parameters of a next-generation Valley economy. Springing from many parts of the process is the notion of an "electronic community" that uses information and communications technologies to solve real regional problems and address real opportunities. Within a year, the fledgling Smart Valley organization is born to realize this vision.

Of course, the timing was right. The year 1992 brought the birth of the World Wide Web; 1993, the Mosaic user-friendly Web browser or navigator. And, of course, there was no better place, technologically, for such an initiative to be born. But it was a new activism that made Smart Valley happen. Collaborative leadership by a team of civic entrepreneurs made the difference. So did strong grassroots participation in identifying community needs and developing solutions. This top-down, bottom-up combination of collaborative leadership and grassroots participation positioned Silicon Valley to capitalize quickly on the information superhighway opportunity and develop an effective, meaningful version of the national information infrastructure in its own backyard.

"There was this ground swell from throughout the community," recalls Seth Fearey. "I had been working with the Computer Systems

Policy Project to champion the concept of the National Information Infrastructure with public policy makers in Congress and the Bush administration. Here, in Silicon Valley, we had a chance to actually build one and show the world how to do it." From every corner of the Joint Venture effort to examine the economy came questions:

- "Why can't we use information technologies to speed up communications within our cluster?" asked the computer-communications group headed by Ed McCracken and Jim Carreker of Aspect Telecommunications.
- "Why can't we use this superhighway to encourage telecommuting?" asked the Physical Infrastructure Group chaired by a combination of leaders from the Sierra Club and the Building Industries Association.
- "Why can't we file for building and environmental permits electronically?"
- (And perhaps most damning) "Why is Silicon Valley ranked near last in the use of computers in our schools?"

For the first time, the region had a mechanism for working out answers. Through Joint Venture, business and public executives talked together about the attributes and shortcomings of Silicon Valley's economic infrastructure. It became clear that both sides viewed information and communications technology as an integral part of economic infrastructure and that these technologies should play a major role in Silicon Valley's vision of economic recovery and community renewal. "While it seems obvious now," explains Fearey, "we hadn't articulated this as a community. We needed to. The Joint Venture coming together was the mechanism."

The first meetings of the Information Infrastructure Working Group were chaired by Shelby McIntyre, chairman of the Marketing Department at the Levy School of Business at Santa Clara University, and by Ralph Gilman, an independent businessman. Seth Fearey of Hewlett-Packard and Bob Ellis of Sun Microsystems brought to the group their experience with the National Information Infrastructure in Washington D.C. and helped the group articulate how an advanced communications infrastructure would enable economic and social benefits. The participants in the initial Information Infrastructure Working Group shepherded by Fearey christened their vision "Smart

Valley"—the vision of an electronic community that brings the full power of information technologies to change fundamentally the way industry, government, and education work together and create advantage through collaboration. The excitement was palpable. Meetings went into the night. The core group grew from ten to one hundred. Says Fearey, "We set up an e-mail reflector to expand our circle and keep the grassroots energy going. We had energy, but weren't really going anywhere. Finally, there came a time when we had to convert our great ideas into action. We needed the help of Silicon Valley's leadership."

At this point, William F. Miller of Stanford University got the call from Jim Morgan of Applied Materials, acting as a civic venture capitalist, trying to get a promising enterprise off the ground. Recalls Morgan, "We needed to ensure all these good ideas didn't go up in smoke. We needed people who could implement." Morgan, Miller, and Bill Davidow put together a list of potential board members and invited them to dinner at Chantilly Restaurant in Palo Alto, the place on whose napkins many Silicon Valley companies had been started. Bill Miller took the responsibility of ensuring a couple of key invitees were available and would come. In addition, he would try to convince John Young, former president and CEO of Hewlett-Packard, to become chairman. Miller also agreed to be vice chairman and would recruit others.

The last of Fred Terman's academic recruits to Stanford, Miller had spent his life in the bridge-building activities typical of civic entrepreneurs. His years at Stanford, first at the School of Engineering, later as provost, were spent strengthening relations to the community. He believed passionately in the power of the third sector—the nonprofits that add much to community life.

Even when he became CEO of SRI International, Miller used his personal networks to start up and advise nonprofit organizations. He understood the delicate interplay between beneficiaries, funding, citizen support, and leadership. Miller's curiosity about the world and his desire to share ideas landed him a spot on the Singapore National Science and Technology Board. Here, he saw firsthand the determination with which this small nation was using information technology to become the Intelligent Island. The essence of the Singapore strategy was to use information technology to solve local problems such as using expert systems to evaluate electronically filed export and building permit applications.

Trained as a physicist, Miller believed the Singapore case provided an "existence proof. I greatly admired their farsightedness. I thought if Singapore could do this, so could Silicon Valley, but never in such a top-down way," recalls Miller. To help recruit and motivate the new Smart Valley board, Miller mailed a *Harvard Business Review* article on the Intelligent Island to ten CEOs. Then, in his systematic, under-stated style, Miller called them one by one to recruit.

The article made a strong impression on Bill Davidow and Regis McKenna, an early adviser to Apple and president of Regis McKenna, Inc. They had envisioned a "wired Valley" for years. Davidow's 1992 book *The Virtual Corporation,* with Mike Malone, in part reported and in part envisioned this evolution. "The virtual corporation produces products and services that are produced instantaneously and cus-tomized in response to customer demand." Virtual corporations would need new infrastructure to manage the relationships of virtual busi-ness. McKenna saw a wired valley as a true community-building tool and believed that if all parties work together to make a major contri-bution to social good, private good would come of it. Davidow, McKenna, Miller, and others, including Congressman Norman Mineta, agreed to serve.

Miller's final call was to John Young. Recently retired from Hewlett-Packard, Young chaired the Computer Systems Policy Project, which was searching for ways to realize the vision championed by Vice Pres-ident Gore and others of a National Information Infrastructure. Young had become excited by Seth Fearey's involvement on behalf of HP in the region. Recalls Young, "I saw that the timing was right, that we could be a beta site for the National Information Infrastructure. We needed to reduce to practice a lot of these ideas that were easy to describe in concept but hard to make work." Young agreed to chair the new Smart Valley board.

As a microcosm of Joint Venture: Silicon Valley, Smart Valley was now positioned to connect people with great ideas to people with real pull. By blending bottom-up community participation with top-down leadership, the new organization could benefit from the best of Sili-con Valley—the vision and tenacity of the citizen entrepreneurs and the pragmatism and connections of the seasoned Valley hands.

Like their counterparts in other communities worldwide, the team of civic entrepreneurs developing Smart Valley drew on their experi-ence as successful business executives. The desire to contribute not money, not name recognition, but their skills developed through their experience is a common and powerful motivator of civic entrepreneurs. Harry Saal gave up his post as chairman of Network General to become executive director of the effort.

All the civic entrepreneurs knew the venture capital industry well. Bill Davidow was a venture capitalist. Regis McKenna and William Miller had served as advisers and board members of venture-backed start-ups for years. John Young, Seth Fearey, and the other board members knew the model well. They adopted it as modus operandi for Smart Valley.

Venture capitalists seed multiple businesses, knowing that some will fail, hoping some will blossom beyond belief. Smart Valley serves as honest broker for many applications-oriented projects at once. Venture capitalists differentiate potential investments on the basis of stage of development and potential for impact. Smart Valley identifies four to six "Flagship Projects" and thirty to forty pilot projects. Flagship projects receive extensive staff support; pilots benefit in other ways from the Smart Valley recognition.

Venture capitalists know that manipulating venture capital is a contact sport, requiring extensive interaction between the financier and the company. Often to the chagrin of start-ups, when venture capitalists invest, they expect to sit on the board. Likewise, Smart Valley takes on a flagship project only if a Smart Valley board member is personally interested in serving on the project's board of directors. Regis McKenna is directly and intimately involved in developing the Public Access Network; William F. Miller, the CommerceNet. Eric Benhamou, CEO of 3Com, brought together eleven companies and thirteen hundred people to look at telecommuting. "We did demonstrations, wrote a handbook, audited results."

While Smart Valley is a story of the captains of high-tech industry demonstrating collaborative leadership to launch a high-profile initiative, Regulatory Streamlining is a story of a small-business entrepreneur and a city manager who systematically and quietly stimulated extraordinary improvements to Silicon Valley's business climate. Together, the two have tapped into a vein of private-sector quality experts ready to bring the quality movement to government permitting.

Chris Greene and Tom Lewcock are clearly not a typical small-business man and bureaucrat. Greene had been a member of the San Jose Symphony board and then worked on the Harvard Community Partners project, which matched Harvard Business School alumni with nonprofits suffering from management problems. He had made substantial contributions to these efforts and was searching for a bigger challenge. He found Joint Venture: Silicon Valley.

Greene decided to "adopt" Joint Venture, and signed on to participate in the Bioscience Working Group. "If it had been academic, I would have dropped out immediately. But, I saw real decision makers, so I stayed involved." His motivations were twofold. "On the personal side, I've always been interested in the history of our country and the way in which it was governed. At that time, I was in the midst of a six-volume biography of Thomas Jefferson. The whole concept of how communities work together for mutual benefit intrigued me. On the business side, my engineering company works closely with the construction industry. To the extent that we could make this area a more competitive region, particularly for high-tech companies over the long term, it would be good for Greene Engineers as well as others."

In the Bioscience Working Group, Greene shared his perspective as design contractor to biomedical companies. He witnessed firsthand how inconsistent interpretation of building codes across cities frustrated companies' attempts to expand in the Valley. The time it took also mattered. Largely, this time lag was a function of the newness of the Silicon Valley region rather than a blatant attempt to thwart business expansions. Chris saw the forest as well as the trees. "Across America there is a very important sense of place, pride of place, and tradition of improving the local community. The Northeast has town halls. The South has hospitality. The Plains has barn raisings. One of Silicon Valley's weaknesses is that we have no tradition. In the past, the Valley was little separate towns that didn't work together. But, as cities grew, they physically bumped right into one another. That, combined with the Silicon Valley ethic of 'everyone working in their own shop,' created real trouble."

In the working-group, idea-generation process, Greene emerged as a champion of a new idea. "We began toying with the idea of a regulatory forum between government and industry that would allow both sides to develop common ground on permitting and other regulatory issues." Jane Shaw, COO of ALZA and chair of the Bioscience Working Group, saw Greene's energy and wanted to help him keep the idea alive and generate support. Jane cleared the way for him to link up with the Regulatory Working Group, cochaired by Tom Lewcock.

In Tom Lewcock, Greene found a kindred spirit with a bent toward public service and a belief in the power of quality processes, customer orientation, and measurable objectives to change government in fundamental ways. Reared in Minneapolis, Lewcock arrived in Sunnyvale in 1977 at the height of the boom time for both business and government. The Valley of that time could not have provided a more awesome contrast to the Minneapolis he left behind. Minneapolis had a long and proud history, centered on well-established companies with a strong tradition of corporate involvement in the community. Silicon Valley was making it up as it went along. Hot new companies on fast-growth tracks held an almost religious belief in unbridled entrepreneurship. Any ties individual executives had were probably, like Lewcock's, to the communities of their birth. Minnesotans cared deeply about their government institutions; many of the new transplants to Silicon Valley probably could not find their city hall.

Lewcock not only managed to "just keep up" but to transform Sunnyvale to a model government reinvented along quality principles. He also introduced a performance-based budgeting system that radically changed how Sunnyvale set goals, measured customer satisfaction, and allocated funds. The system upheld the test of time and changed political leadership. In 1992, Lewcock and Sunnyvale were featured in David Osborne's *Reinventing Government*. In 1994, President Clinton and Vice President Gore paid a visit.

Along the way, however, Lewcock had developed a deep belief that reinventing government was not enough, "that there are a variety of issues that normal institutional frameworks are going to have a very difficult time changing from their present condition—not just because of resource limitation but because there are issues, particularly quality-of-life issues, that go beyond what government can or even should do."

Part of the secret was good, strong government institutions. The other part was collaboration in innovative ways with the people government was supposedly serving. "I believed very strongly that the institution of government is simply not in the same age as the people or industries in the community. The information age has fundamentally changed what government needs to do. Yet government institutions are the last to understand that we are not simply in a different economic time. What this new age is about is collaboration—something bigger than the sum of government and business together."

When Lewcock received a call asking him to cochair a regulatory working group for the Joint Venture process, he was curious and could not think of a reason to say no. His involvement in pioneering model hazardous materials legislation had earned him a reputation as a regulatory guru. His contribution to Joint Venture would be much bigger; Joint

Venture would prove a vehicle for making his new beliefs about the role of government and collaboration in the global information age operational.

From their unique vantage points, Lewcock and Greene knew that unnecessary government delays implementing regulations were the root of the problem, rather than the regulations' substance. Valley companies needed regulatory and permitting processes that moved as fast as Valley businesses did. Companies needed to reduce the duplicative paperwork overhead associated with permit compliance. Almost no one was asking for lower standards. Greene systematically interviewed nineteen VPs of operations in top Silicon Valley companies; all but one agreed that the problem was unnecessary time delays rather than too-strict standards.

Lewcock and Greene convened a small circle that included a lawyer, public officials, business people, and environmentalists—people they had met through the Joint Venture strategy process. In the first year, they agreed to concentrate on permit streamlining. They began to ask some creative questions: If we had this much interest in contributing time to really solving the problem, weren't there bound to be others? Could we talk to private sector quality experts, the people who helped Solectron win the Malcolm Baldrige award or helped National Semiconductor cut chip defect rates? Could we talk them into donating their time to work with public officials to re-engineer regulatory processes? Would it work? Could government change?

Their initial vision: to bring private sector, total quality management experts together with government officials to examine the flow charts for permitting, introduce the concepts of continuous improvement, re-engineer the processes, and monitor results. But a more far-reaching vision also emerged: to turn the local regulatory environment from being a cause of industry locating elsewhere to being a strategic ally in the global, time-based competition high-tech companies face.

By using private sector volunteers and delving into the minutiae of how permits are issued, the re-engineering teams are slashing red tape. Today, 95 percent of permits in Sunnyvale get same-day service; the remainder are issued in two weeks. The Town of Los Gatos cut processing time for business licenses in half. The Santa Clara Valley Water District increased its resolution rate of cases involving leaking underground fuel tanks 400 percent. The list goes on and will grow.

As civic entrepreneurs, Lewcock and Greene have come to believe in the power of neutral community forums to spark collaborative action. Recalls Greene, "It is not a business group helping government to reform, with all the negative connotations that entails. It is a neutral forum to work on problems of common interest. Fundamentally, we are not changing processes per se but transforming the performance capabilities of people."

Tom Lewcock agrees. "There are few people more rigid in their thinking than building inspectors. I began to see them think in fundamentally different ways about their role in the community, about what was possible. This was remarkable. People have made such significant mental leaps and commitments to act in fundamentally different ways than they had before. I'm now a believer that, done properly, collaborative forums can be created where people don't think they really can be. People will commit an amazing amount of time and resources in a pretty passionate way when they're brought together in the right kind of ways."

A final example of the venture capital model in action, deepening commitments to change, is in the area of education. "When I found out that we were hiring high school graduates in Korea to do what some of our college graduates in the U.S. were doing, I realized we had a big problem." With that, Glen Toney, Applied Materials's group vice president for global human resources, sought to organize a coalition of business, education, and community leaders to do something about the declining K–12 education system in Silicon Valley. According to the California Department of Education, less than 10 percent of Silicon Valley public schools are outstanding performers.

Joined by local business and education leaders, including teachers, Toney worked with the group to create a vision that matched the vast scope of what was necessary to keep Silicon Valley a world-class economic region. Together, they formed the 21st Century Education Initiative, under the umbrella of Joint Venture: Silicon Valley Network.

Ed McCracken, speaking for the business leaders involved in the effort said, "It's hard to bring people into Silicon Valley quite often because of the reputation of our school system. The future success of Silicon Graphics and other high-technology companies in Silicon Valley will depend on the existence of a world-class, K–12 educational system. Responsibility for this rests with educational and community leaders and all of our citizens, including me. Silicon Valley helped develop the continuous improvement culture, and we need to share ideas and think together about how it may be helpful in education and other community areas."

McCracken is among many local executives who have come out of the Hewlett-Packard tradition of civic engagement. Each has been inspired by the community perspectives and practices of David Packard, in particular. According to McCracken,

> Packard always viewed business in the broader context. You have four constituencies as a company: shareholders-owners, customers, employees, community. That was part of the HP way, the statement of vision for the company, and it made a lot of sense to me when I grew up in HP with these four constituencies. . . .
>
> Like Packard, our objective here has never been to maximize short-term shareholder return. Long-term shareholder value is the key, and there is nothing inconsistent between that objective and serving our other three constituencies. That is not to say that we don't pay attention to short-term financial performance . . . of course we do. In fact, consistent profitability is precisely what allows us to take care of our customers, create growth opportunities for our employees, and have a positive impact on our communities, all of which in turn are important parts of our model for long-term success. So it is a mistake to view these as "either-or" goals. We think they are highly complementary.

Businesspeople worked with educators to address the long-term viability of their companies. The team took stock of the situation, including conducting a public opinion poll of community attitudes and involvement in education. Although individual schools, teachers, and students ranked as world class, they found that Silicon Valley's overall system of public education did not:

- The community is losing confidence in public education—a perception reinforced by reports of low test scores, high dropout rates, and poor basic skills among many of our students.
- Many businesses are questioning the effectiveness of public education. They are having difficulty finding qualified employees locally. Recruiting professionals from outside the region is problematic because candidates are reluctant to place their children in local public schools.
- Educators themselves have become frustrated with the lack of parental and community involvement and declining financial support for schools.

They found a system that was not working for its participants, its customers, or its funders—the citizens of Silicon Valley. Rather than assign blame, they decided to work together to regain prominence and achieve world-class standards in education.

The team decided that it must be the first coalition of business, education, and community leaders to challenge Silicon Valley to commit itself to building a world-class education system. By the turn of the century, as their mission statement explains, they hope "to spark a local educational renaissance—a new community commitment to build a world-class educational system that enables all students in greater Silicon Valley to be successful, productive citizens in the twenty-first century."

After defining a set of guiding principles (that is, guidelines for world-class standards), the team made the shared commitment to raise and direct resources only to educational improvement efforts that are systemic and sustainable and produce measurable gains in student achievement. They believed that to spark a renaissance would require significant start-up capital, so they set a goal of $20 million in cash, equipment, and in-kind human resources. In less than one year, the team exceeded the fund raising target.

The initiative provides a new focal point for community and corporate involvement in education—an opportunity to join forces and team with schools that have themselves committed to a "systemic change process." What would it take to turn Silicon Valley education around? The team came to the conclusion that what was necessary was a deeper partnership than had ever been attempted (see Exhibit 6.1).

Five Renaissance Teams involving more than fifty schools are now under way, aligning curriculum across K–12 grades, defining specific student outcomes, and creating new assessment methods to measure student progress. The initiative represents a sharp departure from traditional business support for education in Silicon Valley. It is the product of sustained commitment by a team of civic entrepreneurs. Ed McCracken has remarked that "one of my proudest accomplishments has been getting the education initiative started with a lot of momentum, professionalism, power, strength. Of all my Joint Venture activities, that's what I've been most proud of."

They Establish a First-Class Support Team

Although much attention must go to leadership transitions and the deepening of commitments, civic entrepreneurs also work diligently to put top-notch staff in place to support implementation. It is important to understand what they do not do. They do not simply hand over

1. We must build an unprecedented coalition for change.

To produce systemic and continuous improvement in public education, the passion and resources of the greater Silicon Valley community are necessary. If we expect to progress to world-class standards, the effort must assemble an unprecedented coalition of educators, parents, businesses, foundations, and the broader community to support continuous educational improvement across the region. To build this coalition, Joint Venture: Silicon Valley Network's 21st Century Education Initiative and Smart Valley, Inc. teamed up. Together, they signed up most of the large employers in the Valley at the $1 million level, as well as smaller employers and others in the community.

2. We must team with schools for a long-term change process.

As in business, continuous improvement in education requires a long-term commitment to the process of change. The initiative is committing to working with teams of schools for at least three years to design and implement strategies that prepare schools for the twenty-first century in terms of curriculum innovations, staff development, technological capacity, and assessment. The initiative hopes to spark a renaissance by fostering systemic improvement in schools in greater Silicon Valley between 1995 and 2000—directly working with 15 to 20 percent of all public elementary, middle, and high schools in the region. The partners are working intensively with fifteen teams of schools for at least three years each. These groups are called Renaissance Teams:

• *Each team is composed of at least one high school, one middle school, and one elementary school; a "vertical slice."* This requirement is based on the strong belief that for educational improvements to be truly systemic, changes must be made and coordinated across all grade levels.

• *Each team includes a wide range of school and community partners.* Teachers and principals, as well as district administrators and school board members, are working together. Participating from outside the schools are parents and community partners such as business, preschool, higher education, and government. Only with broad community involvement can major, sustainable improvement in student performance occur.

3. We must define and progress toward world-class standards.

Building on national education goals, public-private initiatives, and input from various segments of the Silicon Valley community, the 21st Century Education Initiative defined a set of goals for student achievement, elements of an effective learning environment, and expectations for broad community involvement in education:

• *Each team is developing a unifying vision and plan for progressing to the goals.* Teams use existing process models or develop their own unique approach. The coalition provides assistance in the form of in-kind process experts from some of the Valley's most successful companies, funds for teacher release time, technology experts, and experienced "coaches" who have gone through educational change processes and can provide ongoing technical assistance.

• *Each team is developing measurable outcomes for student achievement and an evaluation plan for tracking progress toward the goals.* Before any additional resources are assigned, a team must have a plan with measurable outcomes and an evaluation system in place. The coalition provides assistance in the form of in-kind assessment and evaluation experts from local industry, educational assessment consultants, technology implementation experts, and information on best practices from around the country.

• *At the end of three years, each team must have strategies in place to sustain their educational innovations.* (Examples: reallocation of resources, new long-term funding sources such as bond issues, or long-term partners from business and the broader community).

Exhibit 6.1.   Implementation of the 21st Century Education Initiative.

the reins of implementation to an expert. Nor do they choose someone who will simply carry out orders given by a strong board of directors. Instead, civic entrepreneurs choose top professionals who are
strong leaders in their own right, good consensus builders, and flexible managers who will make adjustments as they get feedback from
the implementation process.

In Austin, Pike Powers observes that the selection of implementation support is critical. "I pick them because I know that they are
going to finish the job. It may not be pretty or perfect, but it will be
finished. That's who I pick every time. You don't pick the fair-haired
or just for their connection. It's most important to finish."

In Cleveland, staff professionals work as peers to volunteer community leaders, with roles clearly delineated. According to Carole
Hoover, "Volunteer leadership is not apprehensive about having
strong, independent people as staff leaders. They're not interested in
putting you in a box. So, consequently, we get high-quality people as
staffers. Staffers are expected to be leaders too." Al Ratner agrees that
"there is a partnership between what would be called the lay and professional communities. But we don't really consider them lay and
professional communities. We don't separate them. We are literally
equals, with our own particular roles. That is very important, and we
have been blessed with strong people in those positions."

THE DRIVER: PRESSES FOR FOCUSED, MEASURABLE RESULTS

As a driver, the civic entrepreneur ensures that measurable objectives
are set and reached, that implementation efforts avoid fragmentation,
duplication, or rigidity in approach, and that the focus remains on
challenging objectives. Civic entrepreneurs relentlessly ask questions,
reminding all those involved in implementation about the driving
goals and objectives of the effort. They help others keep distractions
to a minimum in the implementation process, while at the same time
remaining open to new tactics that will make implementation run
more smoothly and effectively. Civic entrepreneurs drive implementation by taking the following steps. They:

- Press for measurable outcomes
- Discourage fragmentation and duplication
- Keep the focus on challenging objectives

Advice for Civic Entrepreneurs Acting as Integrators

• *Do* expect to spend significant time finding the right people for implementation, including top-level leadership *and* staff; using the in-kind services of a professional recruitment firm can very helpful at this stage.

• *Do* be prepared for outbreaks of turf competition among process participants, as they try to merge collaborative initiatives into their organization; it may work, but only if the organization is willing to truly transform and be held accountable by the community for results.

• *Do* manage expectations of process participants, since most of them will not continue as champions in the implementation stage; give them a graceful exit or other ways to contribute, and make sure they share in the credit of implementation over time.

• *Do* remain particularly flexible in the early stages of implementation, to allow for experimentation with different approaches and to avoid a preoccupation with organizational structure at the expense of action.

• *Don't* put staff in a separate category; expect them to be civic entrepreneurs in their own right, playing a complementary but equal role to those on their voluntary leadership boards.

• *Don't* get discouraged by implementation setbacks; seldom is the first implementation design the right one, it is a process of trial and error to find the right approach.

• *Don't* be satisfied with commitments only from CEOs; push the commitment to implementation down into organizations, providing tangible opportunities for subordinates to get involved on behalf of their organizations.

• *Don't* stop providing strategic guidance; it is critical that you help new players understand the roots of implementation, the original intention of the process participants.

They Press for Measurable Outcomes

Civic entrepreneurs are constantly asking the question, How can we measure that? Everything that is important should be measured. Civic entrepreneurs have often learned this lesson the hard way in their own business or in other community endeavors. They have experienced perceived successes that cannot be documented because no one thought through how to measure them. They have experienced failures whose lessons are unclear because, again, no one thought through how to measure them. "If you're not measuring your accomplishments and reporting on them, then the interest fades away," according to Silicon Valley's Seth Fearey.

Civic entrepreneurs help their communities set quantifiable benchmarks and relentlessly measure progress toward them. Taking a page from the "continuous improvement" primers of business, they recognize the importance of process and capacity-building objectives but emphasize tangible, bottom-line results. They have learned to balance the need for short-term, highly visible results with the need to work on longer-term issues requiring systemic change.

Civic entrepreneurs insist on structure and explicitness in assessment. Explains Silicon Valley's John Young, "You have to have a business plan; you have to have metrics, and you have to have a time line for results, and they are all fully accountable. You can't get to the next increment of resources until you have proved that you've gotten the results at which you are aiming." Arizona's Alan Hald knows from experience that it is "important to create structures that allow people to feel accountable for results."

Civic entrepreneurs are wary of the superficial application of measurement methodologies. The following story is all too familiar: a community organization or collaborative effort uses the tools of benchmarking to provide the appearance of hard-nosed assessment and rigorous attention to outcomes. Progress is inevitably made on some set of concrete measures, many related to the number of meetings held or information distributed, victory is declared, a new set of measures much like the old set is chosen, and the cycle is repeated. But, are these the right measures? Do they relate to the overarching mission and vision of the organization or collaborative effort? What purposes do they serve?

Civic entrepreneurs realize that assessment or benchmarking of one's own progress can be one of the biggest catalysts or greatest obstacles to effective action. With the right purposes in mind, benchmarking an organization's progress toward measurable objectives can produce positive results. If the exercise is driven by the desire to spark creative ideas, think through strategy, clarify expectations about what's important, set priorities, provide information for continuous improvement, and build credibility and community support, then benchmarking can be a powerful catalyst for action. If the exercise is driven by the desire to maintain control, implement the only "right" solution, discourage deviation from the initial plan, and punish those who don't measure up, then benchmarking can be a powerful obstacle to honest debate and effective action.

Lawyer and civic entrepreneur Sandy Kress of Dallas and his twenty-six–member panel, the Commission on Educational Excellence, realized the importance of measurable outcomes. They proposed a plan to give parents and local educators substantially more control over the budgets, staff, and instruction at individual school sites. In return, results were to be measured by school, with financial rewards for those showing significant improvement, with some of those rewards going directly to teachers. At the same time, teachers who are not performing would be reassigned or removed. And incentives were created for clusters of schools to seek out "enabling compacts" with public and private agencies to ensure that social services would be available to students in need at the school site. Kress and his commission also created an organization to track progress over time. With a strong commitment to accountability, a new bond issue was passed to support the reforms (Peirce, with Johnson and Hall, 1993, pp. 237–241).

In Silicon Valley, civic entrepreneurs have established a rigorous and comprehensive approach to assess progress in implementation. Joint Venture: Silicon Valley pursues an annual process of negotiating memorandums of understanding with its affiliated initiatives by which the initiatives clearly articulate what they intend to accomplish during the next year and what they request from the Network board to get the job done. Exhibit 6.2 describes the components of the MOU.

The most important purpose of the MOU process is to be a focal point for each initiative to clarify periodically its mission, vision, and activities. The process has helped encourage periodic reviews by Initiative staff and boards, which in turn have produced such changes as an overhaul of original measurable objectives, the inclusion of promising new strategic directions, and new organizational strategies to better achieve original measurable objectives (for example, new staff, mergers with other initiatives, new fund raising). The benchmarking process

Highlights of Business Plan
Mission of the Initiative
Organizational Structure
Principal Activities
Measurable Objectives
Budget and Staffing

What the Initiative Expects from the Network
Board Support
Staff/Consultant Support
Fund Raising Support
Communications Support
Lobbying Support
Administrative Support

What the Network Expects from the Initiative
Meeting of Measurable Objectives
Designation of the Initiative as an "Affiliate"
Coordination on Fund-raising
Mechanism for Public Participation
Participation in Network Activities
Establishment of a Code of Conduct Covering Conflicts of Interest

**Exhibit 6.2.   Structure of MOUs Between the
Joint Venture Network and Each Initiative.**
Source: The Joint Venture Way, Irvine Foundation, 1995.

is a catalyst for continuous examination and adjustment to maximize results.

The process has also reinforced a sense of commitment between implementation partners and with the general public. Joint Venture compiles all the Initiative measurable objectives into a *Quarterly Benchmarking Report,* which is distributed to a four-hundred–person Leadership Council and made available to the general public on-line and through the Joint Venture offices. "The MOUs, the orientation toward a strong business plan, the definition of measurable results up front, then reporting out over time—all these are critical," according to Tom Lewcock. "I fear that we would have had less corporate commitment without this results-oriented thinking; they may have backed away."

They Discourage Fragmentation and Duplication

One of the most important roles of the civic entrepreneur in implementation is to fight against the natural forces of organizational fragmentation and duplication. In implementation, it is natural to be tempted by new opportunities and ideas. Some are worth incorporating, but many are diversions to the main thrust of implementation. It is also natural for aggressive organizations to want to participate in and own a piece of the implementation pie. At the same time, both of these tendencies can destroy collaborative community initiatives in their formative stages. Civic entrepreneurs help their communities navigate around these obstacles.

Fragmentation of focus and leaders is a real danger during implementation. Silicon Valley's Neil Bonke recalls how he learned from experience. "I worked for many years in Rochester, New York. I learned the importance of giving back to the community. But, my efforts there were fragmented—working on the community chest or the United Way campaign. Now, I'm involved in a very focused way under a broader architecture called Joint Venture: Silicon Valley." Florida's Larry Pelton warns that communities must identify how to use talent in focused, high-leverage ways: "If someone has the courage to step up, organizations grab them and put them on boards, and they are burned out."

The tendency toward duplication must also be countered. If the issue is popular and the community leadership is supportive, many organizations may vie for a place in implementation. This kind of situation is positive, if civic entrepreneurs keep pressing for collaborative approaches. Otherwise, as Florida's Larry Pelton observes, "Sixteen organizations come up with sixteen solutions to the problem." Florida's Jim Gardner agrees. "Multiple groups work on problems, and they just die. They end up with multiple leaders that compete with each other." The key, according to Arizona's Alan Hald, is to keep people focused on "how to leverage our resources as opposed to compete for a fixed pie."

Cleveland's civic entrepreneurs counter fragmentation and duplication by exercising strong, well-connected leadership at the board level. Explains Richard Pogue, "There is a conscious effort on the part of the business leadership for organizations not to duplicate each other and fall all over each other and get into turf battles. There is a very clear, defined role for each one. This helps an awful lot. Once in a while, we'd have a couple of staff people fighting over turf or something, and at the volunteer level the chairs would just step in and say, 'hey, cut that out.'" Al Ratner emphasizes that "it is the same people. You have these interconnections on boards. All of us are involved in a whole bunch of things. This helps reduce overlap and turf battles, because we'll say 'hey wait a minute' if something like that happens."

In Silicon Valley, Joint Venture: Silicon Valley Network acts as a focal point to encourage cooperation among implementation initiatives. The Network's business plan, approved by its board, includes a section on networking the initiatives. People are given clear expectations that working together is rewarded. With boards for each Initiative and the Network as a whole—including two Network-board liaisons on each Initiative board—Joint Venture is moving toward the Cleveland model of well-connected leadership in implementation. As a result of these different checks and balances, there is little duplication and fragmentation of efforts. In fact, important new collaborations between initiatives have evolved (see Figure 6.1).

They Keep the Focus on Challenging Objectives

When faced with the enormous tasks and obstacles of implementation, and when it comes time to take visionary ideas and turn them into action steps, many community efforts revert to traditional ways. It is natural that, faced with an overwhelming challenge, people will turn to the familiar. Unfortunately, it is at this important crossroads that taking the familiar path does little to address difficult, complex issues facing the community. "The hardest time is when the report is completed, and there is the need to move to implementation," observes Arizona's Jack Pfister. "Translating strategic plans into action, even for corporations, is an extremely hard thing to do. All of a sudden, everybody realizes that change might actually happen. And the mood changes. The governor becomes suspicious. The economic development people do everything they can to go back to doing things the same old way."

Civic entrepreneurs help implementation partners keep their focus on challenging objectives, giving them the courage to choose the more difficult but ultimately more rewarding implementation path. Austin's Glenn West helps keep his community focused on the important challenges. "Economic development is not the 10 percent of time we spend attracting and marketing, it's the stuff we do with schools, transportation, the arts; leadership is a lot more important in the long term. Focus on the right things; get your product in order. There is a tremendous waste of time and resources marketing communities that aren't ready to be marketed."

In Wichita, keeping the community focused on challenging objectives was a careful, gradual process itself. Civic entrepreneurs like

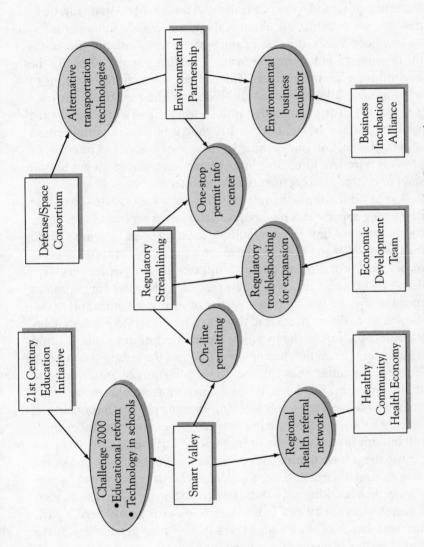

Figure 6.1. Examples of Joint Venture Initiative Cooperation.

Lionel Alford worked on partnerships with the education community, celebrated positive steps along the way, but kept pushing for more change. Recalls Tim Witsman, "WI/SE was the convener. From that, we had superintendents meeting once a month. We made progress, but initial programs were not really systemic change. Gradually, business says we've got to talk about real reform, including standards."

In Silicon Valley, the case of the Smart Valley Initiative illustrates the importance of keeping the focus on challenging objectives. "In the beginning," explains William Miller, "there were multiple visions of what Smart Valley would actually do. Building on the grassroots process, the group concluded quickly that the orientation toward applications was the right one. What good is building an information superhighway if no one is using it?" The need was not to build more physical infrastructure, cable lines, phone lines, and so on but to find ways to use the existing infrastructure better.

The key dilemma—the raison d'être for collaboration—was that developing applications required working across various sectors of the community and dealing with multiple constituencies. "Staying close to the customer" was, of course, the mantra for Valley firms. Yet the customer worlds of citizens groups, educators, and city planners were decidedly new and different. A new type of intermediary organization could accelerate the coming together of multiple community constituencies to define needs and develop information technology solutions. It could bridge the technical and nontechnical worlds. It could ensure that information technologies changed the lives of the many in Silicon Valley rather than the few. The core identity of Smart Valley as an honest broker was born. It was a much more ambitious and challenging objective than simply lobbying for more physical infrastructure.

John Young explains the importance of pursuing this more difficult but important objective of finding applications and helping people use the infrastructure. "When we talk about exotic technologies, what we find, time after time, is that what's key is getting the right people together, breaking old habits, and getting organizations to change. Technology is not an end in itself. Technologists always need a partner, whether it's the city managers to do smart permitting or the school people to change the curriculum."

Smart Valley would not be in the business of providing technical support, offering equipment, or actually installing networks. Clearly, in Silicon Valley—home to half the world's systems architects—this was not the pressing need. The idea instead was actually much more challenging—to broker, to bring together, whatever resources were necessary to create new information infrastructure applications on a project-by-project basis. It proved to have tremendous power and appeal.

Advice for Civic Entrepreneurs Acting as Drivers

- *Do* apply the same discipline and creativity to investing your time, talent, and resources in a civic endeavor as you would with launching a new business enterprise or product line, or a major new initiative for your organization.

- *Do* use your position on the boards of different organizations (or the influence of your own board members who may sit on multiple boards) to encourage collaboration and discourage duplication and fragmentation of effort.

- *Do* propose and support a comprehensive approach to assessing progress in implementation, using multiple indicators and making regular reports to the community.

- *Do* keep challenging your implementation partners to build on successes and assess setbacks, focusing on lessons learned.

- *Don't* accept measurable objectives for implementation that focus on the number of meetings held or other "activities"; keep pushing for real results that are measurable, even if it requires additional investment in surveys or other assessments to produce good data.

- *Don't* let accountability be informal; put it all in writing in the form of a memorandum of understanding or something similarly tangible.

- *Don't* erect artificial barriers between ideas and initiatives once the implementation stage begins; in the stress of focused implementation, don't let people become closed to all new ideas.

- *Don't* let implementation descend to the lowest common denominator; because collaboration is hard work, some will choose the path of least resistance, assuming that "this is all that can be done right now."

CHAPTER SEVEN

Improvement and Renewal
Helping the Community
Change Continuously

The threat of becoming ingrown or irrelevant is real.

—*Pike Powers, Austin*

If we're satisfied with what we've done, we're gone.

—*Al Ratner, Cleveland*

ivic entrepreneurs play two critical roles in supporting their communities as they try to turn short-term implementation successes into a culture that supports a sustainable, continuous capacity for change. They act as mentor, and they act as agitator. As mentor, they formalize support networks and other organizational platforms from which the community can continue working together on important issues, nurture a culture for ongoing development of civic entrepreneurs, and acclimate newcomers into the community. As agitator, they provide the constant reminder that change is a continuous process, encourage scanning their community to keep people thinking about change, and push people's horizon toward a vision of an even better future. Civic entrepreneurs have achieved the following during the improvement and renewal stage:

- Cleveland has repeated its collaborative process many times since the early 1980s, producing an impressive string of major development projects. The city is now applying their approach to more difficult issues such as workforce development and K–12 education.

- Arizona is considering repeating its broad participatory process to refocus the state on important long-term issues. Civic entrepreneurs are also considering applying the process to K–12 educational improvement.
- Joint Venture: Silicon Valley has designed an annual renewal process, which involves the release of a yearly *Index of Silicon Valley* and a community leadership group meeting to catalyze action on priority issues.

THE MENTOR: BUILDS SCAFFOLDING FOR OTHER CIVIC ENTREPRENEURS

As a community tries to solidify the tradition of collaborative problem solving, civic entrepreneurs play the critical role of mentor. They provide the supportive infrastructure—the scaffolding—that will support the people and practices of civic entrepreneurship in their community. Civic entrepreneurs mentor by taking the following steps. They:

- Build platforms for continuing collaboration
- Nurture a lasting culture of civic entrepreneurship
- Reach out and involve newcomers to the community

They Build Platforms for Continuing Collaboration

Civic entrepreneurs build the linkages between networks of business, government, and community leaders. These linkages are often informal and ad hoc at first, as leaders of very different organizations, experience, and perspective begin to explore common ground. The linkages grow stronger and more formal when these leaders decide to work together on a specific implementation initiative. "It's a process—networks spin off networks spin off networks," according to Alan Hald. Or as Ioanna Morfessis, also of Arizona, observes, "It's like the biblical genealogy—this begat that and this and the other—the begat effect, the ripple effect occurs in ways we can't even measure. This open process really galvanized people."

Although important, this informal networking is often not enough to sustain community collaboration. Civic entrepreneurs understand that collaboration is not a one-time event. As Austin's Neal Kocurek observes, "We can be so much better than we are by bringing the business community and other parts of our community together on a continuing basis to move forward."

Civic entrepreneurs play an instrumental role in helping their communities take the next step by helping create a more formal "network of networks," which often means the creation of a new kind of collaborative organization. "It's important to sustain a platform. Times are going to change, and these kinds of activities, if you have that platform available, get fueled with a lot of new energy for the next down cycle," according to Arizona's Bob Moya. "Otherwise, we always seem to be preparing to fight the last war."

In Arizona, the ASPED collaborative process evolved into a collaborative organization called GSPED, which has supported the implementation initiatives of Arizona's industry cluster groups since 1992. "The true measure of effectiveness of these type of initiatives and collaborations is, did it make a difference, and was it sustainable, and the answer is yes," observes Ioanna Morfessis. "In fact, in different forms, these new formal and informal networks that emerged are still making an impact, as are the individuals who were engaged in the process." This evolution was particularly important in Arizona because, as Morfessis notes, "we lacked a civic infrastructure in our community."

At the same time, civic entrepreneurs do not assume that traditional organization forms are well suited to sustain new kinds of community collaboration. In fact, they are instrumental in creating new network organization models, based more on voluntary commitments to shared interests than political jurisdictions or hierarchical management structures. "When Cleveland Tomorrow came together," emphasizes Al Ratner, "it realized two things. One was that it would be a conduit and would assist other people in seeing that things were accomplished. It would use many existing organizations and only get help from new organizations if necessary. Second, we realized at that time we were all white males and that the community had to be the people who made the determination as to what would happen."

Wichita's Tim Witsman believes that, in hindsight, his community might have been better served by creating more of a network organization to sustain its collaborative efforts. "Instead of setting up WI/SE as an operating entity, create it as a virtual organization. WI/SE could outsource to other groups for implementation. It could be more nimble. There would not be a lot of staff reports and worry about organization structure. We would debate the big issues and contract out the work." Florida's John Anderson suggests a similar model. "Once you build relationships, it is possible to connect using electronic networks. An academy could help build leadership and relationships, focusing on professional development. You create an ancillary nonprofit to help train and support economic development professionals."

Larry Pelton, a leader of a Florida regional economic development organization, created a new electronic networking model in 1992: the *Enterprise Network of Palm Beach*. The network helps firms in the region's driving industry clusters—computer-communications, business services, aerospace-engineering, and food-agriculture—gain access to key infrastructure resources. Via the network, local corporate leaders collaborate to solve common training, technology, or financing challenges. Also, training, technology, and financing institutions collaborate to meet the needs of businesses. The electronic network allows firms and institutions to use e-mail and bulletin boards to access information and solve problems in real time.

Across America, civic entrepreneurs are experimenting with different kinds of network organizations to sustain cooperative efforts, link stakeholders, and leverage talent and resources. These new organizations may mark the emergence of new mediating structures of civil society. Michael Sandel (1996) has written that America needs to encourage the development of institutions that help citizens deliberate about the civic consequences of economic arrangements. Civic entrepreneurs are at the forefront of defining new kinds of organizational vehicles to mediate between the economy and community. The working relationships fostered by networks help ensure that regions can respond quickly to threats and opportunities.

These new collaborative network organizations share common characteristics. They:

- Foster continuous communication between industry "customers" and "suppliers" in government and the community

- Serve as neutral forums for surfacing new ideas for continuously improving the economic vitality and quality of life of the community

- Act as catalysts to create and provide initial support to temporary, interdisciplinary teams with a specific charge for action
- Commit to specifying objectives and measuring results over time

By no accident, these principles parallel those developed by the total quality management approach to business. After a decade of successful experimentation with TQM in the private sector, a Total Quality Community analog is emerging at the public-private interface.

Civic entrepreneurs understand that the occasional highly visible collaboration is not enough. They know that networks of people who are comfortable practicing collaboration of one kind today and another kind tomorrow are necessary. This principle is well understood in a region like the Twin Cities, which has created multiple mechanisms to sustain continuous collaboration across generations.

In the Twin Cities, a web of organizations exists for bringing forth civic entrepreneurs and sustaining the social networks between economy and community. All in all, the Twin Cities arguably have the most well-developed civic infrastructure of any metropolitan region in the country:

- The CEO-driven Minnesota Project on Corporate Responsibility identifies ways that companies can involve their employees in a wide range of community projects.
- In 1977, the Minnesota Business Partnership was created to involve top business leaders with state leaders on issues important to the future of Minnesota.
- The Minnesota High Technology Council has focused business leaders on improving the quality of education.
- Minnesota Wellspring creates public-private partnerships for economic development.
- The Civic League provides a communitywide mechanism to raise, discuss, and act on issues of broad concern.

In Silicon Valley, leaders saw each other socially, negotiated with each other, even contributed to philanthropic causes together, but had never been tapped to benefit a broader community. After a nine-month participatory strategic planning process, Joint Venture: Silicon

Valley transitioned from a "movement" overseen by an ad hoc affiliate of the Chamber to a new type of nonprofit organization.

To move from ideas to action and sustain collaboration, civic entrepreneurs created a new type of nonprofit intermediary organization, Joint Venture: Silicon Valley Network. On an ongoing basis, Joint Venture's mission is to "bring together people from business, government, education, and the community to act on regional issues affecting economic vitality and quality of life."

Joint Venture: Silicon Valley Network has also spawned a number of new networking mechanisms to help reconnect economy with community. These mechanisms include the Enterprise Network, which is helping new firms gain access to seasoned executive advisers; the Defense/Space Consortium, which is helping defense firms connect with commercial partners; the Environmental Partnership, which is nurturing environmental start-ups in shared incubator space; and the Economic Development Team, which connects firms that are thinking about relocating or expanding with local economic development resources. The pattern is the same in every case: Joint Venture: Silicon Valley Network is sustaining new social networks that bridge the economy and the community.

Joint Venture leaders recruited state senator Becky Morgan to serve as president and CEO of the new networking organization. Morgan explains her motivation. "I saw the organization as an exciting, challenging opportunity to do things differently. In a state the size of California, I had come to believe that we would rejuvenate it region by region." The Joint Venture: Silicon Valley Network is a way for civic entrepreneurs to work on implementing the first round of ideas identified by the community and address future opportunities and problems as they arise (see Exhibit 7.1).

George McLean, publisher of Tupelo, Mississippi's *Daily Journal* from 1934 until his death in 1983, returned to his hometown after doing graduate work at Stanford University to champion the cause of economic development. "Tupelo might have joined the rest of the South on the path to economic stagnation, distinguishing itself for little other than being the birthplace of Elvis Presley" (Cooper, 1994, p. 1). But George McLean would have none of that. He established a new collaborative organization—a Community Development Foundation. Instead of luring firms with tax breaks, it concentrated on working with the local community college to upgrade worker skills.

Created in 1943 by civic entrepreneur Richard King Mellon, the Allegheny Conference on Community Development has provided a platform for civic entrepreneurs to act as catalysts for change at several critical junctures in Pittsburgh's economic evolution.

After World War II, the conference actively promoted Renaissance I, a renewal effort focused on air quality improvements and downtown development. These efforts helped reshape the Pittsburgh landscape and set the stage for the growth of a bustling commercial and business district—a diversification into business and financial services that fueled a new period of economic growth in Pittsburgh.

Erosion of Pittsburgh's iron and steel industry advantage caused the conference to take strong action again by the early 1970s. It created a new group (Penn's Southwest Association) to attract new firms in other industry sectors to diversify the local economy further. After fifteen years in operation, the association had attracted almost three hundred companies and thirty thousand jobs to the nine counties of the Greater Pittsburgh region.

However, by the late 1970s, Pittsburgh's steel industry was in collapse. Foreign competition had decimated the region's once-formidable comparative advantage. In response, the conference intensified its efforts. A new phase of downtown development (Renaissance II) began and continued through the 1980s. In 1981, the conference developed regional consensus about a long-term economic strategy. It organized nine task forces to develop recommendations.

At the conclusion of the process, the conference committed $3.6 million in seed money to kick off implementation of one hundred recommendations. It also energized other organizations such as the Pittsburgh High Tech Council. It set up the Pittsburgh Cultural Trust to provide ongoing development of the arts, including a $42 million Center for the Performing Arts. And its economic strategy set the stage for an even more comprehensive public-private Strategy 21, which identified further actions to take into the twenty-first century.

By the 1990s, Pittsburgh was on the rebound, with gains in both employment and income. It has established new growth sectors in biomedical research, robotics, and software and assembly. It also scores well on measures of livability (for example, Rand McNally's *Places Rated*), only a short time after serious economic and community dislocation. Although the Allegheny Conference on Community Development and the civic entrepreneurs who lead it cannot take full credit for the rebound, this kind of leadership has aggressively pushed new directions during periods of economic hardship in Pittsburgh.

Exhibit 7.1.   Pittsburgh's Focal Point for Collaboration.

Today, all adults employed in manufacturing are expected to undergo training every five years. "The city's vocational education is envied all around the country. A new IBM computerized-manufacturing training workshop is as advanced as any in America. The county now has the highest income per head in Mississippi, despite having retained much of its rural population" ("Survey: The American South," 1994, p. 12). In 1993, Tupelo brought in sixteen new factories with a total capital investment of $100 million. And collaborative, heavy investment in worker training has enabled the black community to participate in the region's success: the unemployment rates for blacks in Tupelo is half that of blacks in the rest of the state.

Many regions, however, find it much more difficult to move beyond "crisis collaboration." New York City was able to come together quickly to save itself from imminent fiscal disaster in the mid-1970s, but once the crisis had passed, civic entrepreneurship dissipated. Not until David Rockefeller in the early 1980s exerted a new kind of leadership did New York City civic entrepreneurs found a focal point for sustained action. Rockefeller helped create the New York Partnership, which "institutionalized an entirely new concept for New York's business leadership, pulling together more than a hundred CEOs and other major executives from big business, small business, community, and other social service groups" (Katzenbach and Smith, 1993, p. 136).

Chicago has experienced similar difficulties. Civic entrepreneurs H. Laurance Fuller, president of Amoco Corporation, and Duane Kullberg, managing partner and CEO of Arthur Andersen and Company, helped sponsor an assessment of community collaboration in 1986, *The Chicago Project: A Report on Civic Life in Chicago.* They found collaboration difficult because business executives and public leaders did not understand or respect one another. Both believed that the other side was unwilling to engage in ongoing communication and give-and-take. And no one believed that a sustained forum existed for effective interaction between the public and private sectors.

Not all regional organizations are collaborative organizations either. Some regional organizations actually discourage collaboration, sap the energies of the community in nonproductive activities, or act as flashpoints for regional resentments. These organizations do little to build or sustain new social networks and are often counterproductive. They sometimes create new adversarial situations or cynicism among participants about whether anything can be accomplished collaboratively.

In Boston, for example, the role of regional organizations took a different route from that of Silicon Valley. In the 1970s, while the Santa Clara County Manufacturing Group set out to work with government on mutually acceptable solutions to the region's growing quality-of-life problems, the Massachusetts High Technology Council took an adversarial role. Created in 1977, the Council "devoted most of its efforts to lobbying for tax cuts that further undermined the ability of the public sector to contribute to industrial development" (Saxenian,

1994, p. 68). Other vehicles such as the MIT Enterprise Group and the Route 128 Venture Group "served primarily as one-time sources of information and/or contacts for managers, rather than the basis for enduring networks" (Saxenian, 1994, p. 69).

A recent Harvard survey of more than five hundred companies shows that business leaders strongly blame government and the media for the region's woes—a culture of blame that has plagued Route 128 in recent years. "Traditionally, many high-tech companies concentrated on their own industry first and paid little, if any, attention to social responsibility. Their only politics were politics of opposition, largely to taxes, not of vision for the community" (Kanter, 1995, p. 235).

They Nurture a Lasting Culture of Civic Entrepreneurship

Civic entrepreneurship is not a quick fix. It is not easily created. "A collaboration of incompetents, no matter how diligent and well-meaning, cannot be successful," observes Michael Schrage (1990). It takes time. "You must have a power base that stays in place for a couple of decades," according to Cleveland's Jim Biggar. "It doesn't happen in five years." And it means nurturing a culture that supports budding civic entrepreneurs. According to Austin's Neal Kocurek, "The challenge is always more leadership. We need to develop a cadre of strong, committed community leaders. We must leave that legacy."

By nurturing a culture of civic entrepreneurship in their communities, established civic entrepreneurs help create "share of mind" among emerging or future community leaders. Cleveland's approach, observes Steve Minter, is to give "a lot of thought to the selection of leaders so that they will be actively involved. It's a tradition in this community. And, a lot of thought is given to succession planning. It make a great deal of difference in terms of communication and continuity." Austin's Neal Kocurek believes that it is simply the "responsibility of leadership to involve other people and mentor them in the process. I would say why don't you carry this ball and run in this direction. Harold, let's build a civic center here in West Austin. He took the ball and started running, and hasn't stopped."

Wichita is typical of communities struggling with the constant challenge of renewing leadership. "There are a number of younger people with fresh ideas that have to be brought in," according to Lionel Alford. "Too often, we think we have to have the old boys and don't bring the young people into the fold. It's our fault that we haven't done that." Hale Ritchie adds that Wichita is not sure who its future leaders will be. "The newspaper recently asked key people in the community to identify the top ten leaders for the future. Forty to fifty people were nominated, but no one was mentioned twice."

Although many methods are in use to build a culture of civic entrepreneurship, active participation in collaborative community processes is the best training ground. As Arizona's Steve Zylstra observes, "the ASPED/GSPED process has created a base of civic entrepreneurs, a core group that even in a noncrisis will want to play a role for a couple reasons. First, we care. Second, we feel accountable. A number of us feel that we have to keep the momentum going, keep these clusters going." Austin's Pike Powers confirms that "projects are a way to bring people on board, and in the process they become civic entrepreneurs via modeling behavior."

Organizations and communities can also take proactive efforts to build on this experiential learning. "You're not training leaders," according to Arizona's Alan Hald. "Almost always, you're dealing with people who are seasoned leaders in different areas. What you do is bring an individual leader from a business or government form into a civic entrepreneurship form. You're teaching that person a process that creates a different kind of leadership, but it is not a traditional training of leadership as such." Communities can take entrepreneurial people who are leaders in their own area of expertise and help them develop the language, tools, and connections to apply their talent in the civic arena.

Many informal and formal methods exist for nurturing the local culture of civic entrepreneurship. "We are identifying emerging leaders and inviting them to breakfasts without organizational affiliation," according to Florida's Larry Pelton. "It helps incubate leadership." Cleveland's Richard Pogue said, "One device that has been helpful is Leadership Cleveland. This was one of the early leadership programs in the country and focuses on people who will be leaders ten years from now. It's been a great opportunity for the younger people who are going to be in the CEO chairs a few years from now to hear the wise, sage elders tell how it's done. You keep the flame alive by constantly talking about the bad old days and how we got through them, and the new leaders kind of pick it up by osmosis." Adds CEO Jim Biggar, "They build trusting relationships among themselves that may not fully pay off for Cleveland until many years later."

Dennis Mullane, chairman of Connecticut Mutual Life Insurance, knew Hartford was hurting from a leadership vacuum in the early 1980s. "The old order was no longer in place, and no new order was there in terms of community leadership." The old order of corporate leaders—the so-called bishops—passed from the scene as new neighborhood groups grew in strength. But there was little communication among different groups and, when they did talk, they played the blame game.

Mullane led an effort to build a new cadre of civic entrepreneurs, creating a program for them to work together and build their leadership skills. Choosing the American Leadership Forum model, they established a local chapter in 1984. In the past decade, according to expert observers of community collaboration, "Hartford's readiness and capacity for change have been significantly enhanced. Many of the participants have sparked collaborative projects to address specific problems and are regarded by those who know them as important assets in the city's civic infrastructure" (Chrislip and Larson, 1994, pp. 70–71).

Arizona's Jack Pfister believes that his state needs to reinforce its culture for civic entrepreneurship more formally. "Arizona needs a leadership academy, like the War College, to develop corporate people and others into civic entrepreneurs." According to Pfister, "People would come away with more sophistication about leadership in the economic arena. They would have the opportunity to meet and interact with peers. It would be an intensive immersion into the community. We need to develop the next generation of leaders, not just the top. People don't know a damn thing about how the economy works. Even people who are taught economics are taught that it is all about acting alone. Not true."

At the same time, observes Wichita's Hale Ritchie, leadership development efforts are most effective when participants can immediately apply their skills in the civic arena. "People went through the leadership program but really had nothing to do afterward. They want to do more." He also believes that such programs do not produce "the visionary leader who makes it happen, but it does bring in the troops." Moreover, being an economic leader requires a different paradigm, language, knowledge, and networks than being a leader in the arts.

Generic leadership development programs are of less value than more focused, substantive efforts that offer the opportunity to apply newly honed skills as a civic entrepreneur.

In some communities, major companies focus their attention internally to set expectations and provide guidance on how managers should engage in community affairs. "Many corporations teach people as they come up through the ranks that addressing civic issues and providing leadership are important parts of the job, and they put major support under those people to do that," according to Cleveland's Carole Hoover. "It sets precedent, which helps promote sustainability. Economic development has become institutionalized today, and institutionalization is good," observes Austin's Neal Kocurek.

Silicon Valley's Jim Morgan ensures that his company is active in every region in which it has a major operation—and not just as a participant in the local United Way campaign but as a strategic partner in that region's infrastructure development. "We try to do things in each region, whether it's Austin or Japan. We tailor our programs to the culture and customs of each region—in China, we developed a program to provide seed money to support research work, because they have a lot of brainpower but little cash. In Japan, we're focused more on education. In Europe, we work more with the universities and special technical groups."

Ed McCracken shares Morgan's sentiments. "With Hewlett-Packard, I saw the philosophy applied not just to Silicon Valley but to Germany, Grenoble in France, Singapore, or places in Colorado. Wherever the company operated, being part of those communities was a priority from the beginning and not just the responsibility of top management." Arizona's Jack Pfister remembers the change that took place within his organization. "Historically, the utility had been insulated. It didn't understand the community and the world. With deregulation and competition coming, it was time to get over our myopia and broaden our horizon. At performance review time, community leadership was part of our executive requirements. But I now believe you must also train private leaders to engage more effectively with their community."

In the future, we may see a growing trend toward the use of corporate education and training funds to support skill development for civic entrepreneurship, as more and more companies recognize the importance of building economic community wherever they have major operations. For example, California's Pacific Gas & Electric Company created a new core curriculum to train its managers in the principles, practices, and experience of civic entrepreneurship, so they can apply the skills in civic settings across northern and central California. "Businesses understand better today than they used to that what's in the long-term best interest of the entire community is in the long-term best interest of business," according to Austin's Glenn West. However, there still need to be "role models in the community for businesses to understand that, because some businesses grasp that better than others."

Many communities stumble because traditional role models disappear or corporate leadership becomes much more transitory. According to Wichita's Lionel Alford, "The success and continuation depends on who's the leader. If you get someone not well known or who doesn't have the capability of motivating other people, then you are going to see a decline in its focus and effect."

It is unwise to rely on only one or a few sterling leaders. What happens if they retire, leave the region, spend more time on their business, or otherwise opt out? "What happens in Arizona when Jack Pfister and Mark DeMichele are gone?" asks Jack Pfister. "This state is growing, and new people and executives are coming in all the time." Dayton found out when its main catalyst and civic entrepreneur John Patterson, CEO of National Cash Register, retired and removed himself from most civic activities. The result was a splintering of activity among the remaining CEOs, with few newcomers to help out. They gradually spread themselves thin on a variety of small community projects but lacked the time and energy to tackle major issues—suffering from a kind of "compassion fatigue" as one CEO put it (Frey Foundation, 1993, pp. 18–19).

Communities more dependent on branch plant operations and lacking corporate headquarters often find it difficult to sustain a culture of civic entrepreneurship. Tim Witsman notes that Wichita has "lost three people as Chamber chairs due to transfers. Outside ownership and transfer of leadership result in less stability. We need to look more to locally based folks. But this is more a service person who may not have the clout."

In Florida, outside ownership of major employers provides a constant challenge. "In Tampa, years ago we had three locally owned banks. If there was a major civic project, you could depend on those banks getting involved—almost a formula on contributions: 40–40–20. Bank, phone, and power companies were locally owned and leaders got involved," recalls Terrell Sessums. "Today, it's more like a colonial econ-

omy. Business people are more managers than leaders. It's had a blur-
ring effect, more of 'cash register' reaction. Consolidation has been
good for the banks but bad for the local economy. Major decisions are
being made at remote sites."

Outside ownership makes the nurturing of a local culture of civic
entrepreneurship even more important. As John Anderson observes,
"This is fundamental to understanding a new paradigm for Florida. You
have fewer local leaders to get involved. Regional managers get two-year
assignments, travel half the time, work seventy to eighty hours a week.
They are not going to get involved and don't have the authority to
approve funding. It requires more and more people to get involved."

Despite the fact that they are largely "branch-plant" instead of
"headquarters" locations, places like Austin and Phoenix have nurtured a culture of civic entrepreneurship and a growing and diverse
cadre of civic entrepreneurs. In fact, the best civic entrepreneurs know
how to develop diverse teams of people. They have often learned
through experience how to do so within their company. They believe
wholeheartedly that, given the right focus and support, diverse teams
will outperform individuals and hierarchies in dealing with systemic,
continuous change. Austin's Neal Kocurek believes that "it is important that we are a very tolerant place." Instead of building hierarchies,
they build platforms and scaffolding from which others can succeed.

Alan Hald created such scaffolding so new leaders could climb into
community leadership roles in Arizona. ASPED led to a new public-
private partnership, greater involvement of industry in economic planning, and renewed faith in the future. At a time when Arizona was
reeling from the Keating savings and loan scandal and collapsing real
estate industry, ASPED brought to public life a new generation of civic
entrepreneurs such as Steve Zylstra, local manager of an electronics
components company, who spearheaded a rethinking of the state's
technology policies. This new breed practiced diversity and openness,
shunning closed-door dealing that had characterized an earlier era.

Ray Plank, CEO of Apache Oil Company, knew that Wyoming was
in trouble. He loved his adopted state for its rugged beauty, but its
economy and people were suffering in the mid-1980s. No one seemed
to know what to do. He did not have the answer, but he knew that a
new generation of leaders was needed to shake Wyoming out of its
complacency.

Plank put $100,000 of his own money on the table and one by one
challenged young, successful business men and women, who had to

this point focused mostly on their own businesses and careers, to make a commitment to the state's future. Among those recruited was Pete Williams, who later became the chief spokesman for the Department of Defense and a household name during the 1991 Gulf War. The group came together and pushed a set of investments and strategies to start Wyoming moving. But perhaps the biggest payoff from Ray Plank's efforts was the opportunity he gave to a new generation of leaders to take their first swing at civic entrepreneurship. Many are now in leadership positions in business and government in Wyoming.

Civic entrepreneurs often create unconventional means to give voice to new kinds of leadership. They have learned that conventional institutional relationships often raise rather than lower barriers to change. They lock newcomers out of real decision making. New means must be used to ensure the renewal of leadership, civic entrepreneurship, and economic community.

St. Paul is a community trying to reinforce its culture of civic entrepreneurship. It has established a Leadership Initiative in Neighborhoods Program. Thanks to civic entrepreneur Polly Nyberg, community affairs manager for the St. Paul Companies, who pioneered the effort, "Individual neighborhood leaders get grants to help them sharpen their skills with formal or informal study, site visits, travel, whatever seems indicated" (Peirce, with Johnson and Hall, 1993, p. 284).

All these kinds of activities are steps toward the ultimate goal: to establish a local tradition of civic entrepreneurship. Recent research by Robert Putnam has helped explain the power of sustainable collaboration between community and economy. His twenty-year study of the regions of Italy found that their economic performance was closely linked to measures of civic community. According to Putnam, "Civic traditions turn out to be a uniformly powerful predictor of present levels of economic development. . . . In summary, economics does not predict civics, civics does predict economics" (1993, pp. 156–157).

Economically successful regions in north central Italy are based on a "seemingly contradictory combination of competition and cooperation. Firms compete vigorously for innovation in style and efficiency, while cooperating in administrative services, financing and research. . . . A rich network of private economic associations and community organizations have constructed an environment in which markets prosper to promote cooperative behavior and by providing small firms with the infrastructural needs that they could not afford alone (Putnam, 1993, p. 160).

Among American communities, Minneapolis has one of the strongest cultures supporting collaboration and civic entrepreneurship. "The mechanism that transforms narrow self-interest into a balanced state of cooperation among independent individuals is the network of associations, study groups, committees, and other small groups of private citizens" (Ouchi, 1984, p. 204). While each small group typically consists of like-minded citizens pursuing narrow interests, larger groups bring divergent people together to work on issues. The same people participate in multiple groups, remembering sacrifices and repaying debts as time goes on. "It is the connection among self-interest groups and the mutual understanding that the citizenry together can progress while separate interest groups cannot that produces the partnership in Minneapolis" (Ouchi, 1984, p. 204).

Minneapolis is "not a place of do-gooders or altruists but of realistic, self-interested individuals who operate within an institutional network that constrains each person slightly, so that no one can achieve his or her selfish goals by interfering with others. No one person, group, or bureaucrat is wise enough to direct the whole city; indeed, no one does. There is, rather, a stable pattern of repeated exchanges over many years that make social choice and collective action possible, only because each person knows that if he or she yields narrow self-interest to broader interest this time, the corporate memory will see that sacrificial support today will be repaid, somehow, in the future" (Ouchi, 1984, pp. 208–209).

A culture of civic entrepreneurship is a critical ingredient for a wide range of economic communities. A comprehensive assessment of high-growth rural counties across the United States (National Governors' Association, 1988, p. 43) found that "most high-growth counties had a well-organized partnership of local leaders who worked for economic growth and diversification with the support of local government. It was commonly found that one individual plays the role of sparkplug, maintaining the partnership through good times and bad." Like their metropolitan area counterparts, successful rural areas have a culture of civic entrepreneurship that can shift the direction of the community to meet challenges and seize opportunities.

They Reach Out and Involve
Newcomers to the Community

Civic entrepreneurs make an extra effort to involve newcomers in community leadership. This practice helps communities dependent on outside ownership and transitory leadership to acclimate people quickly so they can make a contribution. Even if they leave after a short time, the expectation is set for their position so that the next person to assume that position knows that civic entrepreneurship is part of the job description.

The challenge is never-ending. According to Arizona's Mary Jo Waits, "We have to recognize that our state is rapidly growing, with a lot of new people, and they don't have the information base about the ASPED framework. At the last town hall meeting, when we asked people to raise their hands if they had participated in the ASPED process, less than half had." Pike Powers knows his community faces a similar challenge. "Austin is a transient community—50 percent of the adults have lived here less than ten years, one-third less than five years."

A typical problem is that newcomers remain tied to their original communities. Take Harry Figgie and Richmond, Virginia. Figgie was chairman and CEO of Figgie International, a *Fortune* 500 manufacturer of sporting goods. Based in Cleveland, Figgie grew upset with the deteriorating quality of life and economy and was lured to Richmond by economic developers. They convinced him to relocate. Soon, they began to solicit him for donations for local charities, but he resisted because his ties were with other charities, including those in Cleveland. He was met with growing indifference. He began to feel that they wanted his money but not his involvement. After just six years, he returned to Cleveland (Kotler, Haider, and Rein, 1993, pp. 60–62).

In contrast, some communities work hard to engage newcomers immediately. "When new CEOs come into the job or into town, there is a great interest to get them involved," according to Cleveland's Richard Pogue. "We want new people. It's an expectation." Mayor Glenda Hood of Orlando emphasizes that "whenever there is a new business leader who comes to town, I personally reach out and invite that person to get involved. We mix permanent and transient leadership." In Orlando, the views of new leaders are expected and respected. "We capitalize on the new leadership and the new ideas and energy they bring to the community," according to Hood. "We need to make people feel passionately about the issues."

Austin has taken this openness to newcomers to new levels. According to Austin's Pike Powers, "The community is open to accepting new people. In other places, there is a hierarchy. Here, it is more of a meritocracy than an aristocracy. It is part of what we expect of the company. If you come here, we want you to be a corporate citizen. If you want to be a part of this community, you must become part of the business leadership."

Not surprisingly, Austin takes the acclimation process very seriously. Initially, Austin relied on local civic entrepreneurs like Pike Powers and Lee Cooke to organize and give new civic entrepreneurs opportunities to get involved. With more than a decade of success, Austin is now moving into a new phase, embarking upon a broader leadership development initiative through its Chamber of Commerce to nurture civic entrepreneurship among its newcomers. "Discover Austin is aimed at new CEOs and senior managers. They and their spouses go into an intensive four-month education program, a series of orientations as to how the community works," observes Pike Powers. "This is way beyond the leadership development programs that virtually every community has."

THE AGITATOR: PUSHES THE COMMUNITY'S HORIZON

Civic entrepreneurs are restless souls. They believe there is always a better way to do something, or a brighter future for which to work. They are the enemy of complacency. They are the agitators that keep their communities scanning for new issues and better ways to address them. They are not agitators in the sense of advocating on issues of self-interest. Instead, they are concerned that the community keep challenging its assumptions, asking hard questions, and striving for a better future. Agitators are, according to the dictionary definition, "implements for stirring." Civic entrepreneurs are continuously stirring their communities to improve. Civic entrepreneurs agitate by taking the following steps. They:

- Push for a continuous process of change

- Encourage constant scanning of community issues and trends

- Keep talking about building a better community

Advice for Civic Entrepreneurs Acting as Mentors

• *Do* ensure that your community has at least one collaborative networking organization to serve as a platform for future civic entrepreneurs.

• *Do* explicitly support civic entrepreneurship within your organization or firm, giving emerging leaders the opportunity to learn by doing.

• *Do* challenge and support a new group of leaders to take a fresh look at long-running organizations or activities, or the direction of the community.

• *Do* create a local leadership development program that goes beyond networking and team building to focus and act on key community issues.

• *Don't* assume that the culture of civic entrepreneurship will naturally diffuse across your community; it needs constant nurturing or it will erode.

• *Don't* assign the work of a collaborative organization to an organization that is set up for something else (for example, advocacy); the incentives will be wrong.

• *Don't* do general leadership training; focus your efforts on helping people who have already demonstrated the ability to lead in their own field (business, government, nonprofit sector) to translate their skills to civic endeavors.

• *Don't* assume that branch plant managers and others new to your community cannot become civic entrepreneurs; create a climate of expectation for the position regardless of the individual in that position.

They Push for a Continuous Process of Change

Instead of advocating a particular solution, civic entrepreneurs agitate for a continuous process of change. Although they recognize that the issues may change, they know that the community will be resilient if it has a process for identifying and acting on new issues. "ASPED is institutionalized into the fabric of how we do business now," according to Ioanna Morfessis. "Before, the paradigm was growth as a function of new jobs and new people. That's how people saw economic development. Today, they see it as an integrated process that encompasses virtually every aspect of life in the community—business, economy, community, society, education."

Silicon Valley has experienced a similar change. As Jim Morgan sees it, "Because we now have the ability to bring groups together to work on issues, it lets us do a lot of new things. New opportunities will come up, like multimedia, and we can respond quickly. Clearly, by involving education and other groups you can accelerate a lot of movement. We have a model, and once you have a model you can make things happen." Glen Toney adds that adaptability is key. "We can start on this journey and have it all road-mapped out, and we won't necessarily remain on the road map. Change means you fall off your design and pattern, and you have to keep working to get back on track. It's an effort of continuous improvement."

At the same time, without a continuous movement forward, natural forces will pull communities apart. It is not enough to accept the status quo, because the status quo means falling behind. Wichita's Lionel Alford warns that "time passes and people lose sight of what got you where you are. We have new leaders of WI/SE, which creates new tensions." Tim Witsman adds that "we don't have the same long-term top business leadership—the business folks are less willing to challenge government. Government is taking a stronger role but not as steady a role. Community building takes a long time."

Cleveland's Jim Biggar believes that "it's like a mountain. The forces of erosion are always at work. We speak of ourselves as the new American city where diversity works, but if we lose the ability to do that, or if we lose our public-private partnership, then it slides down and the natural forces are to pull those apart. Left alone, they pull apart. So, the community has to believe, has to have the religion that holds that together. The community has it now, but there will always be more demagogues who say business is no good or incite on the race issue."

Civic entrepreneurs are vigilant for community complacency. "The threat of becoming (a) ingrown or (b) irrelevant is real," observes Austin's Pike Powers. "You need (a) new people and (b) new ideas." Despite Arizona's success, Alan Hald continues to ask questions. "How do you reinvolve large numbers of people? How do we move in a new direction now that we are at our peak and resources are available? For every five people once involved, two are still involved. At the same time, many more people are involved now who were never exposed to the original process and framework."

One of the biggest challenges is to create an environment that welcomes new ideas and leaders. "The biggest obstacle is, 'We did that,'" observes Cleveland's Steve Minter. "Today, a whole new group of people come in and say, 'Let me tell you about these great things.' You have to bite your tongue. You think, 'Hey, we did this X years ago,' and so on." At the same time, Minter knows that this is an important ingredient in fighting complacency. "The reality is that we better be fortunate enough that a new group of people comes along and says you know you didn't accomplish that much, and here's what we need to do now. It's an enthusiasm that makes sense. It needs to be a totally new crusade, instead of, 'We've been through that already.'"

Another major challenge is in overcoming the natural tendency to relax once a crisis has passed. Arizona's Alan Hald reflects on what has happened since the early 1990s. "Once the economy improves, the issues don't seem as important. Instead of preparing for the next downturn, people are basking in the good times. The down times are what spawns innovation, creativity, and energy. When you have surpluses and good times is exactly the time you need to take action, to prepare for or prevent a downturn. The issue is resilience." Hald admits, "We're struggling a bit. Civic entrepreneurship is at its finest in a crisis. When there is no crisis, and it's about maintenance, civic entrepreneurship is tough to do. People say, 'There are other things I'll do because there is no crisis.' It's a challenge we all face."

Fighting community complacency requires constant process innovations. "You have to find new ways to add value," according to Arizona's Steve Zylstra. "When you bring people together on a periodic basis, it has to be worthwhile to them; you have to impart new information and opportunities and new excitement whenever you bring them together." Ioanna Morfessis agrees. "You always need to look for new ways of energizing and helping people think out of the box." In Florida, "the question is not whether there is a sea change and whether we will have a new paradigm," according to John Anderson. "We need a process that allows a continuing dialogue. Not a stop-start thing where people hit a wall and get tired. We need an ongoing experiment." Wichita's Hale Ritchie agrees. "You better be flexible and revisit your mission, and you better be broad-based or you will run out of people."

Cleveland is an example of a community that has kept using its process to delve into more and more difficult issues. "It used to be that we were fighting with Newark for the bottom or top depending on the category; it used to be that we were just trying to hang on, turn our image around, but we can't deal with the deeper issues like poverty," according to Steve Minter. "Now we have had some success, and we are coming back to the question of poverty. We established the Commission on Poverty, went out to twenty-seven business and political leaders, and not a single person said no in 1989—because we were at a different place. Again, we went through the process of establishing the database, establishing the Center for Urban Poverty and Social Change at Case Western Reserve University, in conjunction with Rockefeller University, so that the commission was deciding on its own approaches but building from other than just anecdotes. We can now lay out a strategic plan with some pretty daunting tasks. We don't have all the answers, but we have the beginnings of some of the approaches."

Wichita's civic entrepreneurs are looking for ways to reignite the process. "The only way to do this is to put together the younger group of business and community leaders and have them reevaluate where we are, and they become the new focus," according to Lionel Alford. "You need a fresh piece of paper to take a new look." In retrospect, despite the success of Wichita's efforts, Alford says he "should have asked for a ten-year commitment of funding, not five years. At year eight, I would have put together a different group to restudy and to get the new power structure involved. I'd say, 'You're the new leaders, do it your own way.'" Cleveland has adopted just such an approach. "Cleveland Tomorrow and the Cleveland Foundation have regular strategic reviews every four or five years. We stand back and take a look at what we're doing. That is some protection for constantly renewing your sites," according to Richard Pogue.

Communities like Cleveland understand that continuous process really means building a foundation of trust, a set of expectations that allow people to shift their focus over time to whatever the community needs to address. "In a sense, we've done the easy things, though they were tough to get done," observes Al Ratner. "The kind of issues we're trying to tackle now are the basic issues of how do you attack poverty, what do you do with the schools. I don't believe that it will be all the buildings we have built that will make the difference. We are now all asking ourselves if we can deal with the fundamental issues. But if we hadn't done all the earlier things, we would never even have gotten to do the hard things."

They Encourage Constant Scanning of Community Issues and Trends

Civic entrepreneurs encourage their communities to scan for emerging issues and trends continuously. As a result, an increasing number of communities are identifying quantifiable progress indicators and updating them annually. In spring 1995, the Organization for Economic Cooperation and Development (OECD) held the first international conference on indicators: "Indicators for Urban Policies." An August 1995 inventory noted forty U.S. communities and states in the process of developing community indicators of economic, environmental, and social well-being (Corson, 1995). Scanning efforts in these communities have similar characteristics:

- Typically, the scope of the indicators goes beyond economic indicators to include quality of life, environmental, health, and social indicators. In fact, a core theme is often the interdependence of the different parts of the community.

- The benchmarking stimulates more broad-based discussion and debate about the community's underlying values, long-term goals, and shared vision for the future. Community participation is often crucial to the process of developing the indicators.

The civic entrepreneurs and organizations sponsoring the development of the indicators are not necessarily working to make progress on any or all of them. Rather, they view themselves in facilitating and educating roles.

Under the guidance of Ed McCracken and other civic entrepreneurs, Joint Venture: Silicon Valley Network has quite consciously stimulated debate about the desired future of the Silicon Valley economy and community. Early on, leaders ran up against a dearth of information about Silicon Valley, the economic region. Although all data were collected at the county level, Silicon Valley's driving industries and workforce did not fit neatly into political boundaries, spanning one county and parts of three counties.

Joint Venture sought to become an objective, reliable source of information about the region's economy. This focus was almost immediately expanded at the urging of the public-private Joint Venture board to include quality-of-life indicators. The idea was to develop a series of indicators that would:

- *Educate:* increase understanding among decision makers and the public about how the Valley is doing
- *Monitor:* track progress toward the vision of a twenty-first century community—a community collaborating to compete globally
- *Scan:* identify critical issues that need to be addressed

In January 1996, Joint Venture published the second annual *Index of Silicon Valley* to measure progress toward a "21st Century Community." The document describes, in user-friendly terms, how the Valley is doing on fifteen economic indicators and sixteen quality-of-life indicators. Major categories of economic indicators include job quantity, job quality, and business vitality. Education, environment, children and youth, infrastructure, civic engagement, and livability are the major categories of quality-of-life indicators. The *Index* is updated annually.

The *Index* is developed in cooperation with the thirty-person Joint Venture board and a ten-person advisory board of leading economists. Once developed, the *Index* is presented and disseminated widely in the community to provoke community discussion, particularly about new issues requiring community attention. Feedback from the community in 1995 led to the inclusion of new indicators in 1996, including the arts and self-employment.

In Seattle, civic leaders have sponsored a new community dialogue on progress indicators that has been brewing since 1990. First released in 1993, *Indicators of Sustainable Community* is the handiwork of Sustainable Seattle—a civic forum and volunteer network committed to improving the Seattle region's long-term cultural, economic, and environmental health and vitality. Volunteer leaders of this grassroots, citizens' initiative crafted a highly sophisticated process for involving more than two hundred citizens in identifying twenty quantifiable indicators of whether the region was moving toward or away from sustainability.

The notion of sustainability recognizes the linkages among economic, cultural, and environmental well-being. Sustainable Seattle's working definition of sustainable development stems from the United Nations 1987 report, *Our Common Future.* It is development "to meet the needs of the present without compromising the ability of future generations to meet their own needs" (United Nations, 1987, p. 43).

Through individual meetings, committee work, and four plenary meetings of a 150-person civic panel, people representing business, environmental, government, labor, religious, and education perspectives developed an agreement about what their desirable future would look like (see Exhibit 7.2.).

Sustainable Seattle's innovations are powerful in their simplicity. Not an organization in the formal sense, Sustainable Seattle is a voluntary association administered by Seattle's urban YMCA and guided by a board of trustees that calls itself "steward of the process." The process of developing indicators was highly participatory but structured to end in results. The Indicators product is a tool for people in the network to educate others, track progress, highlight policy trade-offs, and ultimately change behavior.

For *Sustainable Seattle,* good indicators:

- Are bellwether tests of sustainability and reflect something basic and fundamental to the long-term economic, social, or environmental health of a community over generations

- Can be understood and accepted by the community as a valid sign of sustainability or symptom of distress

- Have interest and appeal for use by local media in monitoring, reporting, and analyzing general trends toward or away from sustainable community practices

- Are statistically measurable in our geographic area and preferably comparable to those of other cities/communities; a practical form of data collection or measurement exists or can be created.

Exhibit 7.2.   What Makes a Good Indicator?

Source: Sustainable Seattle, 1993

Jacksonville also provides a good example of institutionalized community scanning. Since 1985, the Chamber has produced an annual update on trends, which reflects extensive volunteer input on what indicators to track. The Chamber has developed a "replication kit" that provides a step-by-step, how-to guide for other communities to use. It emphasizes community involvement as a major key to success.

In Cleveland, the tradition of community scanning is well established. Steve Minter of the Cleveland Foundation notes that it is important to keeping revisiting the same issues, which take on new dimensions and require new responses as time passes. "When the foundation came into being in 1914, it copied Pittsburgh and New York and did community surveys to look at community problems. The very first survey focused on the Cleveland public schools. Others examined the social welfare system, parks and recreation, the need to Americanize new immigrants, and the criminal justice system. In the 1960s and 1970s, many of the issues were the same as they are today. The issues are enduring issues." Whether focusing on new issues or old issues with a new urgency, community scanning is an important ingredient for continuous community renewal.

They Keep Talking About Building a Better Community

Despite their success, civic entrepreneurs keep renewing the vision of a better community. They keep pushing the horizon, articulating an even better future for their community. "On a scale of 1 to 10, we're a 10 on what we've done, and we're a 3 on what we need to get done," believes Cleveland's Al Ratner. "What we've done, we've done exceptionally well. On the other hand, if you spend any time and you see how many people live in poverty in this city, we still have a lot of work to do."

Civic entrepreneurs keep prodding the community to be visionary. "There is no overarching vision for education," complains Arizona's Steve Zylstra. "There are so many groups working on the issue; some are opposed to each other. That's where the GSPED process could really make a difference. If you can do it for the entire economy, why not education?" Wichita's Tim Witsman is vocal about his concern that "two years ago, we began to lose the vision. Business has remained committed to the original vision, but it's been harder to sustain on the governmental side." Silicon Valley's William F. Miller understands the value of vision and the rewards. "There is tremendous pleasure in sharing the power of ideas, seeing people reorient themselves, and then practicing this new thinking."

Fundamentally, the civic entrepreneur is one who sees opportunity in crisis, who feels the need to do better when things are going pretty well, who deeply believes that the community can always be better. "What we were twenty-five years ago, we can't be again, but we can be something better," believes Tom Skornia, a lawyer and one of the early proponents of regional collaboration in Silicon Valley.

Advice for Civic Entrepreneurs Acting as Agitators

- *Do* set expectations that an implementation success always has a next logical step; once people have a taste of success, encourage them to take it further.
- *Do* set the stage for addressing fundamental issues by building trust and a sense of success with tangible achievements.
- *Do* promote periodic identification and discussion of new community issues.
- *Do* keep seeding your speeches, public statements, and private discussions with visions of an even better community.
- *Don't* ever use the phrase, "We already did that"; acquaint people with what has been done, and challenge them to suggest and work on taking the next step.
- *Don't* just release a report on community indicators and trends; engage the community in choosing the indicators, and launch the report with a communications campaign that engages people in discussion about the implications of the indicators, setting the stage for action.
- *Don't* ease off when the economy is doing well; capitalize on good times to focus the community on major investments in the future.
- *Don't* accept that any community issue is unresolvable; find examples from other communities and ignite a debate about how they might apply locally.

"The president of the Ford Motor Company says he has to replace 60 percent of his employees in the next ten years, and he doesn't know where he's going to get the workers. What you understand is not that you have terrible problems but that those are great opportunities," observes Cleveland's Al Ratner. "You can look at things as problems or opportunities. We don't look at the school situation as a problem but as the phenomenal opportunities we are missing for what our city could become. That partly answers the question of how we keep the spirit alive. If we're satisfied with what we've done, we're gone. We have enough work for twenty years, then someone else will figure out twenty beyond."

CHAPTER EIGHT

Conclusion:
Renewing America
One Community at a Time
Speeding the Change Process

There are no simple solutions to our national challenges; no magic formula will set things right. America will have to
renew itself community by community. Civic entrepreneurs will lead
the way, working together to build vital economic communities.
Through trial and error, instinct and observation, new leaders are
learning how to channel the talent of diverse community interests into
shared vision and collaborative action.

We have a choice. We can let the natural forces drive new leaders
to the forefront—as has happened in places like Austin, Arizona,
Cleveland, Florida, Silicon Valley, and Wichita. Over time, more civic
entrepreneurs are likely to emerge. Inevitably, some communities will
thrive; others will fall behind. Alternatively, we can look for ways to
encourage the spread of civic entrepreneurship across America, a
nationwide "scale-up" of effective civic practices that have been prototyped in various communities. If we choose the second option, we
must find ways to speed the learning process for civic entrepreneurs,
which, in turn, will accelerate the renewal process of communities
across America.

ACCELERATING THE LEARNING
PROCESS FOR CIVIC ENTREPRENEURSHIP

Today's civic entrepreneurs have learned their trade working in the trenches. Some have also observed or talked with civic entrepreneurs in other communities. Their lessons point to developing more civic entrepreneurs as a central challenge for sustaining economic communities over the long term. How can we—as business executives, public officials, economic development practitioners, foundation and nonprofit directors, media leaders, and citizens—encourage civic entrepreneurship in more communities? How can this generation of civic entrepreneurs inspire and prepare the first generation of the next century?

We believe that certain actions could stimulate civic entrepreneurship to help build economic community in America's regions. We can do better than let the natural forces take their course. Together, these actions constitute a bottom-up/top-down national agenda for civic entrepreneurship (see Exhibit 8.1). The four cornerstones of this agenda are:

- Recognize civic entrepreneurs: celebrating role models
- Network civic entrepreneurs: learning through linking
- Develop civic entrepreneurs: educating deeper, across generations
- Encourage civic entrepreneurs: supporting collaborative initiatives and organizations

---

Recognize civic entrepreneurs: celebrating role models
   We can create civic entrepreneur team awards.
   We can use the bully pulpit to showcase new American heroes.

Network civic entrepreneurs: learning through linking
   We can build learning networks of civic entrepreneurs.
   We can forge global alliances of civic entrepreneurs.

Develop civic entrepreneurs: educating deeper, across generations
   We can create civic entrepreneur academies.
   We can better leverage corporate civic engagement.

Encourage civic entrepreneurs: supporting collaborative initiatives and organizations
   We can seed new collaborative initiatives.
   We can support collaborative intermediary organizations.

Exhibit 8.1.   A National Agenda for Civic Entrepreneurship.

RECOGNIZE CIVIC ENTREPRENEURS: CELEBRATING ROLE MODELS

Communities, states, and nations should publicly recognize the new kind of leadership provided by civic entrepreneurs. Public recognition accomplishes two objectives. First, it celebrates the fact that civic entrepreneurs exist—that diverse teams of people are doing something out of the ordinary to move their communities forward. Second, recognition provides the opportunity to educate the broader community about what civic entrepreneurs do—the roles they play, their effective practices, how they engage their communities in new ways. Widespread recognition of civic entrepreneurs would provide inspiring role models for new and aspiring civic entrepreneurs to follow.

We Can Create Civic Entrepreneur Team Awards

Recognition could take the form of specific awards. When America's business faced the global competitive challenge in the 1980s, leading businesses recognized that the key to competition was higher quality. The U.S. government established the Malcolm Baldrige Quality Awards to recognize firms that achieve the highest standard of quality. The Baldrige Award has educated businesses about what quality is and how to achieve it. It has served as a rallying point for thousands of American companies to launch, document, and monitor quality improvement programs.

The competitive challenge facing American communities today is as great, and demands as fundamental a reorientation, as the competitive challenge facing American business a decade ago. Our economy cannot be competitive if our communities are weak. In the spirit of the Malcolm Baldrige Award, a national civic entrepreneur award program would showcase the practices of civic entrepreneurs and recognize the results their communities achieve. To reinforce the team nature of leadership, the award would recognize civic entrepreneur teams and community initiatives to build collaborative economies rather than individual leaders. The presence of the award would provide incentives and models for communities to think and act in new ways. An annual event or conference could focus national attention on civic entrepreneurs and their economic communities.

Communities and states could develop their own versions of the national Civic Entrepreneur Team Award, perhaps named after a legendary local figure or team. Similarly, the emphasis should be on using public recognition of civic entrepreneurs as an opportunity to communicate widely the importance of civic entrepreneurship to their own community or state. The media and foundations can play a critical role in profiling effective community leaders and disseminating information about what they do. Both education and inspiration are required.

We Can Use the Bully Pulpit to Encourage New American Heroes

In addition to creating awards, we can establish the bully pulpit as an effective tool to showcase civic entrepreneurs and raise them up as role models. National, state, and local leaders can use the bully pulpit to champion the cause of civic entrepreneurship. A good example is the KickStart Initiative of the U.S. Advisory Council on the National Information Infrastructure, cochaired by Ed McCracken of Silicon Graphics and Delano Lewis, president and CEO of National Public Radio. Complementing recommendations on national policy issues, McCracken helped launch a nationwide effort to spotlight grassroots efforts to apply information infrastructure to community issues. Kick-Start provides a leadership guide to support community efforts to connect to the information superhighway. Follow-up activity is supported by the private Benton Foundation.

Another example is NetDay, a grassroots initiative showcased by President Clinton and Vice President Gore to connect California schools to the Internet. Through community efforts across the state, citizens, businesses, and schools joined together on a single day in March 1996 to connect 30 percent of California schools to the information superhighway. Clinton and Gore personally pulled wire at a California school and recognized the tremendous civic initiative. The federal government did not provide funding but blessed a locally inspired idea and gave it wide visibility, both locally and nationally. Seven months after learning how-to lessons from the California prototype, NetDay went national but maintained its grassroots structure.

The next time a president of the United States, a governor, or a CEO recognizes a hero during a State of the Union address, a State of the State address, or a corporate rally, that hero should be a civic entrepreneur team who is recognized for good works in building economic community (Exhibit 8.2).

If you are a business executive, recognize leaders who leverage their civic involvement in extraordinary ways to benefit the company and the community.

If you are a public official, raise up civic entrepreneurs in your speeches as new American heroes, and encourage more Americans to lead in this way.

If you are an economic development practitioner, recognize the role civic entrepreneurs play in leveraging your effort.

If you are a foundation or nonprofit executive, consider how you could help establish a civic entrepreneur team award at the national, state, or community level.

If you are a citizen, pay attention to the good works being done by civic entrepreneurs and help move it forward.

If you are a media leader, consider how you can profile the people who make things happen in your community and what they do as effective leaders.

Exhibit 8.2.   What You Can Do to Recognize Civic Entrepreneurs.

NETWORK CIVIC ENTREPRENEURS: LEARNING THROUGH LINKING

Civic entrepreneurs tell us that they have learned from their counterparts in other communities. Every team described an initiation process that involved learning who had done what in successful communities and then incorporating these lessons and launching a tailored, homegrown initiative.

Cleveland civic entrepreneur and foundation executive Steven Minter describes a learning process that has been replicated many times over in successful communities. In the 1980s, Minter and others were invited to visit Baltimore. "We were inspired. Some of us became students of Baltimore. . . . This goes beyond just talking about it. You get a common experience, not that we copy them, but a feeling that we can do something like that."

This learning process has been repeated in community after community. Phoenix studied Cleveland to learn about the role of business and civic leadership and studied Florida to learn about industry clusters. An early product of the Arizona Strategic Planning for Economic Development (ASPED) process was a best practices guide for state and local economic development leaders. In Silicon Valley, the San Jose Chamber visited the Austin Chamber in 1993 to learn from that community's success. They came back with the feeling, "We can do that too." And Jim Morgan knew Alan Hald from Phoenix and was inspired by what his team had done. Joint Venture: Silicon Valley Network explicitly built on best practice experience from other regions to create a state-of-the-art process for regional rejuvenation.

This process is a kind of informal benchmarking. The word *bench-marking*, increasingly important in the private sector, refers to "the search for those best practices that will lead to superior performance" (Camp, 1989, p. xi). Civic entrepreneurs search for *dantotsu*, a Japanese word that means the "best of the best." They seek examples of world-class practices or methods from other regions, even from those that look quite different. They then use this knowledge to design effective processes and outcome objectives for their community.

The private sector has learned that effective benchmarking is the ongoing process of seeking out and learning from world-class leaders, not a one-time event. To accelerate civic entrepreneurship, the key questions become: How can we broaden the learning process to other communities? How do we sustain learning as communities and their leaders evolve? How can we systematize the learning process and provide civic entrepreneurs an opportunity to reflect together on what they've learned?

We Can Build Learning Networks of Civic Entrepreneurs

When the world economy dramatically changed in the 1980s as a result of global competition and the collapse of Communism, the World Economic Forum in Davos, Switzerland, took center stage as a forum for the world's economic leaders to meet together on an annual basis to discuss the future directions of the world economy. This forum has provided a network for leaders to learn from each other at times of rapid change. Similarly, many civic entrepreneurs express strong interest in building "lateral relationships" with civic entrepreneurs from other communities. They want to share lessons learned and have a support network.

A Civic Entrepreneur Network could provide an ongoing opportunity for civic entrepreneurs from diverse regions to share experience and benchmark best practices. The Network could use a variety of venues to create a continuous learning community. State or national meetings of the Civic Entrepreneur Network would allow leaders to build relationships and rapport face to face. The Network could manage on-line dialogues, offer interactive learning tools, and promote computer- or video-based conferencing for virtual communication and education. Case studies on community best practices could be prepared by practitioners and shared on a regular basis. The Network could arrange benchmarking visits between civic entrepreneurs in different communities.

One emerging model is the Pew Partnership for Civic Change, an intermediary of the Philadelphia-based Pew Charitable Trust. Since 1992, the Partnership has provided grants to fourteen small communities (less than 150,000 people) to build community by collaborating on projects. Leaders of the projects meet every six months to share lessons learned, and a newsletter updates all participants on progress. In September, 1996, the Partnership announced a new initiative focused on providing training and support for twenty civic entrepreneurs in each of ten communities of 150,000 to 400,000 people. The Alliance for National Renewal, convened by the National Civic League and founded by John Gardner, is networking organizations from the public, private, and nonprofit sectors that are working to build new community leadership.

The goal is to make it easy for civic entrepreneurs to learn from each other. Like commercial entrepreneurs operating in remote environments, civic entrepreneurs can feel isolated. As George Vradenburg III of Latham and Watkins explained, "The problem is that in some communities civic entrepreneurs are not nurtured. Energy dies without support—like drops of water in a desert." Getting to know others who are lending themselves to community leadership and facing similar challenges can enhance their effectiveness and be a source of personal rejuvenation.

We Can Forge Global Alliances of Civic Entrepreneurs

Networks of civic entrepreneurs could certainly include those from other countries. Around the world, the accelerating pace of change and the shortcomings of national economic leadership are prompting economic communities to take their own initiative. Economic regions are beginning to look outward to build mutually beneficial relationships with their counterparts globally. We are creating an era in which the primary linkages of economic communities are not with their host state or nation but with other communities in the global economy.

The regionalization of national economies is fostering growth in the formal and informal networks binding economic communities to one another around the world. Independent of their nation-states, regions are developing alliances to trade and do business, build infrastructure, and exchange ideas and best practices. Each region and its businesses are searching for new complementarities with other regions to help enhance their competitiveness. This "regional internationalism" is a natural consequence of the rising importance of economic regions.

The interesting question that remains, however, is whether civic entrepreneurship defined in the American context occurs, or will occur, internationally. Although industrialized countries face some similar forces of change, the cultural and political traditions shaping the environment for civic entrepreneurship vary widely. After hearing about growing American interest in the concept of social capital, a Singapore official responded, "In Singapore, the government *is* the social capital." Adelaide, Australia, is experimenting with Silicon Valley's approach of involving industry leaders in developing regional economic strategies and new intermediary institutions. The effort is being led by MFP Australia, a quasi-government organization charged with bringing best practices in economic strategy, urban planning, environmental sustainability, and social infrastructure to Australia. In Australia, the business community traditionally looks to government for leadership, and the "tall poppy" syndrome tends to discourage individual initiative. Also, the word *civic* exclusively connotes local government, and the word *entrepreneur* conjures up negative images of the discredited "corporate cowboys" of the 1980s. Nonetheless, civic entrepreneur leaders (called community champions) are stepping outside the confines of their companies and leading collaborative initiatives. The community is transitioning from a consultative to a collaborative approach in regional planning, from an approach where government drives economic strategy to one where government plays a supportive, facilitating role for business. This is evident most particularly in the emerging industry cluster of multimedia, as well as in the transitioning area of defense electronics.

Though leadership will continue to take different forms in different countries, community leaders globally are in fact learning from each other. The opportunity is to move beyond the single visits and sister-city exchanges of the past to form ongoing learning networks. In September 1996, for example, Smart Valley and Stanford University convened Connect '96—the first forum to bring together the world's pioneers of regional electronic communities for the exchange of ideas and experiences on developing regional information infrastructures and applications. Leaders from forty regional initiatives in North America, Europe, and Asia learned from each other in how-to workshops.

The initial conference is sparking wider dissemination of ideas, future conferences, and a more formal learning and exchange network.

Another example of an ongoing learning network is the Global Fellowship network managed by the Ashoka foundation. The Fellowship links more than six hundred "public entrepreneurs" from thirty developing countries so they can collaborate on projects, exchange information, and share their expertise. Each year, Ashoka recognizes and provides financial support to about one hundred Ashoka Fellows—creative problem solvers who are working on projects that address cutting-edge social problems. The Fellowship Resource Center, based in Arlington, Virginia, provides Fellows with organizational networking, research support, access to information resources, and consulting. Though its focus is more social than economic and is strictly developing-country, the Ashoka model is relevant to creating international linkages among civic entrepreneurs (see Exhibit 8.3).

If you are a business executive, reach out to corporate leaders in other communities and nations; learn what they do best, and share it with your community.

If you are a public official, team with local corporate leaders, and visit other communities to benchmark them in person.

If you are an economic development practitioner, help connect your civic entrepreneurs so they can learn from those in other regions.

If you are a foundation or nonprofit executive, determine how you could create a new infrastructure to link civic entrepreneurs across communities.

If you are a citizen, learn how other places build economic community when you travel the globe or surf the Net.

If you are a media leader, do features on best practices and relevant examples of civic entrepreneurship from other places.

Exhibit 8.3.   What You Can Do to Network Civic Entrepreneurs.

DEVELOP CIVIC ENTREPRENEURS: EDUCATING DEEPER, ACROSS GENERATIONS

In the short term, the challenge is to connect existing leaders so they can learn from each other in real time. At the same time, communities and companies are considering how to deepen the skills of civic entrepreneurs and bring the next generation along. Structured educational and leadership development programs could provide aspiring civic entrepreneurs with the perspectives, tools, and connections to play a leadership role in building economic community. Through interactive learning, experience, and reflection, they could become more adept in playing the appropriate role at the appropriate stage of the economic community-building process.

We Can Create Civic Entrepreneur Academies

One model that could deepen the preparation of civic entrepreneurs is that of an academy—a periodic educational experience that introduces and reinforces new skills over time. Arizona's Jack Pfister believes that Arizona needs a new kind of leadership academy to develop corporate managers and others into civic entrepreneurs. The idea would be to take people who have demonstrated capacity for leadership and give them the frameworks, tools, and relationships for being a leader in the economic arena. Pfister explains, "We need to develop the next generation of leaders, and not just when they reach the top. Like a War College, people need intensive immersion and would come away with more sophistication about leadership in the economic arena. They would have the opportunity to meet and interact with peers. People simply don't know how the economy works, what the leverage points are. Even people who were taught economics were taught that it is all about acting alone. Not true."

Many American communities have some sort of leadership development program, often run by Chambers of Commerce. Typically, they focus on exposing participants, often midlevel business and nonprofit leaders, to a broad range of community areas. For example, through eight sessions, an award-winning program in Dawson, Nebraska, exposes future leaders to seven arenas of community life: quality of life, government, law enforcement, education, health, agriculture, and business-industry. Other leadership development efforts focus on the arts or the social services. Some build in a practicum experience. These community leadership programs can motivate future leaders to work for the community and can expose them to a variety of areas in which to serve.

Two shortcomings, however, prevent many community leadership programs from meeting the needs of civic entrepreneurs. First, they tend to focus on developing generic leadership skills and motivation rather than preparing leaders for a particular content area such as the economy. In fact, many programs do not send a strong message about what makes the economy tick. Second, programs tend to focus more on stability and on familiarizing participants with "the way things work around here now." They focus too little on creating change to "what ought to be."

The next-level opportunity, however, is to create more in-depth training for people who want to be civic entrepreneurs—those who bridge the economy and community. These people would benefit by immersion in how their regional economy functions and in the practices of civic entrepreneurship in initiating, incubating, implementing, and renewing collaborative efforts. Rather than interacting just with their peers, emerging civic entrepreneurs should have the opportunity to interact with established civic entrepreneurs and to reflect together about how the nature of economic leadership is changing.

As they have with existing leadership programs, foundations can play a role in developing broader and deeper understanding of civic entrepreneurship. For example, The James Irvine Foundation in California sponsored the documentation of Silicon Valley's experience, describing the guiding principles and operational lessons learned from the Joint Venture: Silicon Valley process (*The Joint Venture Way*, 1995). The foundation is now supporting efforts to disseminate the lessons to other California communities and to test other collaborative regional models. The next step is to provide more in-depth training and coaching for leaders to initiate collaborative efforts in diverse communities and industries. This is being done as part of a new long-term strategy to promote regional collaborative initiatives as an underpinning of sustainable communities.

The Florida Chamber engaged private sector leaders to launch a new privately driven, state economic partnership—*Enterprise Florida*—and to stimulate regional initiatives. John Anderson, the CEO of *Enterprise Florida*, recognizes that a new state orientation must be implemented through community-level activities. Anderson is launching a summit process to help economic development leaders across Florida share in state-of-the-art economic development thinking and tools. This summit process could be the wellspring for developing more civic entrepreneurs in Florida.

We Can Better Leverage Corporate Civic Engagement

Individual companies can experiment with new internal policies and practices that develop civic entrepreneurship, including methods for better leveraging their time invested in community activities. For example, Applied Materials expects its managers to be actively involved in their region, whether it be Silicon Valley, Austin, Germany, South Korea, Japan, or China. The company has relied on the skills and experience of headquarters' "civic entrepreneurs" as well as regional managers, to leverage their community involvement. Hewlett-Packard encourages employees to engage with their communities, both as individuals and as representatives of Hewlett-Packard. The company has sponsored seminars to introduce its stakeholders to new models of collaboration. The goal is to develop leaders both in and outside of Hewlett-Packard who can build bridges between the many economies and communities where Hewlett-Packard operates.

California utility Pacific Gas & Electric is funding joint leadership development training for its employees and local community leaders. The utility has worked with business and community to provide "civic entrepreneur seminars" to prepare local leaders for a stronger role in their economy. In one seminar, twenty-five leaders from diverse sectors discussed the underlying principles that guide civic entrepreneurs and engaged in exercises that helped them apply those principles. In a second seminar, those same leaders were asked to use the practices of civic entrepreneurship to develop a business plan outlining the distinctive contribution of their collaborative organization to the regional community (see Exhibit 8.4).

If you are a business executive, build civic entrepreneurship into your executive development programs and find ways for community leaders to participate.

If you are a public official, work with local companies to create, enhance, or support local leadership development efforts focused on the roles and practices of civic entrepreneurship.

If you are an economic development practitioner, help train your community in the principles of economic community and civic entrepreneur leadership.

If you are a foundation or nonprofit executive, invest in programs, institutions, and the development of training courses and tools for current and next-generation civic entrepreneurs.

If you are a citizen, develop collaborative leadership skills through experience and education.

If you are a media leader, use your medium to provide ongoing education about leadership development and pioneer new tools for the education and motivation of leaders.

Exhibit 8.4.   What You Can Do to Develop Civic Entrepreneurs.

ENCOURAGE CIVIC ENTREPRENEURS: SUPPORT COLLABORATIVE INITIATIVES AND ORGANIZATIONS

A final, and ultimately most important, cornerstone of the national agenda for civic entrepreneurship is to encourage civic entrepreneurs by supporting their collaborative initiatives and organizations. As we recognize, network, and develop civic entrepreneurs, we need also to support directly their efforts to transform fragmented interests into high-performance economic communities. Civic entrepreneurs always do their work through some type of organizational platform, however informal. Typically, this platform is either a new collaborative initiative—a community coming together for the first time—or a collaborative organization—an existing structure for ongoing community collaboration. Ultimately, to accelerate civic entrepreneurship across America we must support the organizational platforms where civic entrepreneurs interact on a regular basis with each other and with their communities.

We Can Seed New Collaborative Initiatives

One of the most difficult challenges is raising initial seed money to finance a collaborative process of change in a community. "Patient capital" is needed, particularly at the two earliest stages of the change process: in initiation and in the incubation of potential actions. The work of these early stages—community education, commitment building, leadership recruitment, idea generation—in case after case has proved essential for securing later tangible results and an ongoing collaborative spirit. Yet many communities find it very difficult to raise funds to support process, when it is unclear what tangible results will follow. In some communities, a deep-pocketed civic entrepreneur steps up and writes a personal or company check. In other communities, an existing organization contributes its time and resources as an initial catalyst. Yet in many communities, both of these options have proved difficult, and at some point cash resources are required. We can expand the avenues by which this early seed funding is secured.

Local and national foundations can play an instrumental role in the early stages of community collaboration and in helping maintain momentum through key transitions. The Cleveland Foundation played a catalytic role in Cleveland's initial rally in the early 1980s and has provided funding and leadership at critical times over the last fif-teen years. The Pew Charitable Trust's grants through the Pew Part-nership for Civic Change have helped small communities launch economic initiatives based on strong local leadership and principles of collaboration. Traditionally, foundation investments have targeted nonprofit efforts to improve quality of life and neighborhood devel-opment. Increasingly, foundations are interested in regional economies as a critical underpinning of quality of life. Just as they have in the past supported leadership development in disadvantaged communities, they have become interested in leadership development for regional economic communities. An opportunity is to link leadership of dis-advantaged neighborhoods to broader regional communities for their mutual benefit.

Associations like the National Council for Urban Economic Devel-opment, National Civic League, and Urban Land Institute can play a role in helping their constituencies apply the collaborative approach in their own communities. They can highlight thoughtful practition-ers of civic entrepreneurship who help connect divergent sectors in their communities. They can provide their members with the language and case examples to make them more effective catalysts for strength-ening economic community.

Corporations of all sizes and from all sectors must play a role in financing the early organizational stages of community collaboration. Support most be both broad and deep. Most communities typically look to a handful of corporations for leadership and resources. Those com-panies that traditionally acted alone should seize the opportunity to work laterally with other businesses to work on fundamental, rather than marginal, change. Group vice president Glen Toney of Applied Materi-als explains, "I have learned the importance of positioning our efforts within a broader educational improvement initiative, making a long-term commitment, and coordinating our efforts with those of other companies and organizations working on educational improvement."

With the realities of government devolution, it would be easy to conclude that federal and state governments have no role in helping build strong economic communities. Also, we have learned the hard way that well-meaning, top-down government programs can undermine and misdirect local initiative. Nonetheless, federal and state governments should play a role in supporting the early-stage organization activi-ties of communities. A new model of "economic federalism" would be based on the principle that economic communities have primary responsibility for choosing their future but that the federal government can help communities realize their future. Through a challenge grant approach, federal and state governments could match funds raised locally to support the early stages of community collaboration. The Office of Economic Adjustment in the Department of Defense, for example, has provided planning grants to communities impacted by defense cutbacks. In some cases, local governments use these grants to build private sector and other community leadership for dealing with changed economic circumstances, instead of just conducting a study. Use of federal funds to build a civic entrepreneur constituency for change should be encouraged.

We Can Support Collaborative Intermediary Organizations of the Civil Sector

Across America, civic entrepreneurs are experimenting with new kinds of organizations that fit between the economy and the community. When civic entrepreneurs start the hard work of implementation, they seek an organizational structure of some sort to support ongoing collaboration. Civic entrepreneurs ultimately need an organizational platform from which they can work. Sometimes, these are entirely new organizations (Silicon Valley, Wichita, Florida, Arizona). Sometimes, existing organizations transform and play a new mediating role (Austin). Other times, a network of organizations together serve as infrastructure for community collaboration (Cleveland).

Whatever their form, these organizations mark the emergence of a new kind of intermediary structure in the civil sector. If the civil sector is the space in which people from business, government, education, and community can work together, these intermediary organizations provide a modicum of structure through which collaborative action can occur. They help sustain collaborative efforts, link stakeholders, and leverage talent and resources. Collaborative intermediary organizations tend to have five key traits. They:

• Practice inclusion
• Achieve high leverage
• Take a long-term orientation
• Are benchmark-driven
• Keep civic entrepreneurs engaged

Although not-for-profit, they are different fundamentally than traditional third-sector organizations designed for social services, arts, or advocacy. Although collaborative intermediaries often build on entrepreneurial strengths of the private sector, they are not a substitute for government. The quality of a mediating structure depends on the quality of the individual civic entrepreneurs working through it.

What can we do to support community efforts to build strong intermediary institutions of the civil sector?

Successful collaborative organizations depend on leadership from private sector civic entrepreneurs. Without private sector involvement, intermediary organizations can lose their important connection to the changing economy. Businesses must provide financial support to sustain intermediaries and serve as both steward and demanding investor. This base of support should be as broad as possible, not limited to the largest companies, and as deep as possible, putting real skin on the table. Business organizations such as Chambers of Commerce and business councils should evaluate what their distinctive contribution can be to building economic community. Some will dramatically reposition themselves to play new roles.

Local governments and economic development organizations need to view these intermediary organizations as partners to accomplish some of their goals. These organizations can amplify their effectiveness by working on certain issues through the civil sector. It is important that public sector organizations support intermediaries financially, even in symbolic amounts. This sends an important signal that government is a true partner in community collaboration. Economic development organizations should resist the temptation to be everything to everyone and consider whether they are best suited to be a collaborative intermediary organization or to be an organizational partner in one.

Just as foundations have a role in supporting the start-up of collaborative initiatives, they can provide critical support to implement initiatives and to maintain the core operations of the collaborative organization. In particular, foundation funding is appropriate for community outreach, as well as for benchmarking progress, evaluating lessons learned, and continuously renewing the collaborative organization and its leaders.

In addition to supporting the early-stage start-up process, the federal and state challenge grants could reward local efforts by helping them expand and evaluate piloted efforts. The collaborative process in Silicon Valley, for example, produced two innovative initiatives with strong civic entrepreneur financial support and leadership—the Smart Valley initiative to develop community applications for the Internet and the 21st Century Education Initiative to spark a renaissance in the public schools. Federal funding leveraged local private and foundation support to implement specific Smart Valley projects and to monitor the success of the school reform efforts. The federal funding did not adversely influence what the community wanted to do but rewarded its self-help efforts. This type of federal-regional partnership is a good model for other places.

The federal government should integrate the themes of economic regions and civic entrepreneurs into federal programs. Federal investments in skills, technology, and physical infrastructure should happen in partnership with collaborative intermediaries and hinge on the strength of local collaboration. Also, steps should be taken to identify and eliminate any federally imposed obstacles to community collaboration. For example, federal mission agencies tend to practice "picket fence" federalism, giving grants to different organizations in a region with little coordination. In many cases, this practice encourages competition, rather than collaboration, among different community organizations. Agencies should consider how they could instead encourage integration and collaboration, particularly in metropolitan regions (see Exhibit 8.5).

If you are a business executive, make a personal or company investment to initiate a local collaborative process, and then stay personally involved.

If you are a public official, offer challenge or matching funding to ignite civic entrepreneurship, and invest public resources in collaborative initiatives that have demonstrated their effectiveness.

If you are an economic development practitioner, sell the benefits of collaboration, and encourage local factions to work together on specific projects.

If you are a foundation or nonprofit executive, invest in start-up efforts that support emerging teams of civic entrepreneurs, and recruit new civic entrepreneurs.

If you are a citizen, play a needed role on a civic entrepreneur team, and champion the need for collaborative forums.

If you are a media leader, make an investment in a collaborative process, challenging other community and corporate leaders to join the effort.

Exhibit 8.5.   What You Can Do to Encourage Civic Entrepreneurs.

Economic communities in the twenty-first century are going to require a strong tradition of civic entrepreneurship. For aspiring regions, identifying and recruiting civic entrepreneurs into economic community building is essential. Civic entrepreneurs will be the key to new global networks of economic communities. They will build relationships among regions in the global economy, forging a new era of regional internationalism. They will be the leading voices in redefining the relationship between regions and national governments, forging a new era of economic federalism. And they will connect to one another and begin to pass on their experiences to a younger generation of civic entrepreneurs.

Today, many Americans believe we have lost our ability to work together, make decisions, and take action on our collective future. Civic entrepreneurs are the new leaders for a new time, who show us that it can be done. With their inspiration and experience, we have learned that we can stimulate wider participation to get action. With their leadership, America will redefine, as it has done many times before, the relationship between its economy and its communities.

~~~ References

"An Economy at Risk: The Phase I Diagnostic Report." Menlo Park, Calif.: Center for Economic Competitiveness, SRI International, 1992.

Blueprint for a 21st Century Community. San Jose, Calif.: Joint Venture: Silicon Valley Network, 1993.

Bradley, B. *Time Present, Time Past.* New York: Knopf, 1996.

Brands, H. W. *The Reckless Decade: America in the 1890s.* New York: St. Martin's Press, 1995.

"Building the School to Work Bridge." Editorial Opinion. *San Jose Mercury News,* Mar. 17, 1996, p. 6c.

Camp, R. C. *Benchmarking: The Search for Industry Best Practices That Lead to Superior Performance.* Milwaukee, Wis.: ASQC Quality Press, 1989.

Chrislip, D., and Larson, C. *Collaborative Leadership: How Citizens and Civic Leaders Can Make a Difference.* San Francisco: Jossey-Bass, 1994.

Cooper, H. "Southern Comfort: Tupelo, Miss., Concocts an Effective Recipe for Economic Health." *Wall Street Journal,* Mar. 3, 1994, p.1.

Corson, W. *Defining Progress: An Inventory of Programs Using Goals and Indicators to Assess Quality of Life, Performance, and Sustainability at the Community and Regional Level.* Washington, D.C.: George Washington University. Rev. draft, Oct. 9, 1995.

Croly, H. *The Promise of American Life.* New York: Bobbs-Merrill, 1965. Originally published 1909.

Cummings, M. "High-Technology Companies: Factors in Site Selection." *Area Development,* Sep. 1995, pp. 111–120.

Davidow, W. H., and Malone, M. S. *The Virtual Corporation.* New York: HarperCollins, 1992.

DeSantis, M. "Leadership, Resource Endowments and Regional Economic Development." Unpublished doctoral dissertation, George Mason University, 1993.

Dodge, W. R. *Regional Excellence: Governing Together to Compete Globally and Flourish Locally.* Washington, D.C.: National League of Cities, 1996.

Drucker, P. "The Age of Social Transformation." *The Atlantic Monthly,* Nov. 1994, pp. 53–80.

Drucker, P. *Innovation and Entrepreneurship: Practice and Principles.* New York: HarperCollins, 1985.

Drucker, P. *Managing in a Time of Great Change.* New York: Truman Talley Books/Dutton, 1995.

Eggers, W. D., and O'Leary, J. O. *Revolution at the Roots: Making Our Government Smaller, Better, and Closer to Home.* New York: Free Press, 1995.

Engelking, S. "Brains and Jobs: The Role of Universities in Economic Development and Industrial Recruitment." Unpublished master's thesis, University of Oklahoma, Economic Development Institute, 1989.

Frey Foundation. "Taking Care of Civic Business: How Formal CEO-Level Business Leadership Groups Have Influenced Civic Progress in Key American Cities." Grand Rapids, Mich.: Frey Foundation, 1993.

Friedman, D. "Are You Ready for the Networked Economy?" *Inc.,* Feb. 1996, pp. 62–65.

Fukuyama, F. *Trust: The Social Virtues and the Creation of Prosperity.* New York: Free Press, 1995.

Galbraith, J. K. *New Industrial State.* New York: Signet Books, 1967.

Gardner, J. W. *On Leadership.* New York: Free Press, 1990.

Gray, B. *Collaborating: Finding Common Ground for Multiparty Problems.* San Francisco: Jossey-Bass, 1989.

Heifetz, R. A. *Leadership Without Easy Answers.* Cambridge, Mass.: The Belknap Press of Harvard University Press, 1995.

Henton, D., Melville, J., and Walesh, K. "Benchmarking Practices, Progress, Performance." *Economic Development Commentary,* 1996, *19*(4), pp. 24–30.

Henton, D. and Walesh, K. "Reinventing Silicon Valley: Creating a Total Quality Community." *Cities and the New Global Economy: Conference Proceedings Vol. I.* Canberra: Australian Government Publishing Service, 1995.

John, D., Batie, S., and Noris, K. *A Brighter Future for Rural America? Strategies for Communities and States.* Washington, D.C.: National Governors' Association, 1988.

The Joint Venture Way: Lessons for Regional Rejuvenation. San Jose, Calif.: Joint Venture: Silicon Valley Network, 1995.

Joint Venture's Index of Silicon Valley: Measuring Progress Toward a 21st Century Community. San Jose, Calif.: Joint Venture: Silicon Valley Network, 1995, 1996.

Kanter, R. B. "The Business of Massachusetts." *Boston Globe,* June 3, 1994.

Kanter, R. *World Class: Thriving Locally in the Global Economy.* New York: Simon and Schuster, 1995.

Katzenbach, J. R., and Smith, D. K. *The Wisdom of Teams: Creating the High-Performance Organization.* Boston: Harvard Business School Press, 1993.

Kotler, P., Haider, D. H., and Rein, I. *Marketing Places.* New York: Free Press, 1993.

Krugman, P. *Geography and Trade.* Cambridge, Mass., and London: Leuven University Press and MIT Press, 1996 (originally published 1991).

Lipnack, J., and Stamps, J. *The Age of the Network.* New York: John Wiley and Sons, 1994.

London, S. *Building Collaborative Communities.* Unpublished paper prepared for The Pew Partnership for Civic Change, Nov. 1995.

Luke, J. S., Ventriss, C., Reed, B. J., and Reed, C. M. *Managing Economic Development: A Guide to State and Local Leadership Strategies.* San Francisco: Jossey-Bass, 1988.

Marshall, A. *Principles of Economics.* Philadelphia: Porcupine Press, 1994 (originally published 1890).

Miller, W. F. "Regionalism, Globalism and the New Economic Geography." Paper presented to Policy Study Group, Tokyo, Japan, Jan. 1996.

Osborne, D., and Gaebler, T. *Reinventing Government: How the Entrepreneurial Spirit Is Transforming the Public Sector.* Reading, Mass.: Addison-Wesley, 1992.

Ouchi, W. G. *The M-Form Society: How American Teamwork Can Recapture the Competitive Edge.* Reading, Mass.: Addison-Wesley, 1984.

Peirce, N. R., with Johnson, C. W., and Hall, J. S. *Citistates: How Urban America Can Prosper in a Competitive World.* Washington, D.C.: Seven Locks Press, 1993.

Porter, M. *The Competitive Advantage of Nations."* New York: Free Press, 1990.

Putnam, R. *Making Democracy Work: Civic Traditions in Modern Italy.* Princeton, N.J.: Princeton University Press, 1993a.

Putnam, R. "The Prosperous Community: Social Capital and Public Life." *The American Prospect,* Spring 1993b.

Rifkin, J. *The End of Work: The Decline of the Global Labor Force and the Dawn of the Post-Market Era.* New York: Putnam, 1995.

Ryan, A. *John Dewey and the High Tide of American Liberalism.* New York: Norton, 1995.

Sandel, M. *Democracy's Discontent: America in Search of a Public Philosophy.* Cambridge, Mass.: Belknap Press, 1996.

Saxenian, A. "The Cheshire Cat's Grin: Innovation and Regional Development in England." *Technology Review,* Feb./Mar. 1988.

Saxenian, A. *Regional Advantage: Culture and Competition in Silicon Valley and Route 128.* Cambridge, Mass.: Harvard University Press, 1994.

Schrage, M. *Shared Minds: The New Technologies of Collaboration.* New York: Random House, 1990.

Schumpeter, J. *Capitalism, Socialism, and Democracy,* New York: Harper & Row, 1962.

"Survey: The American South." *The Economist,* Dec. 10, 1994, p. 12.

"The Sustainable Seattle 1993: Indicators of Sustainable Community: A Report to Citizens on Long-Term Trends in Our Community." Seattle, Wash.: Sustainable Seattle, 1993.

Tapscott, D. *The Digital Economy: Promise and Peril in the Age of Networked Intelligence.* New York: McGraw-Hill, 1996.

United Nations, The World Commission on Environment and Development. *Our Common Future.* Oxford: Oxford University Press, 1987.

Waits, M. J. "Building an Economic Future." *State Government News,* Sep. 1995, pp. 6–10.

Welch, J. F., Jr. "Evolving Industrial Alliances." *The Bridge,* 1987, *17*(4), p. 10.

White, O. "The Real Orlando." *Florida Trend,* Nov. 1995.

~~~ Index

A

Absentee ownership, 65–66, 193
Academies, civic entrepreneur, 217–218
Advocates, 58–59
Agitator role of civic entrepreneurs, 75, 78, 197, 199–207; advice for acting in, 206; continuous process of change and, 199–202; scanning and, 202–205; steps taken in, 197; and vision, 205–207
Agreement building, 73
Ainsley, S., 39, 64
Alford, L., 25, 50, 51, 53, 57, 87, 109, 114, 126, 133, 137, 178, 189, 192, 199, 201
All-America City Award, 146
Allegheny Conference on Community Development, 186
Allen, I., Jr., 103
Alliance for National Renewal, 214
Amelio, G., 136
American Leadership Forum, 190
American Prospect, The (Putnam), 30
Ameritrust, 46, 84
Amoco Corporation, 187
Anderson, J. C., 17, 41, 50, 54, 56, 85, 115, 126, 183, 193, 201, 218
Apache Oil Company, 193
Apple Computer, 43, 104, 136
Applied Materials, 3, 7–8, 39, 43, 47, 82, 108, 115, 156, 166, 219, 221
Arizona, 4–5; civic entrepreneurs in, 30, 37, 55, 57; civic entrepreneurs' commitment in, 87–88, 101; civic entrepreneurs' networking in, 104, 107; civic entrepreneurs' team in, 44–45;

clusters of specialization in, 24–25; demographic change and, 13, 14; in implementation stage, 150, 172, 175, 176; in improvement and renewal stage, 181, 182, 189, 190, 191, 192, 193, 196, 199, 200, 205; in incubation stage, 112, 114, 123–124, 124–125, 131, 132, 133–134, 137, 138; in initiation stage, 81, 85, 87–88, 96–97, 99, 101, 104, 107; leadership development in, 217; raising the stakes in, 96–97, 99; wake-up call in, 85
Arizona Information Infrastructure Initiative (AIII), 124
Arizona Optics Initiative, 24–25
Arizona State University (ASU), 45, 123
Arizona Technology Development Authority, 150
Arthur Andersen and Company, 187
Ashoka Foundation, 216
Aspect Telecommunications, 159
ASPED (Arizona Strategic Planning for Economic Development), 44–45, 122, 123, 133–134, 182, 189, 199, 212. *See also* GSPED
Assessment of situation, 113–114
Atlanta, Georgia, 103
Austin, Texas, 4; civic entrepreneurs in, 29, 37, 53, 57–58, 66; civic entrepreneurs' commitment in, 86, 88–89; civic entrepreneurs' team in, 42–44, 109; demographic change and, 14; globalization and, 8; in implementation stage, 150, 153–154, 156–157, 170, 176; in improvement and

needed for, 72–75; support for, 220–225; and venture capital model, 150, 152, 157–168. *See also* Economic communities

Collaborative intermediary organizations, 222–224

Collaborative Leadership (Chrislip, Larson), 13–14

Comfort zones, reaching beyond, 102–106

CommerceNet, 158, 162

Commission on Educational Excellence, 173

Commitment: of civic entrepreneurs, 86–91; of civic entrepreneurs' friends, 100–102; securing, for implementation stage, 151–168

Communities: absentee ownership in, 65–66, 193; collaborative approach in, 5–6, 71–72; cultures of blame in, 66–67; demonstrating responsibility for, 86–91; forces of change and, 3–4, 6–18; in industrial revolution era, 19–20; making a unique difference in, 54–56; past failures in, 67–68; in progressive era, 20–21; transformed, examples of, 4–5. *See also* Economic communities

Community activists, as civic entrepreneurs, 41–42

Community scanning, 202–205

Competencies, connected community, 25–28

Competition: global, localizing opportunities in, 115–119; globalization and, 7–8, 23–24; information technology and, 11–12; regional, 23–24

Computer Systems Policy Project, 158–159, 161

Connect '96, 215–216

Connecticut Mutual Life Insurance, 190

Constituencies, working with multiple, 102–107

Continuous process of community building, 78, 79, 181–188, 199–202

Convener role of civic entrepreneurs, 75, 76, 77, 129–148; advice for acting in, 147; balancing top-down influence with bottom-up innovation in, 135–141; finding right fit for participants and, 141–145; persistence in, 145–148; setting process rules/discipline in, 129–135, 145–148; steps taken in, 129

Conway, V., 101

Cooke, L., 10–11, 29, 43, 103, 105, 197

Cooper, H., 185

Cornerstone project, 48–50, 122, 125

Corson, W., 202

Crisis: opportunity in, 206; wake-up, 81–84, 85–86

Croly, H., 20

Culture: of blame, 66–67, 80, 90–91, 117–118; of civic entrepreneurship, 188–196

Cummings, M., 27

Cunningham, W., 43, 88–89, 156–157

Cypress Semiconductor, 90, 104

D

Dantotsu, 213

Davidow, W. H., 160, 161

DeBock, J., 89

Decentralization: and diverse leadership, 13–15, 40; and forces of change, 6–7; and networked economy, 11, 12–13; and New Globalism, 7–10; and political devolution, 15–18

Declaration of interdependence, 91–95

DeMichele, M., 192

Democracy's Discontent (Sandel), 21–22

Demographic change, 6; and diverse leadership, 13–15, 40, 92–93

Denver, 139, 146

DeSantis, M., 31

Detroit, 120

Devolution. *See* Political devolution

Dewey, J., 21

de Windt, E. M. (D.), 45, 84, 93, 101–102, 120

Difference, making a, 54–56

Digital Economy, The (Tapscott), 11

Discipline for results, 133–135, 145–148

Dively, G., 46, 101